INVISIBLE
TRILLIONS

INVISIBLE TRILLIONS

How Financial Secrecy Is Imperiling
Capitalism and Democracy—
and the Way to Renew
Our Broken System

Raymond W. Baker

Foreword by Larry Diamond

BK

Berrett–Koehler Publishers, Inc.

Berrett-Koehler Publishers, Inc.
1333 Broadway, Suite 1000
Oakland, CA 94612-1921
Tel: (510) 817-2277
Fax: (510) 817-2278
www.bkconnection.com

ORDERING INFORMATION

Quantity sales. Special discounts are available on quantity purchases by corporations, associations, and others. For details, contact the "Special Sales Department" at the Berrett-Koehler address above.

Individual sales. Berrett-Koehler publications are available through most bookstores. They can also be ordered directly from Berrett-Koehler: Tel: (800) 929-2929; Fax: (802) 864-7626; www.bkconnection.com.

Orders for college textbook / course adoption use. Please contact Berrett-Koehler: Tel: (800) 929-2929; Fax: (802) 864-7626.

Distributed to the U.S. trade and internationally by Penguin Random House Publisher Services.

Berrett-Koehler and the BK logo are registered trademarks of Berrett-Koehler Publishers, Inc.

Printed in Canada

Berrett-Koehler books are printed on long-lasting acid-free paper. When it is available, we choose paper that has been manufactured by environmentally responsible processes. These may include using trees grown in sustainable forests, incorporating recycled paper, minimizing chlorine in bleaching, or recycling the energy produced at the paper mill.

Library of Congress Cataloging-in-Publication Data

Names: Baker, Raymond W., 1935– author.
Title: Invisible trillions : how financial secrecy is imperiling capitalism and
   democracy—and the way to renew our broken system / Raymond W. Baker.
Description: First edition. | Oakland, CA : Berrett-Koehler Publishers, 2023. |
   Includes bibliographical references and index.
Identifiers: LCCN 2022023124 (print) | LCCN 2022023125 (ebook) |
   ISBN 9781523003020 (hardcover ; alk. paper) | ISBN 9781523003037 (pdf) |
   ISBN 9781523003044 (epub) | ISBN 9781523003051 (audio)
Subjects: LCSH: Capitalism—Moral and ethical aspects. | Secrecy. | Corruption.
Classification: LCC HB501 .B2356 2023 (print) | LCC HB501 (ebook) |
   DDC 330.12/2—dc23/eng/20220902
LC record available at https://lccn.loc.gov/2022023124
LC ebook record available at https://lccn.loc.gov/2022023125

First Edition
30 29 28 27 26 25 24 23 22   10 9 8 7 6 5 4 3 2 1

Book producer: Westchester Publishing Services
Text designer: Jane Raese
Cover designer: Matt Avery
Author photo: Elliott O'Donovan

To
Myla, Baker, Shelby, and Ever,
their friends,
and their generation.

Again, the best reason for optimism.

Contents

Foreword, Larry Diamond   ix

Introduction: The Stakes Could Not Be Higher   1

PART I. DEMOCRATIC CAPITALISM AT RISK   5

1   Capitalism's Financial Secrecy System   9
2   Underproductive and Illicit Trillions   27
3   Corruption, Crime, and Terrorism   37
4   Income and Wealth Inequality   52
5   Democracy Weakening   72

PART II. CORRODING THE COMMONS   87

6   Broken Banks   89
7   Covetous Corporations   109
8   Enablers   128
9   Complicit Governments   140
10   International Institutions to the Rescue?   192
11   Hiding in Silos   199

PART III. RENEWING DEMOCRATIC CAPITALISM   203

12   The Precarious State of Democratic Capitalism   205
13   Change: Empowered or Imperiled?   211
14   Restoring Integrity   221

Conclusion: Character Is Destiny   253

Discussion Guide   257

List of Abbreviations   259

Notes   261

Acknowledgments   280

Index   281

About the Author   289

Foreword

In 2005, Raymond Baker published a seminal book, *Capitalism's Achilles Heel*, documenting the problem of dirty, illicit money and what it was doing to our systems of democracy and free market capitalism. The book, based on a decade of research and over 300 interviews in nearly two dozen countries, had a profound impact in demonstrating how global capitalism was going off the rails due to pervasive corruption and illicit capital flows, facilitated and protected by secrecy provisions, scant regulation, and the unfortunate human tendency toward greed. The book gave rise to a movement for "global financial integrity" and an organization of that name that Baker founded the subsequent year. Despite these efforts by a dedicated band of analysts, journalists, and activists, the problem has only mushroomed in scale. Now, we can no longer talk of tens or hundreds of billions of dollars stolen, skimmed, and transferred through illicit or fraudulent activity. Rather, as Baker makes clear in this urgently important new book, kleptocrats, criminals, corporations, and crony capitalists now send invisible trillions coursing through the opaque arteries of global finance. And democracies—not least the United States—are as eager to receive, conceal, and legitimize this diverted wealth as the venal and cunning are to launder and park it.

The result has been an alarming corrosion of democracy and capitalism. Each system—or more to the point, each half of the intertwined system of democratic capitalism—is being dragged down by the relentless pursuit of profit maximization, even when it is immoral (evading the most minimal civic duty to pay taxes on gushing revenues) and frequently when it is blatantly illegal. A complex global industry of lawyers, bankers, consultants, accountants, lobbyists, agents, brokers, and fixers has arisen for one common purpose: to help place trillions of dollars of wealth beyond the reach of public accountability, regulation, and taxation. By making these trillions invisible, untaxable, and (if they are stolen from impoverished publics) unrecoverable, global financial secrecy is dramatically increasing inequality of wealth and income within nations. Worse, as Baker makes clear, economic development is stunted, and inequality is further aggravated by the wasteful, unproductive dispensation of this cornered wealth, most of which is hoarded in various stores of cash or luxury real estate or squandered in obscene displays of conspicuous consumption. As Baker puts it, "the mature megarich are hiding, saving, and playing with their money, while the youthful poor are underchallenged and restless." This mounting inequality is now one of the biggest contributors to the declining functionality of and public support for both democracy and capitalism. As Baker shows and as generations of research on democracy have demonstrated, there is a strong inverse relationship between inequality and democracy.

But the global system of financial secrecy is eroding democracy in another way as well by ravaging the rule of law and, really, any sense of a shared public purpose. As Baker makes clear in this devastating portrait, the current system of global financial and corporate capitalism—as it is increasingly distorted and degraded by the vast inscrutable web of tax havens, secrecy jurisdictions, shell corporations, shadowy corporate subsidiaries, anonymous trust accounts, fake foundations, and falsified trades—is unsustainable. As it moves more and more wealth beyond the reach of public scrutiny and accountability, it is also transferring that wealth from the poor to the rich and from the global South to the North while cleansing much of it of any taint of criminality or corruption. Inequality deepens. Ethics evaporate. Institutions decay. And democracy recedes.

The last 15 years have witnessed a persistent and now accelerating global democratic recession. Since Baker published his first book in 2005 (at what would prove to be the high-water mark for global democracy), levels of political rights, civil liberties, and the rule of law have steadily receded in the world.[1] As the annual data of Freedom House show, the steady post–Cold War progress of freedom in the world came to a screeching halt in 2006, and for every year since many more countries have declined in freedom than have gained (exactly reversing the pattern following the fall of the Soviet Union in 1991). In each decade since the miraculous 1980s, the rate of democratic breakdown (that is, the percentage of the world's democracies that expire) has been increasing, and the first two decades of this century have also seen a marked slowing in the rate at which autocracies make transitions to democracy. As a result, the decade of the 2010s was the first since the third wave of global democratization began in 1974 in which more countries abandoned democracy than adopted it.[2] More countries are also losing rather than gaining ground in control of corruption. My research has shown that deterioration in the rule of law—including transparency, accountability, and control of corruption—has been the leading edge of the broader decline in freedom and democracy.

Paralleling these aggregate trends in freedom and democracy have been alarming shifts in global values, perceptions, and narratives. Democracy remains the preferred form of government around the world, but discontent is mounting with the way democracy is working. A 2020 report by Cambridge University on "Global Satisfaction with Democracy" found that "across the globe, democracy is in a state of malaise."[3] Not surprisingly, countries where rising inequality, political corruption, or corporate malfeasance have been major issues—such as the United States, the United Kingdom, Brazil, Mexico, Colombia, Nigeria, and South Africa—have led the downward trend in public confidence in democracy. All of these countries are deeply, in fact shockingly, implicated in the pernicious system of global financial secrecy that Baker describes in this book.

At about the same time (2019), the Pew Research Center released a survey of public opinion in 27 prominent democracies around the world. It showed not only high and growing levels of dissatisfaction with democracy in most of the countries surveyed but also, like other research, identified weak rule of law as a prominent factor: "Most [people surveyed] believe elections bring little change, that politicians are corrupt and out of touch and that courts do not treat people fairly."[4] Precisely because the trillions of dollars that are being raked, expropriated, laundered, and hoarded across their economies are invisible, ordinary citizens do not see exactly what is happening. But they see the consequences in declining economic performance, rising inequality and elite arrogance, and increasingly corrupt politics. All of these drive democratic disenchantment, political polarization, and rising support for antisystem, illiberal, and authoritarian populists, who then destroy democracy and govern even more corruptly.

Only radical improvements across the globe in financial transparency and accountability and in regulatory capacity and integrity can break this cycle of political decay and despair. Fortunately, Raymond Baker offers a path forward to rekindle a sense of shared public purpose and thereby renew democratic capitalism. The essential starting place is to implement sweeping new provisions for transparency and accountability in a wide range of national and international financial transactions. The ability of corporations to disguise their true beneficial owners must be ended (as it was in the United States for shell banks). Multinational corporations should also have to disclose how they reconcile their tax filings across jurisdictions and how they justify the pricing of their internal corporate trade across borders. Falsified trading across company units to evade taxes should be a crime that is detected and punished. Banks should face closer regulation and stronger anti–money laundering and transparency laws. The auditing functions of modern accounting companies should be strictly separated from the consulting ones to avoid obvious conflicts of interest. The auditing and enforcement capacities of the Internal Revenue Service should be strengthened after a long period of deliberate atrophy. And some reforms of the tax code will be needed (for example through a modest financial transaction tax) to help diminish inequality. Finally, to repeat the core message of this book, no reform strategy can succeed unless it squarely confronts the systemic secrecy that cordons off so much wealth from visibility, accountability, and productive and humane use.

—Larry Diamond

Introduction:
The Stakes Could Not Be Higher

WE ARE AT AN INFLECTION POINT. The two basic components of the democratic-capitalist system are at risk of splitting apart. This poses an existential threat to human progress in the twenty-first century, paralleling the importance of climate change.

How did we get here? How can we prevent this from happening?

An absolutely essential element in fighting a kinetic war or waging a political battle is to understand your opposition, study its strengths and weaknesses. The degree to which capitalism has taken control of the two-part system guiding our lives is inadequately understood. This book addresses this gap and charts a path forward.

Over the last half century, capitalism has created the means by which trillions upon trillions of dollars, euros, pounds, and other stores of wealth can move and shelter invisibly, out of sight and beyond the control of central bankers, revenue authorities, law enforcement agents, and international institutions. With this level of financial secrecy now available to and dominating capitalist operations, riches move inexorably upward, accelerating economic inequality. Rising inequality is directly imperiling—weakening, obstructing, and degrading—democracy.

Across recent decades and particularly over the last 15 years a great many organizations have taken up determined fights against poverty, climate change, terrorism, ethnic division, gender discrimination, money laundering, and corruption and concentrated battles against drugs, human trafficking, wildlife poaching, antiquities theft, resource plundering, cybercrimes, tax evasion, and a multitude of other serious concerns. All of these problems are complicated by and many are direct symptoms of the larger truths now entrenched in the core of the democratic-capitalist

system: motivations and mechanisms moving and sheltering money unseen, uncounted, and unknown. The fact is, organized efforts combating many of our most serious national and global problems cannot
succeed when major parts of the capitalist system are working in purposeful contradiction to such efforts.

Who should care and why?

- The policy arena comprising legislators, government officials, think
  tanks, nongovernmental organizations, and activists needs to understand the financial secrecy system and how it undercuts well-
  intentioned programs aimed at policy innovations and civic
  improvements.
- Scholars and educators need to expose students, particularly at the
  university level, to how capitalism today differs from its roots and
  how many of its routine practices produce inequality, cross into illegality, and threaten democracy.
- Multinational corporations must face up to what has become fundamental within everyday business operations—separating ownership from control, divorcing price from value, and disconnecting
  sellers and buyers. Then dealing with these disjunctures, take pro-
  active steps to assure executives, managers, and staff that in the performance of their jobs they are not committing felony offenses.
- All of us—citizens and consumers—need to grasp that the financial secrecy system created in recent decades impacts the origin,
  quality, and cost of the clothes we wear, cellphones we use, energy
  that powers our cars and heats and cools our homes, rent we pay,
  fees on our bank accounts, movies we watch, jewelry we wear, air-
  planes we fly in, political messaging we absorb, votes we cast, and
  indeed the nature of the democracy in which we live.

Much of what follows draws upon original research and published materials, including my personal observations and experiences across
many decades in the United States and in a hundred other countries. My
earlier book, *Capitalism's Achilles Heel*, delved into dirty money as it impacts the majority of the world living in developing countries. Since the
book's publication in 2005, the concept of illicit financial flows has been
embedded into the global agenda, with 193 countries now committed to
curtailing this problem. I have asked myself many times, "Why not just
leave what I have to say at that?" And the answer is that in recent decades I have observed so many of the issues I confronted in the developing

world and wrote about in *Capitalism's Achilles Heel* coming home to roost in the wealthier world. Widening economic disparities, social unrest, challenges to democracy, violence, even threats of authoritarianism— as so frighteningly demonstrated on January 6, 2021, in Washington, D.C.—are no longer concerns only of "those countries over there." No, these kinds of concerns are now also here, whether "here" is supposedly stable societies in the Americas or Europe or Asia or Africa or else-where. The entire world is affected by perversions arising within capi-talism that are working to undermine democracy.

Throughout these pages, "capitalism" and "capitalist," "democracy" and "democratic," are often presented as conscious realities speaking in their own voices. These tenets are treated as living structures, currently at odds, needing to rediscover the harmonies recognizable in past years. I shift back and forth between these two concepts, as their intertwined relationship is a key component within these writings. Democratic capi-talism is often referred to here as a "system," since its dual components working together establish a systemic linkage that is expected to be mu-tually reinforcing. Instead, capitalism is now subordinating democracy, imperiling the whole system.

Observations and arguments, words and graphs, are laid out as clearly as possible. The climate change issue informs this approach. Scientific research into global warming accelerated in the 1960s and 1970s but took decades to become more broadly understood. United Nations confer-ences weighed in, and Al Gore finally succeeded in securing the issue into global consciousness with his films, speeches, and writings. The young Swedish activist Greta Thunberg stood poised in front of global forums and challenged older generations "How dare you?"

In a similar vein, issues currently surrounding democratic capitalism, particularly issues of widening inequality and rampant illegality, are at the moment principally the purview of scholars and experts. Capitalism and democracy are in growing conflict with each other, yet this confron-tation remains largely contained within the specialized journals of aca-demics and professionals. Instead, learned analyses need to be simplified and extended into mainstream thinking. The gravity of this conflict must be grasped at the popular level, in the same way that climate change is now grasped at the popular level, if it is to be resolved.

This is intentionally a rather short work, conveying a lucid picture rather than myriad details. The focus is on capitalism. Democracy itself has problems that need to be addressed in years to come, but that would be the subject of a different work. Here, I concentrate on the eroding interactions of capitalism with democracy, offering an alternative understanding of the relationship today of one to the other. By the end of this brief journey together, I hope that the depth of the problem within democratic capitalism and the recommended path toward renewal will be evident.

This book takes two avenues into its subject matter, striving to be both informative and evocative, conveying both understanding and feeling, because our intellects and our passions, our heads and our hearts, are required to solve our shared problems.

Permit me to repeat one thing said in my earlier writings. This is not an anticapitalist screed. Democratic capitalism is, in my judgment, the best system yet devised in political economy, but dysfunctions within its capitalist component are undermining the two-part system.

We begin in part I with an explanation of the motivations driving the financial secrecy system and how resulting behaviors are generating and sheltering trillions of dollars in underproductive wealth. This system directly promotes corruption, crime, terrorism, economic inequality, and weakening democracy.

Part II illustrates how these realities further corrode the commonwealth, with chapters devoted to the facilitating activities and impacts of banks, corporations, enabling lawyers and accountants, governments, and international institutions and concluding with the limiting role played in policy silos that are missing the bigger picture.

Thus, the strategic approach taken in parts I and II explains and portrays the continuum of motivations powering, mechanisms operating, and outcomes resulting from ill dealings within capitalism.

Finally, part III brings home the precarious state of our chosen economic and political system. Do the current confluences of pandemic, privation, protests, and political division set the stage for change? How—pragmatically and specifically—do we reset capitalism so that it contributes to shared prosperity and sustained democracy? And in conclusion, the philosophical notion that character is destiny urges that we marshal the power of reason to improve prospects for progress in this age.

Change can and must come if the hinge of political economy is to pivot toward strengthening both equality and justice. Reforming capitalism is a necessary step toward strengthening—indeed saving—democracy. The stakes could not be higher.

PART I

Democratic Capitalism at Risk

WHEN I GRADUATED from Harvard Business School in 1960, I had no idea, not in the furthest reaches of my imagination, that capitalism might someday undermine democracy. The preceding 15 years, post–World War II, marked at least in the United States what was perhaps the highest level of responsible capitalism ever achieved. Veterans retrained for new jobs, employment rose, investment soared, differences between executive and worker salaries were barely 20 to 1, relations between labor and management were generally good, banks and corporations promoted balanced growth, and consumption rose. Hard-won liberty and freedom of enterprise were linked. Every indication suggested that these favorable trends would continue.

But then something happened, as I narrate in the pages of this book. First, capitalism began adopting and then entrenched a new motivation, secrecy, that is now as important as its original motivation, profits. Second, parallel with the growth of this secrecy motivation, mechanisms were created and continue to be expanded enabling income and wealth accumulation in staggering amounts, trillions and trillions, hidden from view, driving oppressive economic inequality. Third, these realities are fostering the noticeable decline of democracy and the relentless rise of authoritarianism.

The simple truth is, capitalism purposefully operating in secrecy and democracy attempting to operate with transparency cannot coexist. Democratic capitalism must change if the system is to survive this century's move toward and perhaps beyond ten billion in global population, most living in economic straits.

Severe imbalance now characterizes the way democracy and capitalism are functioning. Democracy is expected to convey equal political rights, and capitalism should offer fair economic opportunities. Instead, these two guiding tenets are becoming decoupled, no longer functioning in sync. The capitalist side of the equation is running out of control, eroding the social contract, facilitating crime and corruption, evading obligations, maximizing income and wealth inequalities, and thus jeopardizing democracy. I lay the onus for these outcomes primarily on rogue capitalism rather than on a collection of other societal problems.

The original pillars of democracy—popular vote, rule of law, representative legislatures, protection of minority rights—though imperfectly posited and often challenged have not fundamentally changed since their formulation in the late 1700s.

The original pillars of capitalism—making profits, spreading wealth, and generating public goods—are now radically altered. Capitalism has taken on the ulterior motive of masking income in the trillions of dollars annually and wealth in the tens of trillions of dollars cumulatively in the coffers of the richest countries and the richest people.

Earning income and accumulating wealth in a hidden manner explains why economic disparities are soaring. Wealth inequality is exploding in both rich and poor countries. Capitalism increasingly directs its gains into the hands of its most privileged elites. The wealth of the top 1 percent nearly equals the total wealth of the remaining 99 percent. Much of this wealth is in stagnant accounts earning less than or barely the rate of inflation, essentially stored up value, underproductive, rather akin to hoarding currency notes in a vault. This at a time when hundreds of millions of people around the globe, mostly the young, are underemployed. And this at a time when illegal money is closely associated with loss of freedom and civil liberties and declines in the rule of law and accountability in scores of countries.

Income inequality is likewise growing almost everywhere and more so than appears in economic statistics, since income data seldom record what is earned on assets transferred via the financial secrecy system outside of citizens' countries. Both wealth and income disparities are wider than available data reveal.

Balance within the democratic-capitalist system depends on some semblance of an equitable social contract that navigates the space between equal political rights and fair economic opportunities. The ambition inherent in capitalism and the justice expected through democracy are now severely out of balance. Trust, essential to both parts of the system, is weakening. The social contract, however defined or formulated, is fraying.

Democracy is faltering in scores of countries around the world. Authoritarian political elites readily use the financial secrecy system for personal enrichment and find advantage in cultivating and maintaining the democracy deficit.

Rising inequality and weakening democracy contribute to political instability. With little stake in the economies and the politics of their countries, citizens take their discontent to the streets in their own cities and across borders, seeking shelter or joining others of like mind in rebellion and violence.

These trends are unsustainable. Severe imbalances in income, wealth, opportunity, freedom, and security, much of this fostered by a decidedly underachieving capitalist system, will not underpin a peaceful world.

The democratic-capitalist system is at risk. Conventional wisdom holds that the troubles in democracy lie within the mechanisms of democracy itself. I disagree. The troubles within democracy lie primarily within its capitalist counterpart. Capitalism is failing to live up to its stake in the bargain: providing a fair share of well-being for all. Rogue capitalism is on a collision course with democracy, threatening democracy. Rising economic disparity is the fertile field on which political alienation is so often cultivated.

Rebalancing capitalism and democracy is, along with climate change, the most difficult and important challenge facing the world in the twenty-first century, a critical issue around which much of the fate of political economy will turn. Today's flawed two-part system cannot endure through the decades ahead.

We are truly at an inflection point, a historical moment when the democratic-capitalist system that has guided a good part of the world for some 250 years is now threatened by widening economic inequalities, raging financial illegalities, and advancing political authoritarianisms. As currently practiced, our two prevailing doctrines are not working well together and will not get us through the twenty-first century. This book is about improving prospects for the survival of democratic capitalism.

The good news is, we created our problems and therefore we can solve our problems. And we must. We must either reform capitalism or we will weaken democracy. This is the stark choice before us, a pivotal issue in the twenty-first century, a hinge in human affairs going forward. The whole of humanity can rise with a renewal of capitalism's contributions to freedom and liberty.

1

Capitalism's Financial
Secrecy System

THE FINANCIAL SECRECY phenomenon began to accelerate in the 1960s, driven by two global forces. First, from the late 1950s through the 1960s, 48 countries gained their independence. This affected motivations within both ceding countries and the newly independent countries. Former colonial powers, most importantly the United Kingdom and France, sought to hold on to their mechanisms for shifting wealth out of their traditional possessions. And many citizens of these newly independent countries, not altogether trusting their unstable governments, also wanted to get their money out and needed facilitating mechanisms and structures.

Second, multinational corporations, which were quite few in the immediate post–World War II years, began to spread aggressively across the globe and generated contrivances to move their profits in a hidden manner out of distant ventures or risky environments. Growth in global trade enabled shifts of revenues and profits with little oversight by young, unstable governments.

Thus, the financial secrecy system grew in order to serve these two new interests driving the relocation of income and wealth. This system has continued to develop since its modest beginnings in the 1960s to the point that today by some estimates it handles close to half of global trade and financial movements, much of it invisible to governments, central bankers, tax authorities, law enforcers, and legislators.

The financial secrecy system is specifically designed to shift and shelter illicit money. Illicit money is money that is illegally earned, transferred, or utilized. A key point made repeatedly in these pages is that every significant element of this secrecy system has been developed in wealthier Western countries. The mechanisms through which this system operates are not something done to us; these are mechanisms created and expanded by us specifically serving the new motivation within capitalism: secrecy.

Early on, let it be clear that privacy and secrecy in the financial arena are different. I would like my bank account to remain private, as already provided for in law. This does not mean that it should be cloaked in secrecy. If someone with a name similar to mine is suspected of a terrorist act and authorities need to check possibly relevant account activity of me and others, I have no objection. My financial privacy is not above your personal security.

Three sources generate illicit funds: commercial, criminal, and corrupt. The commercial source of illicit money is usually tax evading through trade and capital movements. The criminal source is from drug dealers, human traffickers, counterfeiters, poachers, and more and includes the activities of terrorist financiers. The corrupt component is funds stolen by government officials. The system created to move and shelter illicit money comprises tax havens, secrecy jurisdictions, disguised corporations, anonymous trust accounts, fake foundations, trade manipulations, hybrid entities, and specialized money laundering techniques. Banks, corporations, lawyers, and accountants have devoted hundreds of millions of man-hours to designing, disguising, complicating, and expanding this system to serve the secrecy motive, the motive to move invisible trillions.

TAX HAVENS/SECRECY JURISDICTIONS

Tax havens enable income receipts and wealth accumulations with little or no taxation or regulatory oversight. Starting from just three or four in the 1960s, there are now some 70 to well over 100 across the globe depending on who is counting.

Decisions under British common law laid the groundwork for the tax haven phenomenon. A 1929 case, *Delta Land and Investment Co., Ltd. v. Todd*, solidified earlier decisions that enabled companies registered in the United Kingdom to avoid taxation there if controlled elsewhere. The principle of ownership in one place and management in another place meant that taxes could be virtually eliminated in the country of registration and rather easily manipulated in the country of operation.

Curaçao was granted internal autonomy from the Netherlands in 1954, which enabled it to create a low tax environment for companies incorporated there but not doing business there. In 1955, Curaçao was included in a US-Netherlands tax treaty to avoid double taxation: taxing the same profits twice arising from cross-border investments. US and European corporations by the hundreds established nonoperating entities on the island and then routed transactions through these dummy entities in order to curtail taxes.

Every tax haven services illicit money as a significant part of its business. The Cayman Islands became a tax haven in the late 1950s and today caters to institutional clients and hedge funds. The British Virgin Islands has carved out a niche sheltering Chinese flight capital coming in, incorporating as a foreign entity, and roundtripping back to China. Malta handles Russian and European Union money, specializing in the wealth of oligarchs and kleptocrats. Luxembourg allows the formation of tax-exempt holding companies for foreign assets and earlier facilitated the creation of offshore eurobonds attracting stateless capital. China's 1978 Open Door policy enabled Hong Kong to become one of the fastest-growing tax havens servicing the parent country and other Asian sources of illicit money. Singapore, seeing a great deal of money flowing into its region during the First Indochina War and the Vietnam War, appealed to foreign commercial banks by giving preferential regulatory and tax treatment to Asian Currency Units, tapping wealth floating around hunting for a safe haven. Mauritius services money flowing out of and going back into India, enabling companies to launder money and dodge taxes. Panama leveraged the linkage of its Canal Zone to the United States to become a transit point for ill-gotten gains pouring out of Latin America, a business tapped by Manuel Noriega servicing drug cartels. Bahrain took advantage of Lebanon's civil war to launder money exiting unstable countries in the Middle East. Even the United States gives preferential tax treatment to foreign nationals in order to attract deposits, making this country the biggest tax haven operating anywhere today.

The important point to grasp is that tax havens exist because wealthier countries want them to exist, sheltering profits for multinational corporations and attracting money flooding in from foreign interests. This reality is a principal feature of the financial secrecy system of moving and hiding illicit money.

Most tax havens also operate as secrecy jurisdictions to the point that the two phenomena are now largely synonymous. This means that in addition to providing tax advantages, these jurisdictions also provide the services of bankers, lawyers, and accountants to receive, hide, shelter, disguise, and transmit funds onward, permitting company owners and account holders to remain entirely anonymous.

Switzerland made bank secrecy a matter of law in 1934, appealing to money streaming across the borders of Europe seeking a hiding place. Banking officials themselves were prohibited from disclosing client identities even to Swiss national authorities.

In recent years, a difference has been recognized between "conduits" and "sinks." Conduits gather money and send it on to sinks. A recent study examined networks between 98 million firms connected through 71 million ownership relations.[1] Reportedly, the main conduit countries are the Netherlands, the United Kingdom, Ireland, Singapore, and Switzerland. The Netherlands and the United Kingdom were estimated to handle some 45 percent of the billions a year flowing through the financial secrecy system. Netherlands redirects much of its inflow into European holdings, whereas the United Kingdom transmits much of its inflow into temporary holdings in smaller jurisdictions spread across the globe. The study identified 24 sinks as the most active recipients of these flows, 18 of which are related to the British Commonwealth. Smaller sinks ultimately shift their accumulating millions and billions back into wealthier economies.

The Financial Secrecy Index lists 133 jurisdictions offering secret corporate registrations.[2] This phenomenon, which the founders of the free market system never envisioned, undermines responsible capitalism.

DISGUISED CORPORATIONS

Secrecy jurisdictions permit the formation of entities without revealing ownership.

Panama has more than one million disguised entities on its rosters, most still fully in existence despite the release of the *Panama Papers* in 2016. The Cayman Islands and the British Virgin Islands are home to hundreds of thousands of disguised corporations.

The United States has been the most prolific secrecy jurisdiction for many years. Interstate commerce is largely regulated at the state level. Following the lead of Delaware, every state in the union passed laws permitting company formation agents to establish entities without identifying the natural persons owning the entities. Created at an estimated rate of two million such undertakings a year, America is a preferred destination for illicit money seeking secrecy and shelter. As of this writing the Treasury Department is drafting regulations that will change this reality, hopefully enabling government authorities to identify each entities' substantial partners and shareholders.

Often referred to as shell companies, disguised corporations appear in many variations. Front companies do some legitimate business in order to shelter other segments of illegitimate business. Bearer share companies are owned by whoever holds the share certificate, providing an ideal avenue for money laundering. Law firms maintain thousands of "shelf" companies, preregistered and sitting in inventory awaiting the needs of clients. Additional variations providing measures of secrecy include British Nominee Companies, International Headquarters Companies, Dual Resident Companies, Open-ended Investment Companies, Irish Non-Resident Companies, English Limited Partnerships, Cayman Islands STAR Trusts, and more. Protected "cell" companies and "segregated portfolio" companies allow individual participants to "rent" a piece of a multiowner entity. Captive insurance shelters give large and small entities a means of transferring money out of accumulated profits, thus providing mechanisms for income deferral and tax evasion.

ANONYMOUS TRUST ACCOUNTS

Trusts, with a long history in English common law, usually do not require legal registration where established. Identities of settlers and beneficiaries are generally not required by regulatory authorities. The parties to the trust may themselves be disguised corporations, further burying identifications under layers of secrecy. Settlers and beneficiaries may in fact be the same, undercutting the original intent of trust law. With Jersey, Guernsey, the Cayman Islands, the British Virgin Islands, the Cook Islands, St. Kitts and Nevis, Niue, and others active in the anonymous trust business, "flee clauses" have been agreed across jurisdictions, allowing trusts to be relocated instantly if identities of settlers or beneficiaries are sought. Some asset protection trusts can make stolen money safe, beyond legal recovery.

Disguised corporations, anonymous trusts, and other secrecy mechanisms enable transactions that separate sellers and buyers who purposefully intend to remain unknown to each other.

FAKE FOUNDATIONS

You can establish a charitable foundation, donate your money to your charitable foundation, and designate yourself as the beneficiary of the charity of your foundation, escaping taxes and oversight. Panama established the Private Interest Foundation, stating specifically that "the charter or bylaws specify one or more beneficiaries, which may include the founder."[3] Liechtenstein created the Anstalt in 1928, combining the functions of the trust and the foundation and eliminating personal identifications from official records. In the United States tens of thousands of foundations have been created over the last two decades, with a growing record of abuses from secret ownership, high fundraising costs, employment for family members, personal expense reimbursements, and even fraud in distributions.

FALSIFIED TRADES

For the first 150 years of the free market system, equity investments and trading profits were distinct business activities. Equity, such as purchasing shares, was invested. Trade, such as buying and selling, was conducted. In the most basic illustration, trade generated profits that appeared on the income statement. These profits then accumulated as equity in the retained earnings account on the balance sheet. Taxes would be paid and dividends remitted. This straightforward scenario, however, is no longer the case. Equity investments and trading profits are today conflated concepts.

To put it simply, abusive transfer pricing enables multinational corporations to transfer profits within trade transactions between subsidiary and affiliated entities. This transfer pricing obviates the need to accumulate profits, pay taxes, and remit dividends. All these steps can be avoided via the mechanism of transfer pricing in trade transactions. Set the price; move the profit. No earnings accumulating, no dividends, no taxes, no increases in the equity account. This process may very well break laws in one jurisdiction or another, but this is unimportant if the multinational corporation is not caught or enforcement is weak.

The process is straightforward. Instead of selling item X between entities within the same corporation at its accurately calculated, legitimately valued price of $100 as would exist in arm's-length transactions, it can instead be sold for, say, $50 or $150 depending on the direction in which profits are to be relocated. There are four ways to accomplish this, most easily illustrated by considering transactions between subsidiaries A and B in two different countries belonging to a single parent corporation.

To Move Money Out of Subsidiary A and Into Subsidiary B:

A sells to B at $50	A loses $50	B gains $50
A buys from B at $150	A loses $50	B gains $50

To Move Money Out of Subsidiary B and Into Subsidiary A:

B sells to A at $50	B loses $50	A gains $50
B buys from A at $150	B loses $50	A gains $50

Misinvoicing of the sale of goods and commodities, in other words trading at invoice prices that differ from legitimate values, exploded in the 1960s and 1970s as multinational corporations all over the globe avoided the pesky process of actually accumulating earnings in far-flung investments, paying taxes to foreign governments, going through the unnecessary process of declaring dividends, and remitting profits back to the parent company. However, this misinvoicing of goods and commodities ran into a problem beginning in the 1980s and 1990s as world market pricing data began to become available, enabling foreign governments and customs departments to sometimes recognize misinvoiced merchandise transactions.

So, starting in the 1980s and continuing very aggressively today, multinationals make greater use of intellectual property, services, and intangibles as preferred transactions for misinvoicing. Licenses, royalties, patent rights, management fees, interest expense on intracompany loans, insurance, research and development, advertising, head office expenses, and more are hugely exaggerated in order to eliminate taxes and remittance complications in foreign investments. The shift occurred because it is almost impossible to see an invisible item as misinvoiced, and no good comparative data are available. Virtually every multinational, multibillion-dollar, multiproduct corporation uses trade misinvoicing to shift money across borders. The process has become completely normalized in international business.

Today, multinational corporations' manipulation of the pricing of intellectual property moves hundreds of billions of dollars invisibly around the world. Techniques used are extremely sophisticated and utterly bizarre, sometimes involving more than 30 interlaced steps and, for fully detailed explanations, beyond the scope of this book.

Tax avoidance schemes surrounding intangible assets are built on four foundations. First, tax havens provide the sinks into which money can go to escape revenue collectors. Second, differing national tax systems can be exploited for available loopholes and pathways. Third, the concept of economic substance, that is, the notion that transactions should have real purpose other than tax or title shifting, is largely unenforced in legal and auditing procedures. And fourth, royalties, licenses, user fees, management services, even depreciation, etc. can be shifted with the click of a computer key.

What has happened since the 1960s is that price and value have become entirely different, entirely separate concepts. In billions of transactions, prices do not conform to values. Value is one thing; price is a fiction used to shift money from one place to another. This new normal sits at the heart of much of capitalism's operations today.

BLACK HOLES, SANDWICHES, AND MALTS

The story of the financial secrecy system now begins to be a bit complex, exactly as intended by its creators and operators so that legislators, regulators, and citizens will have difficulty grasping its intricacies and therefore will shy away from trying to curtail its machinations. Some brief insights into the construction of trade manipulations, the core of the system, will, however, be useful.

Bermuda, which decided decades ago to make money by moving money, is a common repository of intellectual property rights, sometimes referred to as the "Bermuda black hole." So, a US company can sell intellectual property, such as the operating system for a cell phone, to its wholly owned, Bermuda-based subsidiary for a low price. This Bermuda subsidiary is in fact incorporated in Ireland but supposedly "managed" in Bermuda. This entity operates as a holding company, holding the intellectual property rights of the parent. This Irish holding entity establishes a second Irish operating entity and licenses this second entity to sell intellectual property rights at a high price to other buyers, including in other countries. These buyers pay the second Irish company for the cell phone and its included operating system (i.e., the intellectual property). This second Irish company accumulates revenues, pays fractional taxes in Ireland, and then remits the revenues to the original holding company subsidiary supposedly managed in Bermuda. Bermuda charges no taxes on corporate income. The net effect is huge untaxed profits for the US parent company accumulating in Bermuda, essentially untaxed revenues generated from business activities in dozens of other countries, and minimal taxes paid in Ireland. The two Irish entities give this scheme the name "double Irish."

A variation on the scheme adds a "Dutch Sandwich" between the two Irish entities. Because consumers in Europe and elsewhere around the world are buying cell phones with the included intellectual property, it is useful to have another European subsidiary, a shell company in the Netherlands, that collects these revenues and then remits to Ireland. Since both the Netherlands and Ireland are members of the European Union, the Netherlands collects no withholding tax on these revenues. And for US tax purposes, these entities "check the box," confirming to the Internal Revenue Service (IRS) that they are effectively a single entity and that therefore the royalty payments flowing between them are disregarded.

The "Double Irish with a Dutch Sandwich" generated hundreds of billions of dollars of profits minimally taxed for primarily US corporations since the 1990s. Ireland, under pressure, overturned the scheme somewhat in 2015, with a five-year grace period to users to seek other avenues.

The "Single Malt," a variation on the "Double Irish," immediately emerged. Under this scheme, instead of a Bermuda-managed holding company, a Malta-managed holding company can be created. This entity channels intellectual property payments to the Irish operating entity. With treaties between the two nations avoiding double taxation, this mechanism accomplishes the same tax-avoidance purpose, though the mechanism is also under scrutiny as of this writing.

Attacks on the "Double Irish" and the "Single Malt" led Ireland to go a step further to preserve its tax haven status. Most recently emerging is the "Capital Allowances for Intangible Assets" (CAIA) scheme. This scheme permits the purchase price for intangible assets to be amortized over a period of years, in the same way that the purchase price of machinery is depreciated over several years. Intangible assets are defined broadly to include trademarks, copyrights, know-how, patents, designs, software, secrets, and more. Thus, an Irish subsidiary buying intellectual property from its parent can write off the cost of that purchase against taxes across, say, five or more years. If the parent company loaned money to that subsidiary to make the purchase, then the interest on that loan, often exorbitantly high, can also be written off over several years. After those years have run, the same exercise can be repeated with a new round of purchases of newly developed intellectual property. While Irish authorities are careful to say that this is not a tax avoidance scheme, some law firms in the country are allegedly marketing CAIA as exactly that. The mechanism has already distorted Ireland's statistics, creating huge differences between gross national product and gross national income.

LEGAL OR ILLEGAL?

Are these sorts of trade manipulations of goods, services, intangibles, and intellectual properties legal or illegal? In most countries, such activities are illegal if they undercut taxes or violate anti–money laundering laws of the home jurisdiction but are not necessarily illegal if they undercut or violate such laws in other countries.

Yet even this reality is beginning to change. There is another category of laws that are often violated: laws against schemes to defraud. In the United States, for example, cases are being decided against perpetrators of trade manipulations in which US mails and wires are used in a scheme to defraud another party, regardless of whether that party is domestic or foreign, private or government. As enforcement of such laws progresses within the trade arena, the difference between tax evasion, which is illegal, and tax avoidance, which takes advantage of marginally legal loopholes, will shrink. In other words, when trade manipulations are used to defraud another party, whether American or foreign, whether another private company or a government revenue department, this can constitute a felony offense. More on this in later pages.

Seeing how easy it is for multinational corporations to manipulate trade documentation, local businesses in all regions of the world do exactly the same thing. Agreements are made with suppliers to overinvoice trade transactions, so that upon payment the misinvoiced amounts will then be deposited into foreign bank accounts. Or underinvoice transactions, thus avoiding customs duties and value-added taxes in the importing country. These transactions deprive local economies and local governments of resources needed for infrastructure, health, and education.

Some think that trade manipulations are done only or mainly for the purpose of tax evasion and avoidance. This is largely correct when the activity is between wealthy countries trading in hard currencies. But the motivation is different in transactions between poorer and wealthier countries. Here the motivation is focused less on tax manipulation and more on converting soft currencies into hard currencies. Both multinational corporations and local firms have many ways to manipulate taxes in their developing country operations, so tax evasion through trade is not the primary aim. Getting money out of weak, inflation-prone soft currencies into dollars, euros, pounds, and other hard currencies is by far the more common goal.

Even within the borders of a single nation, businesses use trade misinvoicing to avoid internal taxes. With state taxes at different levels in America, companies shift profits from one jurisdiction to another to curtail avoidable payments to state treasuries.

Companies can also misinvoice their trades by misstating the volume, weight, quality, or purpose of transactions. In other words, the price can pass inspection while the physical basis of the transaction is manipulated.

Trade misinvoicing has become the principal operating mechanism within the financial secrecy system. The structures of tax havens, secrecy jurisdictions, disguised entities, and more are set up to handle money transferred in a hidden manner predominantly through the nearly invisible process of trade manipulations.

STRETCHING OPACITY

Each of more than 200 legal jurisdictions around the world has its own set of laws. What one country prohibits another may permit. Operators of the financial secrecy system have devoted decades to discovering and exploiting differences in laws and regulations, taking advantage of available ambiguities.

Responsible governments have gone to considerable lengths to avoid double taxation, exchanging treaties by the thousands so that profits taxed in one country are not taxed a second time in another country. But double nontaxation is growing, sheltering profits that are not taxable anywhere.

Lawyers, accountants, and bankers, particularly since the early 2000s, have created an endless range of hybrids, enabling manipulation of tax laws to facilitate evasion or avoidance. A hybrid entity is intended to be fiscally transparent for tax purposes in one country but not fiscally transparent for tax purposes in another country. In normal commercial transactions, one company's expense payment is another company's revenue receipt. When using hybrids in cross-border dealings, this distinction can be eliminated. An expense paid by one company can avoid being treated as revenue by another company. Or an expense paid by one company can at the same time be treated as an expense by the other company. In tax circles, the first example is called a "deduction/noninclusion mismatch." The second example is called a "deduction/deduction mismatch." These and other mismatches can be created through the use of hybrids in trade transactions, asset transfers, equities, debts, and more. They produce the same outcome: economic activity conducted in the shadows with little or no taxes collected by governments.

Another mechanism for avoiding taxes is the corporate inversion whereby a company sells itself to a subsidiary in a low-tax country. Executive operations can remain in the original country; just the legal headquarters is relocated, and the whole entity now has increased profits at the expense of the government in the original and principal place of business.

Opacity also surrounds lawyers' pooled accounts. Lawyers can put clients' funds into accounts they manage along with other clients' money, disguising their separate identities behind attorney-client privilege. White-shoe firms were found to have handled hundreds of millions of dollars that were stolen from Malaysia, addressed further in a later chapter. One estimate put the amount held in law firms' pooled accounts for clients at around $36 billion.[4] This practice is one of the reasons the Financial Action Task Force (FATF), anti–money laundering watchdogs based in Paris, gave the United States low ratings on five categories of regulations on American attorneys.

Other major avenues facilitating opacity and trade manipulation are free trade zones, also called special economic zones. These locations usually provide duty-free and tax-free incentives to investors, supposedly to encourage manufacturing and import-export activities. An estimated 4,300 exist around the world.[5] The United States has more of them than any other country, nearly 200 according to an industry association, plus by some estimates another 500 subzones.[6] All over the world these zones freely let goods in and poorly monitor goods out, driving smuggling and tax evasion. Panama, Ciudad del Este (in the Tri-Border Area nestled between Brazil, Paraguay, and Argentina), United Arab Emirates (UAE), China, and nearly 70 other countries have free trade zones. No country is known to adequately monitor such sheltered activities.

MONEY LAUNDERING

In the minds of many, money laundering is associated with organized criminal activity. True, but some of the techniques are used by otherwise respectable people as well.

Cash is king in the drug trade. Deposited into banks in small increments, it remains largely undetectable. Hidden within other physical goods, currency is easily smuggled across borders. Cash is likewise a principal mechanism powering human trafficking, animal poaching, organ sales, antiquity smuggling, and most other avenues for crime.

Asset swaps move ownership across borders. A company registered in one country can simply exchange its shares and become owned by a company registered in another country, perhaps a tax haven, shifting value abroad. Similarly, a service performed in one country can be compensated for with a payment given in another country, all quite opaque to prying eyes. Fake insurance claims move money across borders in international transactions. A credit card can be established in one country and used for illegitimate transactions in another country. Or a bank can take your money into a concentration account, lump it together with other funds, and shift it abroad, giving you access in another country.

Interest rate manipulations illustrate how capital and trade have become interfused. A parent company can loan money to its overseas subsidiary at an extraordinarily high rate of interest, thus allowing trading profits to be extracted through principal and interest payments. A variation on the intent is thin capitalization whereby the capital investment is minimal and the foreign subsidiary is loaded with debt to be paid off at a high interest rate, again using a capital transaction to shift what would otherwise be a trading profit.

Businesses can also use derivatives for the same ends. A parent and a subsidiary can enter into a derivatives contract, structured so that anticipated price or interest rate movements will lead to one side of the contract requiring payment to the other side, moving money across borders.

CAPITALISM'S NEW MOTIVATION

The preceding seeks to encapsulate an understanding of the financial secrecy system as briefly as possible. Two fundamental points are made repeatedly. First, every element of this modern phenomenon used today was developed within wealthier Western countries; not a single element was developed by criminals, drug dealers, corrupt government officials, or others who are often blamed for misusing financial openness. Second, the entirety of the system is designed to move money out of the hands of the poor and into the hands of the rich, out of the caches of criminals and into legitimate accounts, and out of the domains of the corrupt and into the spheres of the respectable. No part of the system provides economic benefits to the vast majority of humanity.

Secrecy is a self-sustaining motivation that drives behavior and functions quite apart from simpler notions of greed. I have known many businesspeople, bankers, lawyers, accountants, and others functioning within the financial secrecy system that I did not regard as personally greedy nor sense that they were intentionally facilitating the greed of others. On the contrary, for them the right thing to do is secrete and shelter money so it will not be subject to confiscation, lawsuits, taxes, spendthrift relatives, pleas for alms, and other demands. For them, the financial secrecy system, whether its patently illegal or thoroughly obtuse mechanisms, is serving a greater good. Such justifications propel trillions upon trillions of dollars across national and state borders, undermining the capitalist system and its contributions to societies.

Or should we just stick with the facts and avoid murkier notions surrounding motivations? Joe Biden, when he was running for president of the United States, said often that in politics it is a mistake to attribute motives to your opponent. In one-on-one encounters, this is normally sound advice. But what is being addressed here is an entire system, a financial secrecy system specifically designed to disguise and move money for the benefit of the few at the expense of the many. Curtailing this reality has to take into consideration what drives this reality. The profit motive in capitalism has been spoken of for more than two centuries. This fully justifies delving into the new secrecy motive now guiding capitalism. Supporting this view is the argument of Paul Krugman, distinguished economist and Nobel Prize winner, who says,

> Don't be afraid to talk about motives. . . . If you're having a real, good-faith debate, impugning the other side's motives is a bad thing. If you're debating bad-faith opponents, acknowledging their motives is just a matter of being honest about what's going on. . . . [Y]ou deal with the world you have, not the one you want.[7]

In the middle of this financial secrecy world that we have created sits the mechanism of falsified trade. Manipulations of trade, whether by price, quantity, measure, or other devices, are by far the most frequently used instruments within the financial secrecy system. Generating money through manipulating trade transactions then links to every other part of the system via tax havens, secrecy jurisdictions, several kinds of disguised entities, and

FIGURE 1.1 Financial secrecy system
Source: Author's illustration.

money laundering methods. Finally, openings left in national laws facilitate movement of money through the financial secrecy system and ultimately into the coffers of the rich, both corporations and individuals.

Other commentators have addressed particular components of the financial secrecy system in greater detail. What has not been emphasized, however, is that every single component of the modern shadow financial system has been developed for the specific purpose of serving capitalism's new, over the last half-century, secrecy motivation. This is a profound change from the intentions of Adam Smith and other original thinkers and designers of free market ideology. We are experiencing a new motivation within capitalism, a major break in concepts and operations arising across recent decades. What is depicted above did not exist before the mid-twentieth century. This book contributes toward understanding the motivations and mechanisms now operative within capitalism and explains and illustrates the impact these new realities have on prosperity and peace the world over.

Two facets of the shadow financial system predate modern design: the hawala system and Chinese flying money.

Hawala enables money or value to be handed over in one place and handed out in another place with no actual transfer. A hawala dealer in one country will receive money and then cooperate with another hawala dealer in another country to pay out money. Such arrangements are often entered into by family members in one country transferring small amounts to other family members in another country. The hawala dealers on one or both sides of the transaction will take small commissions for their services. They keep track of how much money they have handled for each other, and when balances tip too far on one side or the other they settle accounts between themselves. In settling such imbalances, dealers often resort to the modern financial secrecy system to arrange transfers through trade misinvoicing or money laundering techniques. Sometimes feared by security officials in richer countries as an invisible means of terrorists' financing, the vast majority of hawala transactions are instead small personal remittances between relatives.

Chinese flying money—*fei-chien*—operates on very much the same principle. With Chinese cross-border investment, trade, and construction growing exponentially in recent years, the technique is moving huge sums out of partner countries and into Chinese coffers. Construction materials going in and resource exports coming out are manipulated in quantity and value or through outright smuggling in order to shift revenues across borders by cooperating dealers on the two sides of transactions.

As the modern shadow financial system grew in the 1960s, drug dealers in the 1970s realized that these new secrecy systems were ideally suited for shifting their money, and they stepped into the same structures being made available to the corporate and the corrupt to move their disguised proceeds. In the 1980s other transnational criminals, seeing how easy it was for the drug dealers, they too stepped into the same mechanisms to move their money. In the 1990s and the 2000s terrorist financiers, seeing how easy it was for drug dealers and assorted criminal syndicates to move their money, they too stepped into mechanisms available within the financial secrecy system to secure and position resources both within countries and across borders to bankroll their attacks.

Stressing again, every single component of the modern shadow financial system as depicted in figure 1.1 has been developed in wealthier countries precisely for the purpose of serving capitalism's new motivation: moving, secreting, and sheltering income and wealth in a hidden manner. This is not something foisted upon the richer countries; it is something created by the richer countries. The system is designed to shift money from poor to rich, from criminal to legitimate, from corrupt to respectable. And it does so very efficiently every single day.

Many people believe that bad actors as discussed in succeeding chapters are solely responsible for misusing our good intentions. On the contrary, bad actors are taking advantage of structures we created, in fact structures we frequently operate for the criminal and the corrupt. Secrecy breaks the normally operative laws of supply and demand and undermines theories of growth and equity. We are not dealing with unfortunate outcomes but rather with willful intents.

No short survey such as this can cover adequately all the means available for generating, relocating, and hiding dirty money. What is stressed in preceding pages is the breadth of these activities and the depth to which they have become embedded into the capitalist system's operations. What is described is not how capitalism was intended to work. What is described is how the system works today using every conceivable mechanism to facilitate the new motivation at its core—secrecy.

Now, step back for a moment in order to grasp the three fundamental forces laid out here that have changed capitalism:

- Ownership is delinked from control, utilizing multiple entities.
- Value and price are different concepts, facilitating trade manipulations.
- Seller and buyer can be disguised, unknown to each other and to regulators.

With these three realities firmly entrenched in capitalism's modern modus operandi, our economic system is functionally beyond oversight by anyone.

Some halting progress in curtailing the worst of capitalism's ills is being made, as will be addressed later in this book. But legislators and authorities have not understood a basic truth. You cannot regulate secrecy. You cannot regulate a secret system. Trying to do so is a contradiction in terms. If you do not know what I am doing, how do you stop me from doing it? Law enforcement against money laundering, corruption, tax evasion, and other illicit financial dealings has notably failed because enforcement efforts, laudable as they may be, hardly begin to address the multiple manipulations utilized within the financial secrecy system. What can work and is explained later in the book is transparency and accountability, measures aimed at curtailing the motivations driving the financial secrecy system. Transparency and accountability can eliminate or reduce secrecy far, far more effectively than trying to regulate financial activity while secrecy remains protected.

Most worrisome of all, development of this structure supporting financial secrecy has enabled capitalism to separate itself from democracy, to operate outside competent control of democracy—governments and the people they govern. In this clash, rogue capitalism is winning and embattled democracy is losing, a point driven home in chapters following.

Repeating an earlier point, in order to win the battle for change, it is necessary to understand the elephantine, enigmatic forces opposing change.

This financial secrecy system, this structure that has been created to shift and hide revenues and profits, serving this new motivation within capitalism, this motivation for secrecy, for invisible and unaccountable trillions of dollars of income and wealth, circumventing taxes, driving inequality, impoverishing billions, empowering criminals, enriching despots, what has been done over the last century and especially the last half-century, different from the past, this is without question the ugliest chapter in global economic affairs since the wretched years of lawful slavery. Let us hope that it will not take an equal number of years to change. Like slavery, the costs of ill dealings within capitalism are staggering, to which we now turn.

2

Underproductive and
Illicit Trillions

C APITALISM WORKS BEST when it spreads benefits effectively and
fairly to all segments of society. This is most definitely not what we have
had in recent decades. Instead, we have altered the capitalist system in
order to condone invisible operations precisely designed to concentrate
advantages among the most privileged elite. Cumulatively, tens of trillions
of dollars accrue to the wealthiest individuals and corporations, a considerable portion of it through aggressive use of the financial secrecy system.
Thus, the poor are hugely disadvantaged, driving economic inequality
and threatening democracy, as subsequent chapters make very clear.

BROAD MONEY

Globally, some $120 trillion is sitting in cash and cash-equivalent ac-
counts, most of it earning less than or barely the rate of inflation and
some of it even sheltering in instruments producing negative returns.

Without getting deeply into definitions, economists generally measure
liquid assets as "narrow money" and "broad money." Narrow money is
currency in circulation and demand deposits. Currency means notes and
coins. Demand deposits are essentially checking account balances held
by the private sector, national, state, and local governments, and state-
owned enterprises. Thus, narrow money is basically the medium of easy
transactional exchanges. Estimates place the global total of narrow
money at about $36 trillion, measured in US dollars.

Broad money includes narrow money and adds savings deposits, money market funds, certificates of deposit, and short-term repurchase agreements. These slightly less liquid assets are therefore a means of holding wealth without significant risk. Broad money at the end of 2021 was about $120 trillion measured in US dollars. This is not the measure of total global wealth but of just that part of accumulated wealth which largely represents stored value, stored in the safest possible investments, earning little or no interest or even negative interest. It is hard to make the case that this $120 trillion is working to maximize advantages in the democratic-capitalist system.

Across the global population of 8.0 billion people, $120 trillion would be about $15,000 per person. For a family of four, this would be around $60,000. Only a tiny fraction of humanity has access to such immediate resources. If each person on Earth had savings of $15,000, there would be far less economic strain arising from the COVID-19 pandemic and far fewer people waiting for unemployment checks or dependent on food banks.

Some amount of money has to sit idle, providing the float necessary to pay cash for purchases and write checks. In the absence of better measures this might be roughly the figure for narrow money, $36 trillion. So, much of the rest of broad money, around $84 trillion, is amassed but not invested in assets with any real degree of earning power.

The growth of broad money has in recent years outpaced growth in the global economy, meaning that more money is being stockpiled than is effectively utilized. Figure 2.1 shows this divergence, which began at the time of the 2007–2008 financial crisis and has continued since.

Where does all this money come from? Two sources provide most of the funds: corporate profits from the private sector and surpluses from the treasuries of major exporting countries. Much of the growth of broad money finds its way into US dollar accounts. The United States has the largest current account deficit of any country; thus, the US economy needs massive amounts of incoming money to balance its domestic funding requirements. The global financial secrecy system is a prime mover of these trillions into US coffers as well as the coffers of other hard-currency countries.

Some of the flows through the financial secrecy system come illegally out of developing countries into wealthier countries. Misinvoicing of trade, explained in the last chapter, is the most frequently used mechanism that can be reasonably analyzed from available data. Estimates place illicit financial flows impacting developing countries conservatively at close to $1 trillion annually. And this does not include cash, drugs,

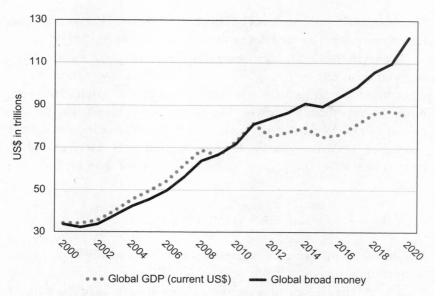

FIGURE 2.1 Growth of global GDP and broad money
Source: Prepared by the author using World Bank data.[1]

human trafficking, and other subterfuges that do not show up in data. More on this in the next chapter.

For decades Americans and Europeans have been persuaded to see themselves as extremely generous to the developing world with foreign aid, private investment, and military assistance. Reality is the opposite. Data indicates that more money appears to be flowing out of the developing world into Western accounts than is flowing via Western generosity into the developing world. Africa is particularly hurt by this phenomenon, with annual outflows—permanent outflows—likely exceeding $100 billion a year and perhaps much more, making Africa in all probability a net creditor to the rest of the world. In other words, it is not always the rich supporting the poor; often it is the poor supporting the rich. The financial secrecy system is designed to accomplish this outcome and performs its role with great effectiveness.

Much of the money flowing through the secrecy system goes into and out of tax havens. Estimates going back to the 1990s, at that time unsupported by good data, suggested that perhaps half of all international financial transfers pass through tax havens somewhere between initiation and completion. Evidence supporting this magnitude has emerged in recent years, indicating that 40 percent of all multinational corporation profits are booked through tax haven entities.[2] And for US corporations the estimate is 55 percent booked through tax havens.[3]

Data on the stock of money sitting offshore in tax haven accounts start, very conservatively, at $7 trillion.[4] If definitions are broadened to include unrecorded assets invested in or shifted through tax havens, then estimates rise to perhaps $36 trillion.[5] These caches, as explained earlier, are primarily motivated by desires to accumulate wealth in a hidden manner and only secondarily by desires to evade or avoid taxes. The financial secrecy system serves this primary motivation as its first order of business.

RIVERS OF NO RETURN

One might assume that at least the portion of broad money in safe short-term instruments—some $84 trillion—is earning good interest. Not correct. Much of it is earning interest at below the rate of inflation. Take the United States, as depicted in figure 2.2. Interest on short-term Treasuries is often below inflation rates. In other words, the difference—that is, the effective yield—is in negative territory.

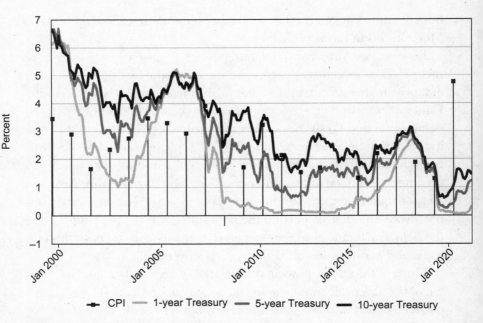

FIGURE 2.2 Treasury rates and consumer price index
Source: Prepared by the author using Treasury and CPI data retrieved from the Federal Reserve Economic Data.[6]

Then we have the phenomenon of negative interest rate securities, which are instruments that require you to accept a loss in order to put your money in. These securities appeal to investors wanting completely risk-free holdings even though they are declining in value. In 2020, Bloomberg estimated these securities at some $18 trillion globally.[7] Why would anyone do this when a government bond paying interest is pretty safe itself? Consider a bucket with a small hole in the bottom. A trickle of water may escape through this hole in the bottom, but this is unimportant as long as you can keep pouring more water into the top. In the same way, the constant availability of capital to add to negative interest rate accounts overrides the loss of interest on these accounts. The financial secrecy system facilitates such flows, adding to principal accumulations rendering interest rate and inflation losses of little or no concern for holders of these instruments. Arguments about the ultimate utility of financial instruments that simply store value weaken in the face of trillions of dollars of instruments intentionally losing value.

Recognize that some economic assets are purposefully unproductive. They may have collateral value or sentimental value but sitting idle they have no immediate economic benefit to their holders. For example, gold in India is commonly viewed in this way. Gold is important as security for low- and middle-income households, particularly for women. Indians hold about 25,000 metric tonnes of gold worth some $1.5 trillion, the highest level of any country. In fact, this equals about 40 percent of India's gross domestic product (GDP). If a young girl needs a laptop to progress in school, her mother may not be willing to sacrifice her gold dowry to enable the purchase. For the country as a whole, continued gold imports at hundreds of metric tonnes every year drain foreign exchange reserves. The Indian government has tried repeatedly to monetize gold, drawing small holdings out of hiding places, converting them to rupees, and shifting wealth into banks, bonds, and productive investments. Inserting a trillion-plus dollars into the economy could have a transformative impact.

RUNNING ON IDLE

Larry Summers, former US Treasury secretary, succinctly stated that "saving has become overabundant, new investment insufficient."[8] Since saving and investment must balance, the question is saving how and investing in what?

A global savings glut is evidenced by broad money now at some $120 trillion, or alternatively the $84 trillion excess above narrow money.

A defining (and frustrating) aspect of our era is that there's too much money—both ready cash and cheap or free borrowing capacity—in the hands of the wrong people. In a world awash in money, investors struggle to find returns and often settle for nothing. Strange as it seems, . . . money in the 21st century simply doesn't know what to do with itself.[9]

What could be done with some of these trillions? Build hospitals, provide vaccines, educate children, repair infrastructure, clean up the environment, pay for alternative forms of energy, and expand peace building. One comparison is offered here, to youth underemployment. Figure 2.3 plots the growth of broad money and the number of youths not in school or without meaningful jobs, indicating that more than 100 million young people are struggling to find productive work, and this was before the pandemic put tens of millions more out of work.

This depiction may understate real unemployment and underemployment because nations and individuals often hesitate to admit their

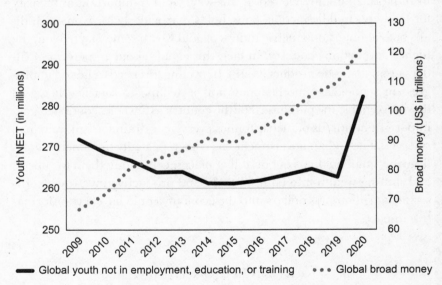

FIGURE 2.3 Youth not in education, employment, or training versus broad money

Source: Prepared by the author using data from the World Bank and the International Labour Organization.[10]

actual straits. For example, an urban shop of 100 square feet with six or eight employees, perhaps family members, might report that each is fully engaged. In reality, that shop could function as effectively with two or three employees. Social status and national pride get in the way of accurately compiling employment data.

The fact is that the mature megarich are hiding, saving, and playing with their money, while the youthful poor are underchallenged and restless. Languid wealth is a negative outcome of current capitalism, generating so much money that cannot or will not be used more constructively. This at a time when hundreds of millions of people around the world are idle and frustrated.

STILL BIGGER NUMBERS

Nor is broad money at $120 trillion and growing the biggest number meriting attention. Derivatives—credit default swaps, options, futures contracts, and the like—currently have a notional value of close to $600 trillion, which is about seven times global GDP.[11] US banks are exposed to some $200 trillion, most such derivatives contracts protecting interest rate movements but also foreign exchange transactions and price movements in equities and commodities.[12] Central banks and governments do not effectively control most of the derivatives market, making these instruments ripe for cascading collapse. While many worry about the sheer magnitude of these contracts, others estimate that the market risk of these instruments may be closer to $15 trillion, which is still huge.[13] The investor Warren Buffett described derivatives as "financial weapons of mass destruction."[14] Another commentator noted:

> The world of finance has become taken over by derivatives—investment plays that create no new jobs, create no new businesses, and spawn no new inventions, cures, or technologies.[15]

And $600 trillion is not even the biggest number meriting attention. Currency trading normally runs around $6 trillion a day, or about $1,500 trillion a year—that's one-and-a-half quadrillion dollars a year—more than 18 times global GDP. Algorithmic trading by preprogrammed computers buys and sells currencies constantly, leading many investors to call for greater transparency and regulation particularly in order to avoid the kind of "flash crash" that earlier occurred in the US stock market. Even John Maynard Keynes, certainly one of the world's smartest economists, lost money trading currencies.

So, we have broad money at more than $120 trillion, derivatives at $600 trillion, and currency trading at $1,500 trillion. Capitalism, making ample use of the financial secrecy system, accumulates and toys with vast sums of money, which as any rational analysis would confirm need to be more productively utilized. The simple truth is that the world has far more money than it usefully employs, and this is putting the point as politely as possible.

CRYPTO, DIGITAL, TOKENS, AND COINS

Playing with excess wealth goes on. Cryptocurrencies—bitcoin and ethereum being the most well known—now total some 10,000 in number. Originally conceived of as payment mechanisms, many have become simply opportunities for financial speculation, that is, stored value held in the hope that someone else will buy at a higher price. Like gold sitting in a vault, never touched, most cryptocurrencies are electrons sitting in a computer, never touched.

> Crypto, like gold, is built on a collective belief about its value. But so to an extent are all asset prices. And crypto is moving past the point where it can be considered its own self-contained world.[16]

Combined values of cryptocurrency transactions, highly volatile, hit $15 trillion in 2021.[17] Specialized money laundering services have arisen, calling themselves mixers, tumblers, and foggers. Cryptocurrency gambling sites are in the hundreds. Crypto crime exceeded $14 billion in 2021.[18] Some corporations are developing internal cryptocurrencies, which could become used in external trading. An Australian study concluded that close to half of crypto transactions examined had illegal purposes.[19] Criminals use cryptocurrencies to do business across borders, completely unseen, and domestic and foreign terrorists are already detected among users. Ransomware attacks, such as the one launched against Colonial Pipeline in the United States, demand crypto money in payment. Cryptocurrencies are often combined with derivatives trading, sometimes with speculators leveraging their plays as high as 125 times their original investments.[20]

Cryptocurrencies are the troubling subcomponent of the broader category of digital currencies. These are currencies without physical notes, existing only in electronic form and requiring user identification. Going digital in trade transactions is not inherently problematic, and many forms of electronic money exist, most convertible into currency notes. More arise every day, both regulated and unregulated. Most are subject to hacking and online theft. Central banks the world over are studying the issuance of digital currencies, well regulated and backed by national currencies, in part to meet the challenge posed by unregulated cryptocurrencies.

> Instead of withdrawing paper money from an ATM and putting it in your wallet, you could withdraw a Digital Dollar into a digital wallet on your smartphone. The promise of such innovation is easier access to money, reduced costs, faster transactions, and enhanced monetary functionality.[21]

Crypto tokens can represent units of value within a cryptocurrency exchange. Nonfungible tokens, or NFTs, represent ownership of a digital asset, such as a painting or a video. Like rare baseball cards, NFTs can have values in the millions. Stablecoins can be pegged to a particular currency or, with greater risk, to a debt instrument. Hundreds of variations on ways to deal in the crypto and digital worlds are constantly popping up.

Decentralized finance, or "DeFi," will undoubtedly grow. Regulatory efforts are tentative, and ways forward are uncertain. Secret currencies, added to broader financial secrecy mechanisms, bode ill for a capitalist system already weakening as a responsible partner with democracy.

Bank of America put the risks as follows:

> Cryptocurrencies challenge the ability of governments to levy taxes and to control capital flows. . . . Encrypted private wallets with digital assets that can be transferred across borders would seem to undermine the monetary sovereignty of every nation-state.[22]

UNSUSTAINABLE

So, this is the overarching financial reality today. Tens of trillions of dollars in broad money, a large portion of which is underproductive. Hundreds of trillions of dollars in derivatives, gambling speculatively on narrow price movements. One-and-a-half thousand trillion dollars in currency trading, far beyond what is needed for efficient market pricing. And cryptocurrencies threatening to take invisibility beyond any levels thus far seen.

Insert these realities into a world plagued by a health pandemic and suffering an economic meltdown, conditions that will no doubt be repeated again in different forms in future years. The world's wealth is not in the right places, adequately contributing to shared interests.

To make the point again, capitalism operating secretly and democracy operating openly are incompatible and unsustainable. This will become increasingly clear in the chapters that follow.

3

Corruption, Crime, and Terrorism

T HE FINANCIAL SECRECY system generates and moves tens of trillions of dollars. So what? So, these massive sums of money contribute directly to some of the most debilitating ills damaging the global community. The enormity of the harm done to shared safety and security is laid out in broad terms in this chapter, with specific examples illustrated in part II. Recall what has been said in preceding pages: Every single part of the modern financial secrecy system that moves and hides illegal and illicit money was originally created and is now principally operated by the upper echelons in wealthier countries.

CORRUPTION

The term "corruption" is usually directed toward nefarious activities involving government officials who enrich themselves through bribery and theft. There is nothing new about this phenomenon, but what is new is its pervasiveness and scale. By most estimates, corruption continues to rise. An analysis of 20 years of the World Bank's Control of Corruption Index showed that 85 percent of countries had worsened or not improved.[1] Similarly, Transparency International's Corruption Perception Index indicated worsening or stagnating positions in 65 percent of countries covered.[2]

The International Monetary Fund (IMF) in 2016 conservatively approximated global corruption at $1.5 to $2.0 trillion annually. This combines both petty corruption that remains within a country and grand corruption that normally transfers money out of a country, helped along by the financial secrecy system. The domestic component is the larger, but at least that money stays home. Grand corruption almost always takes money out, disappearing into the financial nether world. Local corruption is fought primarily through efforts by governments and civil society organizations, whereas grand corruption requires integrated actions by forwarding and receiving nations. And this is where pledges to deter grand corruption are failing in the wealthier countries for a simple reason: massive inflows of money from poor countries make the wealthier countries wealthier still, albeit at the expense of some of the poorest people on Earth.

To its credit, the United States has pursued many cases of grand corruption utilizing the Foreign Corrupt Practices Act (FCPA). Over the last four decades, the government has imposed more than 660 FCPA enforcement actions, most commonly against oil and gas companies, the pharmaceuticals industry, manufacturers, and technology firms.[3]

The key to understanding grand corruption is to recognize that Western operatives in the financial secrecy system facilitated virtually every single case documented or alleged across the past half century. Attaching blame to "those corrupt countries over there" tells only half the story.

Real Estate

A favorite channel for facilitating the flow of corrupt proceeds into Western economies is real estate, especially into cities well established as money laundering centers. Researching the market in England and Wales in 2015, Private Eye identified £170 billion worth of properties registered in the names of offshore companies in the preceding 10 years and estimated that a more accurate figure is likely past £200 billion.[4] A later study by Thomson Reuters and Transparency International's UK office found 44,022 land titles just in London that were owned by foreign companies, with 91 percent of them registered in secrecy jurisdictions.[5] Inflows of hot money have driven prices of homes and flats in London out of sight, rising twice as fast as incomes.

Amsterdam, taking advantage of pre-Brexit assets fleeing London and the Netherlands' leniency toward suspect money, estimates receipts of €12 billion into real estate in 2017.[6] One official lamented that "we don't know whether it is regulated money or not." He went on to say that

> money laundering in property definitely leads to . . . price increases. Citizens with a low or average income are driven out of the city. . . . This is problematic for teachers, nurses and police officers.

An estimated €100 billion annually is laundered in Germany, with some €30 billion going into real estate.[7] As an official noted,

> I know of one company in Berlin that is owned on paper by a Cypriot law firm, which owns 7,000 apartments in Berlin. . . . Real-estate money laundering . . . is high value investment . . . through . . . shell companies and complex investment structures.[8]

Spain's housing bubble burst in 2007, and prices in most areas are still below earlier highs. Russians, Middle Easterners, and Africans have poured money into Costa Brava and Barcelona, with Spanish officials asking virtually no questions about the origins of funds.

Canada is receptive to hot money leaving China, especially following the handover of Hong Kong in 1997. Vancouver is a preferred destination.

> What you have is a huge pool of very wealthy people who want to hedge against uncertainty back home. Combine anxious money—a lot of it—with a beautiful gateway city that has limited space to build, low property taxes, lax regulation on capital flows, and wealth-friendly immigration programmes, and you get a market like this one.
>
> [G]overnment officials have refused to admit that foreign capital is making it impossible to buy a house in Vancouver.[9]

A panel of experts estimated Canada's money laundering problem at C$46 billion, of which some C$7 billion went into and through British Columbia real estate.[10] Transparency International found that corporations spent C$28 billion over 10 years on more than 50,000 properties in the greater Toronto area, with most of the purchases made through disguised corporations with unknown owners.[11]

For decades, the United States has been the most attractive market for laundering through real estate. Southern Florida in particular services corrupt and criminal money stolen in other countries. A small sample of headlines across just six months in 2019 underlines the ongoing reality:

> "The Big Problem of Dirty Money in Miami Real Estate."[12]
> "Russian Allegedly Involved in Major Tax Fraud Bought South Florida Real Estate."[13]
> "US Government Sells Palm Beach Home of Convicted Venezuelan Money Launderer."[14]

"Former Ecuadorian Official Accused in Bribery Scandal Has Ties to SoFla Properties."[15]

"FBI Establishes Permanent Task Force to Investigate Corruption and Money Laundering in Miami's Real Estate Market."[16]

Again, these are just a few reported instances over only six months. Florida has had much the same problem for 40 years. Why did it take the Federal Bureau of Investigation so long to get serious?

Now, New York, and Louise Story and Stephanie Saul of the *New York Times*. A months-long investigation into one property, the Time Warner Center, found 200 shell companies registering ownership of condos, which by 2014 comprised 80 percent of transactions.

> On many deeds, the line for the buyer's signature is left blank, is illegible or is signed by a lawyer or other representative. Phone numbers are registered under lawyers' names; the owner's line on renovation permits is signed by Time Warner staff members; tax statements are addressed to the L.L.C.s. And because most of $5 million or more of the sales are in cash, there are few mortgage statements . . . that might identify an owner or trigger scrutiny.[17]

Florida and New York are not the only places affected. For residential purchases of $5 million or more across the United States, First American Data Tree found that almost half were executed by unknown buyers.[18] The Financial Crimes Enforcement Network (FinCEN) within the US Treasury Department reported in 2017 the results of data compiled for New York City, Miami, Los Angeles, San Francisco, San Diego, and San Antonio, indicating that 30 percent of real estate transactions have suspicious origins "in which shell companies are used to buy luxury real estate in 'all-cash' transactions."[19]

Global Financial Integrity calls US real estate a "kleptocrat's dream." GFI policy director Lakshmi Kumar states that real estate

> provides a really easy way to hide ill-gotten gains with little oversight and few questions asked. If you're a criminal, why would you not choose a method that allows you to flaunt your wealth openly, but also hide its illicit nature?[20]

University of California, Berkeley, economist Gabriel Zucman similarly asks,

Why do we allow a great chunk of Manhattan and London to be owned by faceless shells, potentially hiding criminals and money launderers?[21]

And the same can be asked about other cities including Honolulu, Sydney, Melbourne, Singapore, Dubai, and more. The fact is that corrupt and criminal money flowing from abroad into high-end real estate not only hurts countries out of which the money departs but also affects the affordability and character of cities into which the money arrives. A loss on both sides of the bargain.

Leaks

While governments are often slow to address large-scale corruption and endemic crime, whistleblowers can sometimes push the envelope. Since 2007, startling discoveries have poured out of caches of documents held close by bankers and lawyers. Some of the leakers are seeking to sell information for personal gain; others are serving more noble purposes. The International Consortium of Investigative Journalists (ICIJ), founded by the Center for Public Integrity in Washington, D.C., in 1997, became independent in 2017 and continued its extraordinarily explosive reports.

ICIJ released *Offshore Leaks* in 2013, drawing upon 2.5 million secret records spanning nearly 30 years detailing information on 130,000 offshore accounts belonging to companies and individuals in 170 countries and territories. *Swiss Leaks* emerged publicly in 2015, releasing data stolen several years earlier on 100,000 bank customers across 200 countries. *Lux Leaks* was released in November 2014 with exposure of favorable tax rulings in Luxembourg arranged by PricewaterhouseCoopers (PwC) and was followed the next month with a second release covering similar arrangements by the accounting firms Ernst & Young (EY), Deloitte, and KPMG.

For example, Disney allegedly set up a 34-step process and

> gathered ownership of at least 24 of its subsidiaries in France, Italy, Germany, the UK, Australia, the Cayman Islands, and the Netherlands under the umbrellas of two newly created companies—Mickey Mouse moving money in circles across the globe while transforming it from cash to debt to equity and back.[22]

Le Monde reported that by 2021, tens of thousands of offshore companies in little Luxembourg held assets of more than €6 trillion.[23]

Continuing its exposés, ICIJ produced the *Panama Papers* in 2016. It was the product of a massive leak that revealed the 40-year inner workings of Mossack Fonseca headquartered in Panama, exposing information on 214,488 offshore entities in 200 countries serviced by more than 14,000 banks, law firms, company incorporators, and assorted middlemen. The band kept playing with the release of *Bahamas Leaks* later in 2016, comprising 25 years of listings of 175,000 companies and trusts and their directors' filings with the Corporate Registry in Nassau and two financial service providers. The *Paradise Papers* followed in 2017, demonstrating how the law firm Appleby and a corporate services provider, Estera, in Bermuda allegedly helped hide billions of dollars belonging to 25,000 entities for people in 180 countries. *Luanda Leaks* followed, revealing alleged corruption in Angola.

Focusing on the United States, *FinCEN Leaks* emerged from the ICIJ in 2020, drawing upon thousands of Suspicious Activity Reports (SARs) lodged with the Financial Crimes Enforcement Network. Documents created and filed by nearly 90 financial institutions provide insights into questionable transactions by more than 10,000 organizations and people in 170 countries. Just from this cache alone, the five biggest filers in recent years are listed below:[24]

Institution	Number of SARs	Amount Flagged
Deutsche Bank	982	$1.3 trillion
JPMorgan Chase	107	$514 billion
Standard Chartered	232	$166 billion
Bank of New York Mellon	325	$64 billion
Barclays	104	$21 billion

The *Pandora Papers* capped off 2021, combining the work of 600 journalists associated with 150 media outlets in more than 100 countries analyzing nearly 12 million pages of documents, the largest such collaboration ever. Investigators focused particularly on 15 US states housing more than 200 US trusts that provide secrecy services rivaling, even exceeding, what is available in the world's most notorious tax havens. In South Dakota, for example, trusts can avoid state taxes and exist in perpetuity with beneficial owners never revealed, explaining why some $360 billion of suspect money linked to more than 300 officials and celebrities in 40-plus countries is managed there, under the disbelieving visages of George Washington, Thomas Jefferson, Abraham Lincoln, and Theodore Roosevelt carved into Mount Rushmore. The ICIJ is unsparing in its criticism:

> In an era of widening authoritarianism and inequality, the *Pandora Papers* investigation provides an unequaled perspective on how money and power operate in the 21st century . . . enabled by the U.S. and other wealthy nations.[25]

The ICIJ has consolidated its several releases into searchable spreadsheets. With appropriate caution, the organization notes that "we do not intend to suggest or imply that any people, companies or other entities included in the ICIJ Offshore Leaks Database have broken the law or otherwise acted improperly."[26]

Brooke Harrington, after nearly nine years of embedded research, wrote *Capital without Borders: Wealth Management and the One Percent.* In two interviews, she said the following:

> People who claim to love capitalism and care about capitalism thriving should be very worried about this, because what this concentration of capital in an increasingly small group of people's hands means is that the economic system is ossifying.[27]

> We are reaching sort of French Revolution levels of inequality and injustice.[28]

The "sort of" can be left out of the above statement. Capitalism has reached a point where change is necessary for its survival. This will become increasingly clear in later chapters.

CRIME

Tens of thousands of stories appear each year about transnational criminal activity, yet rarely do these stories go to the logical endpoint. Criminals are in business not to pursue a particular activity but to make money, and the financial secrecy system is the great facilitator of their enormous profits. Expanding and accessing this system has enabled cross-border crime to accelerate much faster than increases in global GDP.

The following is a good estimate of the annual retail value of 11 categories of criminal activity.[29]

Counterfeiting	$923 billion to $1.13 trillion
Drug Trafficking	$426 billion to $652 billion
Human Trafficking	$150.2 billion
Illegal Logging	$52 billion to $157 billion
Illegal Fishing	$15.5 billion to $36.4 billion
Illegal Mining	$12 billion to $48 billion
Illegal Wildlife Trade	$5 billion to $23 billion
Crude Oil Theft	$5.2 billion to $11.9 billion
Small Arms/Light Weapons Trafficking	$1.7 billion to $3.5 billion
Trafficking in Cultural Property	$1.2 billion to $1.6 billion
Organ Trafficking	$840 million to $1.7 billion
Total	**$1.6 trillion to $2.2 trillion**

Transnational organized crime in these forms is about $2 trillion a year. And this does not include cybercrime, credit card fraud, identity theft, and other opportunities presented by the digital age, for which good data are not available. Estimates, however, suggest that cybercrime may exceed the total of all the above.[30]

Counterfeiting
Counterfeiting represents half this estimate, spread across pharmaceuticals, tobacco, alcohol, electronics, luxury goods, and more. And $1 trillion may be a considerable underestimate, since well-established manufacturers are very reluctant to admit that a substantial percentage of products bearing their brand names may be fake. One-quarter of the world market for pharmaceuticals could be fake, with India and China the dominant producers, endangering the lives of millions of people. Counterfeit cigarettes in the tens of billions pour out of China, India, Dubai, Mexico, the Philippines, and elsewhere. Johnnie Walker whiskey appears with fake labels. Microsoft, Apple, HP, and other manufacturers of electronics have battled counterfeit clones found on shelves in wealthy and poor countries alike. Knock-off Rolex watches and look-alike Gucci handbags are available at a tenth the price of the authentic items. Meanwhile, the producers of these bogus goods line up at banks that are more than willing to accept billions in deposits from such fraudulent activities.

Drugs

A half-trillion-dollar business, the global drug trade gets more law enforcement and press attention than any other form of crime. Yet efforts to curtail the origination and flow of drugs show little success. As laid out in the US Central Intelligence Agency's "World Factbook," nearly every country is involved with illegal drugs as a cultivator, producer, supplier, transshipment point, gateway, consumer, or money launderer.

Missing from efforts of the Drug Enforcement Administration (DEA) in the United States is intense concentration on the money. Drug kingpins with limitless product to sell succeed in laundering virtually every dollar of their profits into the global financial system, made easy by the secrecy mechanisms explained in chapter 1. For decades, DEA's emphasis on the product and its consequences has been overriding; emphasis on the money has been inadequate.

Drugs are addressed again in the following pages on Guatemala, Venezuela, Myanmar, and the United States. A question is posed in chapter 10: "How do you curtail the supply of something that is in endless supply?" And the answer is given in chapter 10.

Human Trafficking

While statistics vary, several sources agree that at least 21 million people around the world have been trafficked, producing an estimated $150 billion a year in revenues for the perpetrators. This is the traffickers' profits, without attempting to calculate the diminution in productivity for uprooted children, women, and men in the countries from which they come. And the numbers trafficked and revenues generated also do not include the figures for human smuggling, because the smuggling side of this sordid business is usually done with the agreement of the individual trying to get into another country. The Asia-Pacific region and the wealthier countries of Europe and North America are primary destinations for those trafficked for exploitive labor or sexual activity. Once smuggled into their destination countries, these individuals often must surrender their travel documents to their employers, making escape nearly impossible. Unlike the drug trade, human trafficking kingpins often live in the countries into which their product arrives, then operate front companies and run enforcement gangs. The reality is frightening: at a minimum, 21 million people in the twenty-first century existing in conditions tantamount to slavery, duplicating the worst horrors of earlier times.

Illegal Logging

The largest component of resource theft, illegal logging, is devastating the forests of scores of countries in South and Central America, Central Africa, Southeast Asia, and Russia, leaving behind minimal revenues for those exploited and for their governments. From Amazonia an estimated 50 to 90 percent of timber is cut without authorization. From Indonesia, some 50 percent, and from Russia, with the world's largest conifer forests, 25 percent. For the world as a whole, 14 to 33 percent of timber is illegally harvested. And even these figures do not cover the whole of deforestation, which is a larger concept including cutting that has some vague level of official permission to create farming and grazing land. In the first 15 years of this century an estimated 300 million hectares of tree cover were eliminated, which is almost the size of India, or more than the combined size of Alaska, California, and Texas. Besides losses to biodiversity, this level of destruction by torch and chainsaw contributes to around 15 percent of greenhouse gas emissions.[31]

Consider the Amazon rainforest further. It comprises 64 percent of Brazil's territory, stretches into eight other countries, and is home to 390 billion trees and more than 50 million cows. Jair Bolsonaro, elected president of Brazil in 2019, apparently sees this vast resource as his country's ticket to wealth. So, he has sacked environmental officials, weakened enforcement, and rejected the world's condemnation of massive fires set to clear land, "giving free rein to agribusiness giants, mining corporations, and developers big and small."[32] Global Witness, which has examined illegal logging for decades, alleges that funding for Brazilian agricultural projects in the Amazon comes from Deutsche Bank, Santander, Blackrock, American Capital Group, and others.[33]

Lamenting such developments, Ricardo Galvão, a prominent Brazilian science official fired by Bolsonaro, said, "If the Amazon is destroyed, it will be impossible to control global warming."[34]

Unregulated Fishing

At least we still have the oceans. That is, until off-the-books fishing depletes this global resource. Referred to as illegal, unreported, and unregulated fishing (IUU), this part of the industry is estimated to account for 15 to 35 percent of the world's total fishing production. Thirty-three countries provide flags of convenience to fishing vessels, even including countries that are wholly landlocked.[35] Disguised entities own many of these vessels, so there is no trace of who is doing the fishing and who is selling the unregulated cargo. Crew members are sometimes enslaved for years, never setting foot on land. Waters off West and East Africa are particularly hard hit by trawlers from Europe and Southeast Asia. Drawing on 40 measures, the Global Initiative against Transnational Organized Crime found China to be the country most prevalent in and vulnerable to IUU fishing.[36] Unlike drug cartels that are accustomed to losing 40 percent or more of their product, virtually every illegally caught fish finds an unconcerned buyer and an unwitting consumer.

Organ Trade

With forests and fish succumbing to illegal activity, at least we still have our own bodies—that is, until someone wants an organ transplant and is willing to buy the needed anatomy at whatever cost. This is a business of well over $1 billion a year. The top five organs are kidney, liver, heart, lung, and pancreas, roughly selling for about $100,000 each. Annually, perhaps 12,000 illegal transplants are performed worldwide. Organs are harvested from the dead and even from the not quite dead, with donors receiving perhaps $5,000 to $20,000 and the recipient usually paying six figures. Kidneys account for about two-thirds of illegal organ sales because the human body has two, and thousands of desperate people and jailed criminals are forced to give up one. Syrian officials estimate that across the years of the civil war thousands of refugees have sold a kidney to stay alive or pay for passage out.[37]

Wildlife

Illegal wildlife trade is estimated at $5 billion to $23 billion annually. Between 2010 and 2012, 100,000 African elephants were reportedly killed for their ivory, and another report focusing on 2015 data estimates that 30,000 or more are killed annually.[38] China has been a huge consumer of illegal ivory. Rhino horn, supposedly a cure for cancer, hangovers, and compromised virility, has led to the slaughter of more than 1,000 rhinoceroses a year from 2011 through 2015. Lions and tigers are raised in captivity and slaughtered in Africa and Asia for their bones, claws, teeth, and skulls, supposedly valuable in aphrodisiacs and medicines. Gorillas, chimpanzees, pangolins, meerkats, iguanas, falcons, parrots, and even boa constrictors earn little money for the poachers, while percent markups for the retail sellers are in the thousands. The global supply chain stretches from the interiors of Africa, Latin America, and Southeast Asia via shipping and airline linkages and through corrupted ports and customs authorities to clandestine sellers and openly operating shops and then to the banks that readily take in deposits from known criminals.

Resources

Plundered oil, minerals, and gemstones easily find their way into international markets. A definitive study of oil theft, known as "bunkering," in the Niger Delta combining satellite imagery, interviews with scores of individuals illegally tapping pipelines and exporting crude oil, and reports from industry executives placed the figure above 240,000 barrels a day, an enormous loss to Nigerian government revenues.[39] Globally, theft of crude oil alone is conservatively estimated at $12 billion a year, and when further combined with theft of diesel fuel and gasoline, these crimes deplete resources in Colombia, Mexico, Venezuela, Russia, Iraq, Syria, Indonesia, and dozens of other countries. Drug cartels have become active in this growing line of business.

Theft and underpricing of solid minerals have plagued producing countries for more than a century. The Democratic Republic of the Congo (DRC) is the most exploited country. Copper, cobalt, zinc, tin, and tungsten remain underpriced and undercounted as they depart the country for industrial markets. Coltan, an ore that includes the strategic mineral tantalum used in billions of cell phones, is mined, transported across borders, and officially recorded as coming from countries that in fact have no such local production. Gold is illegally mined in Peru, Colombia, and Venezuela in quantities estimated as high as 90 percent of total production. Ghana has often turned a blind eye to foreign miners who bribe local officials, set up industrial-scale operations, and export gold at no value. Diamonds? The greatest example ever seen of undervaluing exports is the case of diamonds out of South Africa, which were recorded at zero value year after year for a century, finally ending when Nelson Mandela came to power in 1994.

Many more forms of criminal activity benefit from the shadow financial system that moves, shelters, and legitimizes ill-gotten gains: ocean piracy, illegal weapons trade, auto theft, extortion, kidnapping, antiquities smuggling, and more, plus the contributions of the twenty-first century such as cybercrimes, identify theft, credit card fraud, ransomware attacks, and the like. The important point made repeatedly is that every element of the financial secrecy system is designed specifically for the purpose of facilitating corrupt, criminal, and commercial dirty money. This is why the system was created; this is why the system is continuously upgraded and extended. All the modern instruments within the system have been developed in the wealthier countries by financial, corporate, and government interests. The system is doing precisely what it is intended to do.

Is there any bright spot within such a depressing litany? Yes, terrorist financing is addressed next, a good story quickly told.

TERRORISM

After the September 11, 2001, attack on the United States, which killed 2,977 victims at the World Trade Center in New York and the Pentagon in Washington, D.C., and near Shanksville, Pennsylvania, the United States immediately launched greatly enhanced efforts to go after terrorist financing. And it worked. Movements of money by terrorists situated outside the United States have been largely—not quite completely, but largely—pushed out of the legitimate financial system. This success well demonstrates what can be accomplished with political will and dogged determination. Four key components working together made this happen: the Patriot Act, tasking of multiple agencies, pressure on the rest of the world, and access to SWIFT interbank transaction data.

First, in the immediate weeks following 9/11, US senators Carl Levin, Chuck Grassley, Paul Sarbanes, Benjamin Nelson, Jon Kyl, and Mike DeWine pushed to include strengthened anti–money laundering legislation in the Patriot Act, going so far as to threaten its passage as a whole unless these provisions were incorporated. Citibank, JPMorgan Chase, and the American Bankers Association vigorously opposed the pending restrictions on their financial liberties, in the case of Citibank literally screaming in the halls of Congress. To no avail; the Act passed, giving the United States new tools to fight money laundering.

Among these measures is a flat-out prohibition against transactions through foreign shell banks, banks in the thousands functioning without identifying their owners. The Patriot Act says that no US bank can receive money from a foreign shell bank and no other financial institution in the world can send money to the United States that it has received from a foreign shell bank, and these prohibitions apply even to wire transfers that might hit New York correspondent banking accounts for a split second before flitting off somewhere else, and if any such transfers intentionally or accidentally occur, money can be seized from the foreign bank's correspondent account. Instantly, shell banks went out of business all over the world. Thus, a major element that had been a significant part of the financial secrecy system was almost completely taken off the table.

Second, the US government exponentially expanded efforts to track and block terrorist financing. This required a fresh approach. Traditional mechanisms of money laundering—dirty money made clean—are often the opposite in terrorist financing, which is usually clean money made dirty. Terrorist financing was coming from state sponsors, charitable donations, legitimate trade, construction profits, and more. Fighting this needed new tactics. Accordingly, the United States created the Terrorist Finance Tracking Program and designated 51—*fifty-one*—organs of the government to go after this single component of dirty money, stretching from Treasury to Customs to the National Security Council to intelligence agencies to military commands and more.[40] The work of these 51 agencies, departments, and commands within the US government focusing on this aspect of the puzzle is the key reason why the far greater part of terrorist financing has been forced out of legitimate banking channels.

A short note: If the United States seriously wants to curtail drug trafficking, as discussed in the preceding section, appoint 51 agencies of the government to go after drug money. Not the product; the money. Drug cartels are not in business to smuggle drugs; they are in business to make money. Seize their money; evaporate their business.

The third component of fighting terrorist financing was pressure, serious pressure, exerted on foreign governments and banks to both assist the United States and adopt their own programs and procedures. More than a dozen international conventions, guidelines, and groups already existed, decidedly underperforming in anti–money laundering efforts. Treasury Department officials and US intelligence agents were heavy-handed in dealing with recalcitrant governments, particularly in Europe and the Persian Gulf, and forced cooperation. The pressure tactics ruffled a lot of feathers, and they worked. Today, international collaboration in fighting terrorist financing is both broad and deep.

The fourth component of success was gaining access to data from SWIFT, the Society for Worldwide Interbank Financial Telecommunications, a cooperative based in Belgium with US offices. The financial information, not the money, facilitating wire transfers typically goes through SWIFT, the preferred intermediary between correspondent banks. With such information, US officials could begin to see who is sending money to whom. Leaning hard on the officers of SWIFT, US counsels quickly negotiated a confidential agreement that, via submission of a subpoena and later with approval of an auditor, the cooperative would provide data on specified types of transactions deemed suspicious by some of the 51 agencies focusing on terrorist financing. In 2009, the European Parliament likewise negotiated an agreement with SWIFT on cooperation in data mining. Thus, terrorists were on notice that wire transfers were no longer among their viable options for sending money around the world, the last major piece in curtailing their use of the legitimate financial system.

Senator Charles Grassley has continued his decades-long leadership on these issues: "The best way to stop terrorism is to get them where it hurts most: the pocketbook."[41]

Today terrorists are heavily constrained, still operating locally but largely dependent on self-financing, as with ISIS and Boko Haram; on state support as with Hezbollah, which receives funding from Iran, Syria, and other countries; or on third parties, as have aided Hamas in recent years.[42] Financial constraint is the reality that has moved terrorists into criminal pursuits and, parallel, into alliances with criminal gangs to the point where the two activities are now often conjoined or nearly indistinguishable. Terrorists are into kidnapping, extortion, oil and minerals theft, antiquities smuggling, drug trading, and more. Criminal gangs exploit terrorist tactics to control their territories and markets. Over the last two decades criminals and terrorists have found more synergies than conflicts, ensuring that they will be around for a long time to come.

A final word on corruption, crime, and terrorism, at least the financial realities surrounding some of these activities, the subject of this chapter. Each of these illegal activities is currently fought with law enforcement approaches, going after the perpetrators with legislation, investigation, intelligence, police, courts, and civil actions. Each poses its own form of threat to the democratic-capitalist system, necessitating enormous expenditures of time and money in pursuit of safety and security. But law enforcement is dreadfully compromised when the financial secrecy system is working so widely and determinedly to handle trillions of dollars of corrupt, criminal, and commercial dirty money shifting and sheltering around the world. What is required is, yes, law enforcement but, more importantly, a systemic approach that replaces the secrecy system with one that operates with transparency and accountability. Practical measures to accomplish this will be addressed in chapter 14.

In the next subject—on economic inequality—law enforcement has a smaller role to play, and systemic change has by far the larger role to play. Income and wealth disparities are dividing the world, requiring renewal within capitalism if it is to survive with its companion, democracy.

4

Income and Wealth Inequality

ALICE RIVLIN, FOUNDING DIRECTOR of the Congressional Budget Office, former vice chair of the Federal Reserve Board, and for years an economic scholar of renown at the Brookings Institution in Washington, D.C., had this to say just before her passing in May 2019:

> When we look deeply at the political and cultural divisions cleaving the United States, we consistently find extremes of inequality adding fuel to these fires. Stark differences in current economic security and future prospects bring fear, distrust, and resentment. A truly great country . . . would rise to the challenge to heal the wounds of hate and division by giving all Americans opportunities to participate in a growing economy that offers them shared prosperity.[1]

Income and wealth inequalities have been problematic across the globe for decades. Capitalism, as it has come to be pursued through widespread use of the financial secrecy system, is a principal contributor to economic divisions. The global financial crisis of 2007–2008 and the global pandemic beginning in 2020 underline the urgency of resolving inequities that are now so evident and so threatening to prosperity and progress.

POVERTY

Before going forward into income and wealth inequality, commentary on poverty is appropriate. The world knows how it should be dealing with poverty, and the urgency to do so is morally compelling. The extent of poverty has declined globally, with startling reductions achieved in the last quarter century. Capitalism is attuned through charitable instincts to exert at least some modest efforts toward ending poverty. But capitalism frankly does not know how to curtail widening inequality, and inequality is the far greater threat to democracy. Ending poverty is a vital but insufficient step for achieving a more sustainable world. This book is about changes required within capitalism if it is to contribute its full share toward the continuance of democracy.

Having said this, a few points about poverty are appropriate here. In 2018 the World Bank reported that across the 25 years from 1990 to 2015, the number of people living in extreme poverty, defined as $1.90 or less per day in purchasing power parity, declined from some 2 billion to 736 million, that is, from 36 percent to 10 percent of the world's population (not including South Asia). Much of this progress occurred in East Asia and the Pacific region, with China achieving dramatic change, lifting hundreds of millions out of poverty. Sub-Saharan Africa, unfortunately, is moving in the opposite direction, with the number living in extreme poverty rising from 278 million to 413 million across the period, half of them children, with oil-rich Nigeria leading the way. Taking the broad view, François Bourguignon, former chief economist of the World Bank, draws the picture as follows:

> For the first time since the Industrial Revolution two centuries ago, economic progress is moving more quickly than population growth, . . . overwhelmingly because of accelerated growth in average income per capita in the developing world. This is a stunning turn of events.[2]

Additional measures of poverty indicate that a quarter of the world lives on less than $3.20 a day, and almost half of the world lives on less than $5.50 a day. Multidimensional definitions of poverty encompassing education, consumption, and access to infrastructure paint a much more extensive picture of poverty than can be conveyed in monetary measures alone and indicate that half the poor within this broader definition are under 18 years of age. Societal poverty lines, which the World Bank introduced in its 2018 analysis and take into account hundreds of measures, interpret poverty as relative to the communities and nations in which it exists. By this measure, nearly 30 percent of the world is living in poverty. Even pre-COVID, the Food and Agriculture Organization said that three billion people around the world cannot afford a healthy diet.

FIGURE 4.1 Deaths due to violence and poverty (in millions)
Source: Compiled by Professor Thomas Pogge, Yale University. Used
with permission.

Yale philosopher Thomas Pogge estimates that 18 million people a
year die of poverty-related causes. This is about 50,000 a day, more than
2,000 an hour, more than 30 a minute, more than 60 since the reader
began turning the pages of this chapter. The comparison in figure 4.1 to
examples of violent deaths in previous cataclysms drives the point home.
Some longtime observers find the enormity of this reality, particularly
when compared to more widely recalled conflicts and tragedies, the most
compelling case for curtailing extreme poverty.

For many people there is an unfortunate side effect arising from the
focus on poverty. It detracts from focus on the separate problem of inequality. It makes the richest and most ardent within capitalism think
that aiding the needy is the extent of responsibility toward the world's less
fortunate. The positive duty to be charitable sufficiently overrides any negative duty to do no harm. The comforting argument is, help the poor become somewhat better off, and the rich can rise to unlimited heights.
Capitalism has no answer to rising inequality and therefore asserts that
only poverty is important. This kind of thinking, carried deeper into the
twenty-first century, will undermine the democratic-capitalist system.

INCOME INEQUALITY

Inequality has been with us forever, addressed in cogent and troubled
writings by Plato, St. Thomas Aquinas, Hobbes, Rousseau, and scores
of other early thinkers. The world has survived, so why worry? Because

they were writing when the world had fewer than 1 billion people, and today the world has 8 billion people, rising to a predicted 10 billion people or more by the end of the twenty-first century (figure 4.2). This is a quantitative and qualitative difference. Put aside any idea that the past is adequate prologue for the future. In this century of staggering income and wealth disparities, those who feel disadvantaged and downtrodden will force change, and those who are exceptionally fortunate must accept and encourage change. The combination of population pressures and economic motivations will be unrelenting.

As population soars, capitalism drives inequality. Globalization, technology, and financial deregulation are frequently cited as explanations for the separation between rich and poor. Each of these realities is important, but underlying all explanations is capitalism's new motivation for secrecy and the structures created to facilitate secrecy, mechanisms that are dedicated to moving and hiding illicit and opaque income and wealth.

With this structure in place, more countries are experiencing rising income inequality than falling income inequality. Gini coefficients, a measure of inequality preferred by economists, reveal the same conclusion in each of four careful studies of this phenomenon as depicted in figure 4.3. Quite simply, citizens across the globe are correctly sensing that inequality is widening and that for many, personal prospects are narrowing.

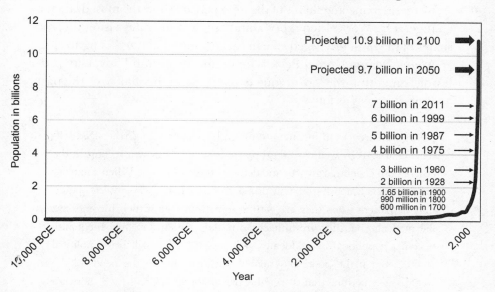

FIGURE 4.2 World population over the last 12,000 years
Source: Max Roser, Hannah Ritchie, and Esteban Ortiz-Ospina, "World Population Growth," OurWorldInData.org.[3]

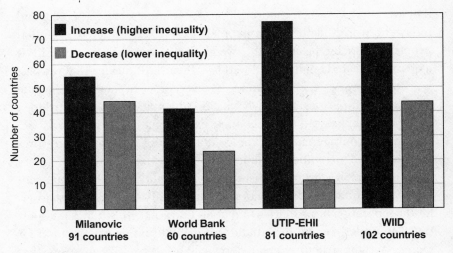

FIGURE 4.3 Countries with changes in income inequality (by source)
Source: Prepared by the author using data from Branko Milanovic, the World Bank, the University of Texas Inequality Project, and the World Income Inequality Database.[4]

Increases in income shares of the top 10 percent of the population are evident in major countries, as shown in figure 4.4.

Increases in income shares of the top 1 percent show the most dramatic change. The World Inequality Database demonstrates rising income shares of the most privileged elite in each country analyzed in figure 4.5.

Angus Deaton, Nobel Prize winner and Princeton University professor, lamenting the "grotesque expansions in inequality of the past 30 years," argues as follows:

> [L]arge differences in income are fueled by . . . and can further feed self-serving actions by well-placed groups to increase their own income at the cost of both economic growth and democratic governance. When whatever growth exists is not shared, new problems arise. Those who are left behind may be patient when they are getting something, but if their incomes are flat or declining, they are unlikely to remain patient for long. Inequality becomes a political issue. Ideally such dissatisfaction will bring political change. But if the political system is sensitive only to the needs of the wealthy—something that is arguably true in the U.S. Congress—there is a direct threat to political stability and, ultimately, to democracy itself. If the main political parties offer nothing to those who are excluded, they may turn to political remedies or candidates that threaten liberal democracy.[7]

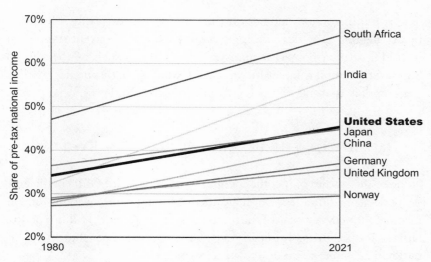

FIGURE 4.4 Share of income held by top 10% (1980–2021)
Source: Prepared by the author using data from the World Inequality
Database.[5]

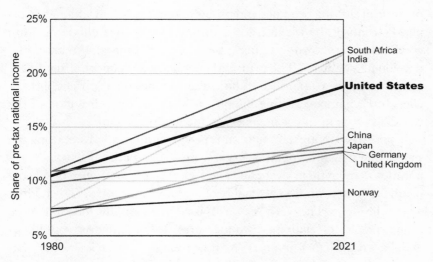

FIGURE 4.5 Share of income held by top 1% (1980–2021)
Source: Prepared by author using data from the World Inequality Database.[6]

    Two broad conclusions are generally agreed: income differences be-
tween many countries are declining, while income differences within many
countries are rising. The decline in between-country incomes is particularly
driven by rising national incomes in China, India, and other Asian states as
these nations adopt technologies and move toward middle-class status.

The rise in income differences within countries is certainly influenced by astonishing growth in the billionaire class and apparent stagnation in middle-class incomes in many richer countries such as the United States. Stagnation is sometimes disputed; what is not disputed is a belief, a perception, that stagnation is real, affecting lives and prospects.

IMPACT OF THE FINANCIAL SECRECY SYSTEM

None of the studies of income inequality, whether with Gini coefficients or by decile or quintile groupings, adequately take into account hidden income, the very purpose of the financial secrecy system. Trillions of dollars are stashed invisibly outside of citizens' countries, not showing up in national accounts or taxpayers' filings.

Thus, the financial secrecy system directly links to inequality. The most commonly utilized element within this secrecy system is trade misinvoicing, the deliberate mispricing of cross-border trade for the specific purpose of shifting revenues and profits across borders in a hidden manner. Percentages by which trade is misinvoiced correlate to rising Gini coefficients, as shown in figure 4.6 covering 58 emerging market and developing countries. The principal operating component of the financial secrecy system—falsified trade—draws money out of dozens of countries, further impoverishing billions of people. For each region of the world, as trade misinvoicing goes up, inequality goes up.

The secrecy motivation now entrenched within capitalism, using the supporting structures of tax havens, secrecy jurisdictions, disguised corporations, anonymous accounts, and more, is a direct cause of income inequality that degrades the quality of life for women, men, and children across the globe. The word "cause" is used intentionally, meaning more than a simple correlation of two measures. Taking hundreds of billions of dollars out of emerging market and developing countries, accumulating to trillions of dollars permanently transferred into wealthier countries, leaves poverty and inequality in its wake.

For half a century beginning in the 1960s, Western development experts, those scholars and practitioners engaged in efforts to bring economic prosperity to poorer nations, failed to put both sides of the development equation on the table: total money in and total money out. A collective ethos within the discipline focused on aid and investment going into developing countries and completely failed to ask what is com-

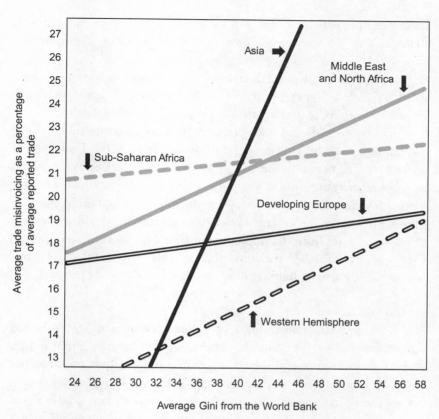

FIGURE 4.6 Trade misinvoicing between reporters and partners versus inequality (2012–2016)

Source: Global Financial Integrity. Used with permission.

ing out of developing countries. Not that they ignored available data; they did not ask the right questions.

How is this possible? Other branches of the economics profession were admirably asking the right questions within their spheres. Yet, with tens of millions of people dying of economic deprivation and hundreds of millions of people living lives of utter desperation, how does a focused group of development professionals disregard something so basic? Well, this much is going into developing countries; how much is coming out of developing countries? A few early papers guardedly attempted to address flight capital, money invested abroad, without making an effort to determine how much was legal and stayed on the books of countries from which it came and how much was illegal and disappeared from any record in the countries from which it came. The question has been asked many times, "How did such a basic deficit in the discipline occur over so many decades?" No answer has ever been offered.

Jean-Paul Sartre, twentieth-century existentialist, speaks of "the moment at which the question transforms the questioner."[8] For virtually the entire community of development experts, this moment never arrived.

There was one notable exception. A Burundian economist, Léonce Ndikumana, and his colleague, James Boyce, both at the University of Massachusetts, began in the late 1990s to address the illicit component of money emerging from developing countries. Others advanced their work a few years later, and today a number of analysts are coming to grips with magnitudes and methodologies surrounding the measurement of resource flows from developing countries. The World Bank and the IMF, addressed further in chapter 10, are, with extreme reluctance, tiptoeing into the arena, half a century too late for billions of people.

Wealthy Countries Too

Nor is this an issue limited only to developing countries. Across the last half century trillions of dollars have poured out of wealthy countries into secrecy sinks, hiding and sheltering money and evading and avoiding taxes. Economic titans in past generations at least kept their money at home. Today, megawealthy titans and major corporations take much of their money abroad. Trickle-down economics does not work when streaming-out economics is the norm.

A growing group of analysts is finally focusing on economic inequality in both richer and poorer countries. Thomas Piketty's book *Capital in the Twenty-First Century*, first appearing in French in 2013 and since translated into 40 languages, has sold 2.5 million copies worldwide. Piketty merits singular praise for asking the right questions, the hard questions, and then courageously addressing these questions with answers couched in orders of magnitude. Chastising his fellow economists (case in point, development economists who for 50 years failed to ask the right questions), he persuasively argues that "economics should never have sought to divorce itself from the other social sciences and can advance only in conjunction with them."[9]

Addressing the world's richest nation, Piketty says:

Since 1980, however, income inequality has exploded in the United States. The upper decile's share increased from 30–35 percent of national income in the 1970s to 45–50 percent in the 2000s. . . . [T]he United States may set a new record around 2030 if inequality of income from labor—and to a lesser extent inequality of ownership of capital—continue to increase as they have done in recent decades. The top decile would then claim about 60 percent of national income, while the bottom half would get barely 15 percent.[10]

Not all the causes of income inequality are hidden from view. Everyone knows that executive pay has exploded since the end of the 1950s. The Economic Policy Institute (EPI) based in Washington, D.C., produced the analysis in figure 4.7, showing CEO pay at the top 350 US firms at 351 times worker pay, up from less than 20 times worker pay in the post–World War II era, lauded by Tom Brokaw in his book as "The Greatest Generation."

Commenting on its 2020 analysis, EPI states that

escalation of CEO compensation, and of executive compensation more generally, has fueled the growth of top 1.0 percent and top 0.1 percent incomes, generating widespread inequality.

[An] implication of rising pay for CEOs and other executives is that it reflects income that otherwise would have accrued to others: What these executives earned was not available for broader-based wage growth for . . . workers. It is useful, in this context, to note that wage growth for the bottom 90 percent would have been nearly twice as fast . . . had wage

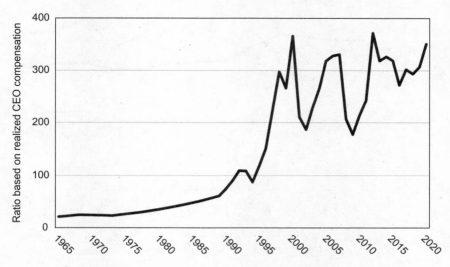

FIGURE 4.7 CEO-to-worker compensation ratio (1965–2020)
Source: Chart prepared by Lawrence Mishel and Jori Kandra, Economic Policy Institute. Used with permission.[11]

inequality not grown. Most of the rise of inequality took the form of redistributing wages from the bottom 90 percent to the top one percent.[12]

As billionaire and millionaire classes get richer, workers receive a declining share of national income, a phenomenon experienced in major countries since 1980 and, as illustrated in figure 4.8, since 2014. Deborah Hargreaves, studying both the United States and the United Kingdom, nails the importance of this issue:

> It is time for the business sector to listen to the moderate voices for reform or reap the consequences of growing inequality, anti-business sentiment and possibly more dramatic clashes. If we don't rise to the challenge, the fundamental trust that makes a liberal market democracy function could be damaged beyond repair. We run the risk of sleepwalking into a dystopian future of extreme income disparities and the unrest that could bring.[14]

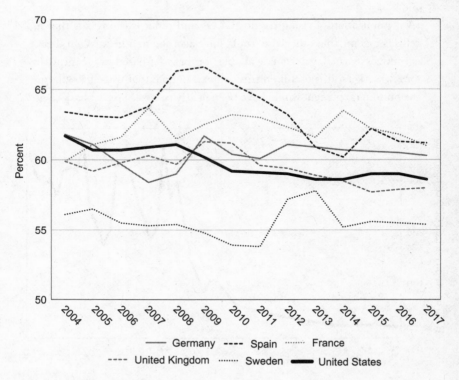

FIGURE 4.8 Labor income share as a percentage of GDP
Source: Prepared by the author using data from the International Labour Organization.[13]

Fading Optimism

The American dream of living better than one's parents is withering. Creatively utilizing tax and census data, a team of Stanford, Harvard, and University of California, Berkeley, scholars led by Raj Chetty produced an extraordinary analysis showing that, whatever one's income group at birth, chances are strong that income levels would be less than that of their parents. Hardest hit are those born in the sample years 1960, 1970, and 1980, with only about a 50–60 percent chance of exceeding the income level of their parents, as shown in figure 4.9.

Explaining further the import of their findings, Chetty et al. state that

> children's prospects of earning more than their parents have faded over the past half-century in the U.S. The fraction of children earning more than their parents fell from approximately 90 percent for children born in 1940 to around 50 percent for children entering the labor market today. . . . [16]
>
> [Income] mobility fell particularly sharply in the industrial Midwest, where rates . . . fell by 48 percentage points in Michigan and about 45 percentage points in Indiana, Illinois, and Ohio.[17]

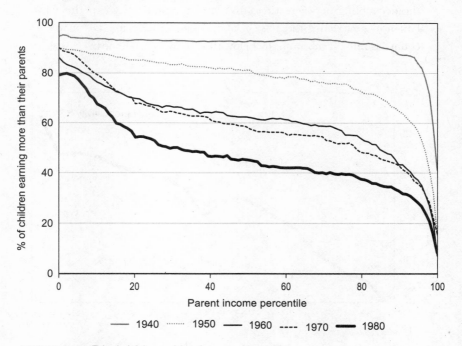

FIGURE 4.9 Diminishing odds of upward mobility
Source: Raj Chetty et al., "The Fading American Dream: Trends in Absolute Income Mobility since 1940." Used with permission.[15]

The *New York Times* effusively praised this analysis:

> Research has shown that people's happiness is heavily influenced by their
> relative station in life. And it's hard to imagine a more salient compari-
> son than to a person's own parents. . . . [This is] a portrait of an econ-
> omy that disappoints a huge number of people who have heard that they
> live in a country where life gets better, only to experience something quite
> different. Their frustration helps explain . . . Americans' growing distrust
> of nearly every major societal institution, including the federal government,
> corporate America, labor unions, the news media, and organized religion.
> In the industrial Midwestern states . . . going backward is the norm.[18]

"Going backward" is certainly not the result of working less and producing less in the United States, and this is also true in many more high-
income countries. The value of what workers are producing outstrips
their participation in these gains (figure 4.10). The *Global Wage Report
2018/19* states that

> the decoupling between wages and labour productivity explains why
> labour income shares (the share of labour compensation in GDP) in many
> countries remain substantially below those of the early 1990s.[19]

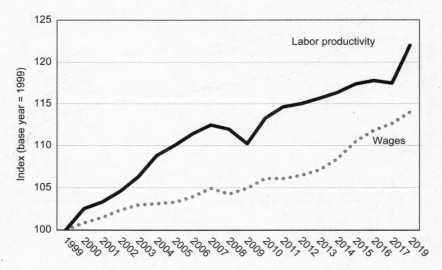

FIGURE 4.10 Trends in average real wages and labor productivity in
high-income countries
Source: Chart from the International Labour Organization.[20]

Singling out the United States, an Economic Policy Institute analysis demonstrates a widening gap between workers' productivity and pay (figure 4.11). Post–World War II years were quite stable, with separation beginning in the early 1980s and continuing since.

Economic analysts typically prefer to ask "what" based on hard data rather than "what if" based on conjecture. In a stunning piece of work, an economist and a mathematician at Rand Corporation joined forces to examine the relatively modest levels of income disparities in the United States in the post–World War II years and asked what if such modest levels of disparities continued up to the present, that is, rising in proportion to GDP. What they found was that

> the rate of income growth at the median of the distribution was less than one third of the rate of growth of real per capita GDP. Unlike the growth patterns in the 1950s and 1960s, the majority of full-time workers did not share in the economic growth of the last forty years, . . . did not share in the benefits of economic growth to any significant degree.

From 1975 to 2018, the difference between the aggregate taxable income for those below the 90th percentile and the equitable growth [consistent with GDP] totals $47 trillion.[22]

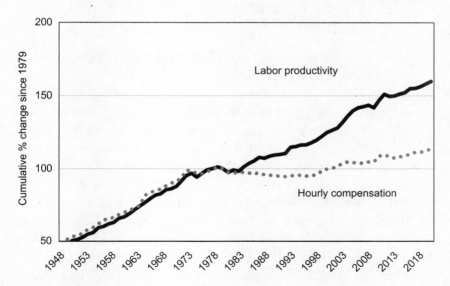

FIGURE 4.11 Productivity growth and hourly compensation growth (1948–2019)

Source: Chart by Lawrence Mishel, Economic Policy Institute. Used with permission.[21]

In other words, 90 percent of US workers are cumulatively $47 trillion behind where they would be if they had just held their own as the economy grew. Add two more years and this can no doubt be rounded to $50 trillion. Commenting further on this study, two analysts put it bluntly:

> Whatever your race, gender, educational attainment, urbanicity, or income, the data show, if you earn below the 90th percentile, the relentlessly upward redistribution of income since 1975 is coming out of your pocket.[23]

Emmanuel Saez and Gabriel Zucman, both at the University of California, Berkeley, also delve into the "counterfactual" question:

> If macro growth had been equitably shared from 1980 to 2018, the average pre-tax income of the bottom half of the income distribution would have been 57 percent higher in 2018 that it was in actual fact.[24]

Especially hard hit are millennials, those born between 1981 and 1996, called "the unluckiest generation in U.S. history":

> The Great Recession pushed young workers a few steps down the wage ladder. Research shows they never recovered. . . . It's happening again, to many of those same young workers.[25]

William Gale at the Brookings Institution, together with other colleagues, agrees:

> Substantial economic inequality has been an enduring fixture of millennials' adulthood. While every generation faces its own unique opportunities and challenges, many people feel that the obstacles facing the millennial generation are especially acute.[26]

Decades of working hard and sharing less, coupled with growing frustrations of younger generations, have now caught up with the United States and other countries. Severe economic inequality exacerbates perceptions of other differences, including those of race, gender, and origin. Shared economic prosperity, if real, can moderate the impact of such differences.

But this reality—income inequality—is not the worst of the picture. Wealth inequality is far greater, threatening stability within and across nations.

WEALTH INEQUALITY

The wealth of the Walton family, controlling shareholders of Walmart, is increasing at $100 million a day. Newly hired Walmart associates are reportedly paid about $100 a day. Is this capitalism performing at its best—$100 million a day versus $100 a day?

For those Americans who hold much of their wealth in stocks, the 40-year run-up in share prices has been stunning (figure 4.12). For those who are dependent on an hourly wage, grounds for decades-long angst are real.

Thomas Piketty points out that wealth inequality is always more than income inequality and has been throughout history. "The distribution of capital ownership (and of income from capital) is always more concentrated than the distribution of income from labor."[28] In his starkest statement, Piketty says that "the consequences for the long-term dynamics of . . . wealth distribution are potentially terrifying."[29]

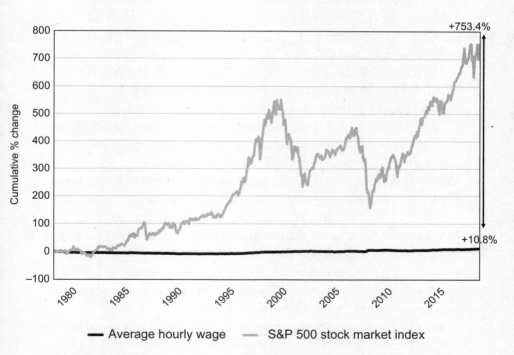

FIGURE 4.12 Stock market growth versus wage growth (1979–2019)
Source: Chart prepared by Institute on Taxation and Economic Policy, using Federal Reserve economic data and S&P 500 historical data. Used with permission.[27]

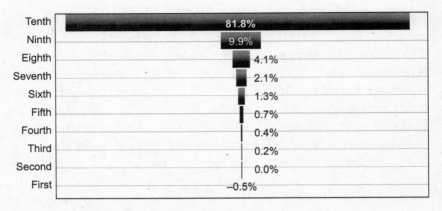

FIGURE 4.13 Share of global wealth (by decile)
Source: Prepared by the author using Credit Suisse data.[30]

The best depiction of wealth inequality is provided in funnel charts as in figure 4.13, derived from Credit Suisse's 2021 Global Wealth Report. Nearly 82 percent of global wealth belongs to the top 10 percent, leaving only 18 percent of wealth for the bottom 90 percent. In fact, Credit Suisse indicates that the bottom 10 percent have a negative net worth, with debts exceeding assets.

Currently, global wealth is more than $400 trillion, tripling in real dollars in the last 20 years. Of this, the wealthiest 1 percent alone are now pushing toward half the total (figure 4.14).

And even these wealth measures are probably underestimated because they may not take fully into account money stashed in secret outside citizens' countries of origin. Gabriel Zucman and colleagues combined information from the previously mentioned *Swiss Leaks* records of HSBC Private Bank holdings, the names of account holders revealed in the *Panama Papers*, and income and wealth records from three Scandinavian countries: "[A]bout 90–95% of all individuals on the HSBC list that could be matched to a tax return did not report their Swiss bank account."[32] Focusing on the wealthiest: "We find that the top 0.01% of the wealth distribution . . . evades about 30 percent of its taxes. . . . [R]esults found in Scandinavia are likely to be a lower bound for most of the world's countries."[33]

Broadly, these researchers estimate that about 10 percent of global GDP is held in offshore havens, which currently would amount to about $8 trillion. The Organisation of Economic Co-operation and Development (OECD) recently reported an estimate of $11 trillion.[34] James Henry produced substantially higher figures in 2013, estimating that $21 to $32 trillion is in "hidden financial assets held offshore." He goes on to comment as follows:

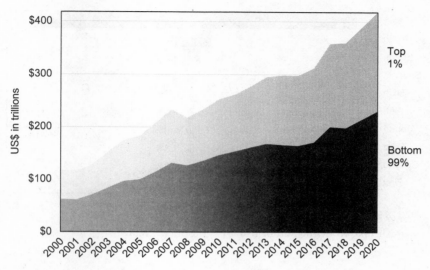

FIGURE 4.14 Global wealth of top 1% versus bottom 99%
Source: Prepared by the author using Credit Suisse data.[31]

> This hidden offshore sector is large enough to make a significant differ-
> ence to all of our conventional measures of inequality. . . . For most coun-
> tries, global financial inequality is not only much greater than we
> suspected, but it has been growing much faster. . . . [T]his offshore
> sector . . . is basically designed and operated, not by shady no-name
> banks located in sultry islands, but by the world's largest private banks,
> law firms, and accounting firms, headquartered in First World capitals
> like London, New York, and Geneva.[35]

Quite possibly, even likely, all three sets of estimates are short of the
mark. The financial secrecy system, in business for half a century, shelters illicitly generated and often unseen wealth in the tens of trillions of
dollars, powering inequality in its wake.

This chapter began with a discussion of why the main focus is on inequality rather than on poverty. Figure 4.15 demonstrates what global
wealth would look like if we took money from the top decile and allevi-
ated the poverty of the entire lower half of the world's population, making every one of these almost 4 billion people in the bottom five deciles
financially equal to those in the sixth decile.

Notice that economic inequality is hardly changed. Instead of owning 82 percent of the world's wealth, the richest 10 percent would then
still own more than 76 percent of the world's wealth. The point is that

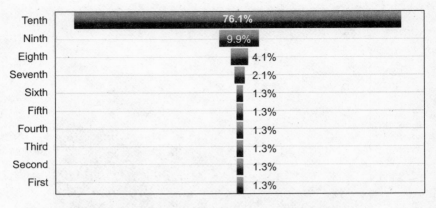

FIGURE 4.15 Share of global wealth (with bottom six deciles equal)
Source: Prepared by the author using Credit Suisse data.[36]

addressing poverty alone does not solve the problem of inequality. Marginally alleviating poverty for the poorer half of the world, those living on just a few dollars a day, is completely laudable and absolutely urgent. But it does not solve the problem of the clash between capitalism and democracy, a clash driven in large part by bewildering levels of economic inequality. Concentrating on the bottom of the scale cannot substitute for changing the top of the scale. Far more equitable sharing of the world's bounty is necessary if the democratic-capitalist system is to survive.

With 82 percent of the world's wealth currently at the top of the scale in the hands of the top 10 percent, recall the description of the financial secrecy system in chapter 1. This is a system created and expanded over the last half century specifically for the purpose of moving money from the bottom to the top, poor to rich, criminal to legitimate, and corrupt to respectable. This is the intent of the system, not an unfortunate outcome. It does exactly what it is designed to do, and democratic capitalism is thereby threatened.

OTHER VOICES

In addition to multiple indices published annually, a vast literature surrounds issues of income and wealth inequality as well as disparities in many other conditions of human existence. A few quotes suggest the richness of scholarship and commentary focusing on the problem.

Fight Inequality: "We are at an extreme point in history. . . . The inequality crisis is fuelling injustices in land, health, education, taxation, worker's rights, women's right and human rights."[37]

Wall Street Journal: "Economics has no accepted theory of inequality—no scientific understanding of the mechanisms and processes that create it. Until recently, wealth distribution was regarded by many economists as a minor issue compared to growth."[38]

New York Times: "The solutions that have currency seem calculated to spare corporations and the wealthiest people from having to make any sacrifices at all, as if there is a way to be found to tilt the balance of inequality while those at the top hang on to everything they have."[39]

Darren Walker, president of the Ford Foundation, asks the right questions:

Make no mistake, the exploitation of our democratic-capitalist system is intentional. Too often, the powerful and privileged who might stem the callousness and corruption seem largely to ignore it, avoid it, minimize it or, worst of all, maximize it for their own gain. As our system falters under the inequality it has produced, as society seems increasingly strained by—and susceptible to—ever-widening gaps, those of us who have benefitted from this inequality need to look in the mirror and ask why. Then we should ask how we fix it, with justice as our objective.[40]

Paul Krugman, Nobel Prize winner and commentator, opines, that

these days almost everyone has the (justified) sense that America is coming apart at the seams. Political polarization has marched side by side with economic polarization, as income inequality has soared.[41]

As Joseph Stiglitz states,

Economic inequality translates into political inequality, which leads to rules that favor the wealthy, which in turn reinforces economic inequality. . . . It is not just our economy that is at stake; we are risking our democracy.[42]

And so it is to democracy that we now turn.

5

Democracy Weakening

WE HAVE THUS FAR TRAVERSED the following ground:

Capitalism has over the last half century taken on a new
motivation: secrecy.

In pursuit of this motivation, an elaborate and far-reaching financial
secrecy system has been created and expanded.

This system is generating, moving, and sheltering hundreds of
billions of dollars annually, accumulating to trillions of dollars,
much of it in underproductive accounts.

Corruption, crime, and terrorism are facilitated and amplified by
this system.

Even worse, the financial secrecy system greatly increases income
and wealth inequalities in both richer and poorer countries.

However, even with all the above, most notably with the reality of swelling economic inequalities, the greatest threat arising from these combined truths that have become fixed firmly within capitalism is to democracy itself.

Democracy has its own shortcomings, particularly as practiced in the United States. The difference between the Declaration of Independence's second line asserting that "all men are created equal" and the US Constitution's compromise that a slave should be counted effectively as three-fifths of a person—without the vote—secured economic ahead of moral concerns, weaving a democratic deficit into the nation's fabric. America is still struggling today with this foundational problem. But the operative words here are "still struggling today." America has at least—through legislation on voting, education, and civil rights—recognized its deficit and strived to enact corrections and protections, very much challenged at the moment and certainly an ongoing project. The same cannot be said about inequality, the reality of which is supported in legislation and has been grossly accelerating for the better part of a half century.

I have observed firsthand dozens of countries where democracy is eroded by widening inequality. This chapter presents data on some of these realities while focusing on what economic disparities mean to democracy. Repeatedly asserted is the argument that we cannot strengthen democracy amid increasing inequality. Stopping and then reversing the advance of inequality is a necessary step toward enhancing democracy. Furthermore, as chapter 14 lays out, ending the climb and changing the direction of economic inequality is achievable with deliberate legislative measures.

Repurposing capitalism can be accomplished more quickly than remolding democracy. And time is short.

INEQUALITY VERSUS DEMOCRACY

The linkage between rising inequality and falling democracy is clear. Gini coefficients, measuring income inequality as explained in the last chapter, can be matched to various indices of democratic strength. Freedom House in Washington, D.C., has for years measured democracy across a range of variables, then consolidating several points of data into overall ratings. Figure 5.1 plots Freedom House's "Freedom in the World" measures for 195 countries and 14 territories against Gini coefficients provided in the "Human Development Index." The downward trend line demonstrates lower democracy scores in countries with higher Gini coefficients. Or, to put it the other way, higher inequality correlates to lower democracy.

Supporting results are obtained across many variations in similar analyses. No matter what data is used or how the data is analyzed, the linkage between higher inequality and lower democracy is, with only a few exceptions, commonly seen across the globe.

Does this linkage exist because the high number of poor countries introduces bias into the data? No. The correlation of higher inequality and lower democracy holds within Freedom House's subcategory of free countries, as demonstrated in figure 5.2. Included among countries with increasing inequalities and falling freedoms are the United States, the

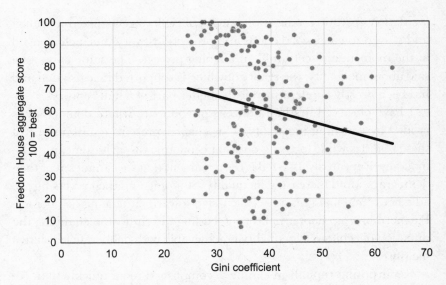

FIGURE 5.1 Democracy versus inequality (all countries)
Source: Prepared by the author using data from Freedom House and the
Human Development Report.[1]

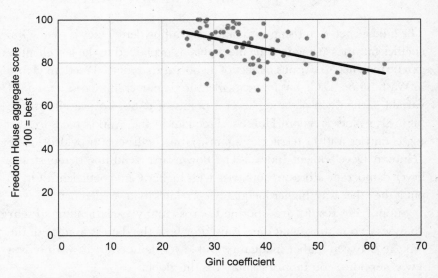

FIGURE 5.2 Democracy versus inequality (free countries)
Source: Prepared by the author using data from Freedom House and the
Human Development Report.[2]

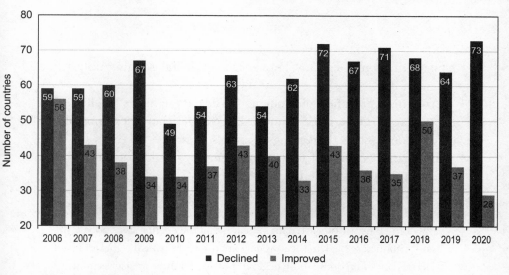

FIGURE 5.3 Fifteen years of democracy decline
Source: Chart prepared by Freedom House. Used with permission.[3]

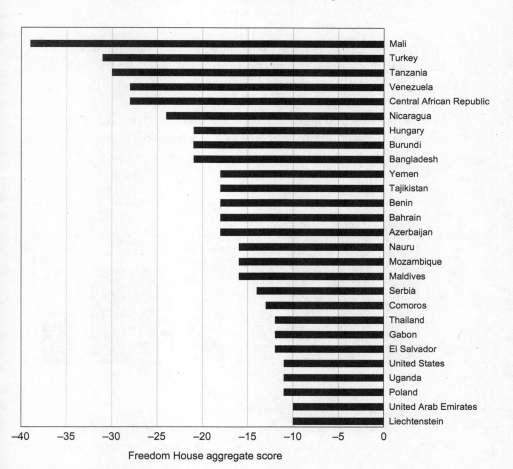

FIGURE 5.4 Largest 10-year declines in freedom
Source: Chart prepared by Freedom House. Used with permission.[4]

United Kingdom, Germany, France, Denmark, Italy, Spain, Austria, and others.

And this is not a new phenomenon. The data in figure 5.3 shows that for 15 years straight, more countries have experienced declining aggregate freedom scores than rising freedom scores.

Dramatic declines in freedom are occurring in countries across every region of the world, as depicted in figure 5.4.

A Congressional Research Service report summarizes as follows:

> Freedom House's historical data indicates that the decline since 2005 is the most sustained setback to the gradual expansion of political rights and civil liberties since Freedom House began reporting on these measures in 1972.[5]

AMERICA

Not only is the decline of liberty happening outside the United States, it is happening in the world's premier democracy as well. The United States clearly exhibits lower rankings in its freedom scores than many other wealthy countries (figure 5.5).

The Economist Intelligence Unit categorizes the United States as a "flawed democracy," noting that America's ranking in its democracy index declined from 17th place in 2010 to 26th place in 2021.[7]

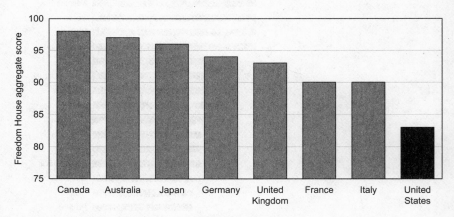

FIGURE 5.5 US democracy compared to its peers
Source: Data from Sarah Repucci and Amy Slipowitz, "Freedom in the World Report 2021: Democracy under Siege," Freedom House. Used with permission.[6]

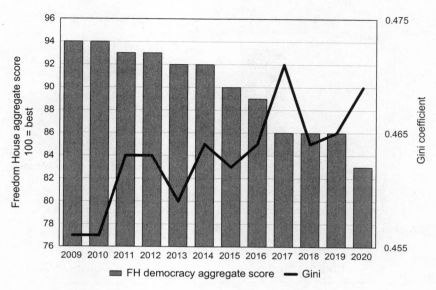

FIGURE 5.6 Changes in US democracy and inequality
Source: Prepared by the author using data from Freedom House and the US
Census Bureau.[9]

The Fragile States Index, compiled since 2000 by Fund for Peace, puts
the United States in 29th place among nations, declining for years in fra-
gility rankings, with the measure for economic inequality particularly
worsening.[8]

Most dramatically, income inequality in the United States has been rising as democracy ratings have been falling. Figure 5.6 shows data on US
Census Bureau Gini coefficients rising in inequality for ten years, as Freedom's House democracy ratings for the United States decline over ten years.

Stark differences in economic well-being were on display in the 2016
US presidential election. Analyses by the Brookings Institution show that
the Democratic candidate won only 472 counties across America, but
these accounted for 64 percent of the nation's GDP, while the Republican candidate carried a whopping 2,584 counties, which totaled only
36 percent of GDP (figure 5.7).

The trend toward higher-output counties voting Democratic accelerated in the 2020 presidential election, moving from the 64 percent, as
shown in figure 5.7, to 71 percent, as shown in figure 5.8.

Pew Research Center interviews demonstrate that since September 11,
2001, public trust in the federal government has been declining among
Republicans and Democrats alike, as figure 5.9 shows.

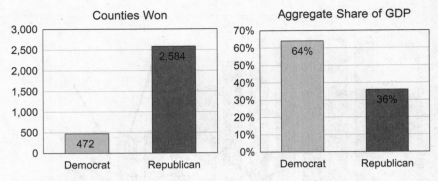

FIGURE 5.7 High-output America versus low-output America, 2016 election
Source: Prepared by the author using data from Mark Muro and Sifan Liu, Brookings Institution.[10]

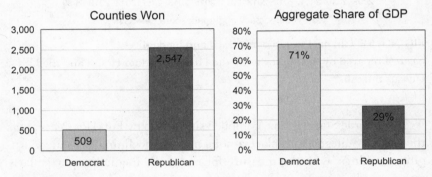

FIGURE 5.8 High-output America versus low-output America, 2020 election
Source: Prepared by the author using data from Mark Muro et al., Brookings Institution.[11]

IDENTITIES OR ECONOMICS?

Rich debate surrounds the question of what is causing political divisions in America and some other major countries. Broadly speaking, two competing explanations are offered: identities and economics. Are evident divisions based primarily on, for example, race, religion, age, or gender or primarily on real and perceived inequalities in incomes and opportunities?

Those advocating identity politics as the principal cause of division find succor in the 2018 book *Identity Crisis.* Analyzing the 2016 election in America, the authors make the central argument that "economic anxiety had been decreasing, not increasing, in the eight years before 2016."[13] Therefore, they conclude, with rising faith in the economy, anxiety linked to economic concerns could not be the cause of voter discontent.

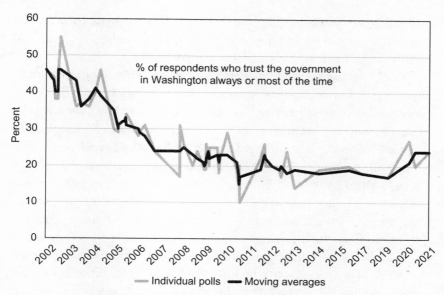

FIGURE 5.9 Public trust in the US government
Source: Pew Research Center.[12]

Eight years before 2016 was 2008, the onset of the "Great Recession," when the entire economy of the United States was fearing disaster. Factories closed, banks stopped lending, homes were repossessed, mortgages dried up, workers lost jobs, and retirement accounts dwindled. Any poll of economic concerns that starts from the rock bottom of 2008 has only one way to go—up—so making a case that since 2008 economic prospects were improving and therefore economic anxiety was not a significant factor in the election is both a fallacious use of statistics and a misreading of the national psyche.

Ryan Cooper, writing in *The Nation*, criticizes *Identity Crisis*, noting a far more extensive study as follows:

> A 2015 paper . . . that examined 140 years of political history in 20 advanced countries (including more than 800 elections) found that financial crises are associated with a 30 percent rise, on average, in the vote share of extreme right parties. . . . [A]re we really to believe that every single one of those countries had a purely coincidental postcrisis outbreak of racism and extremism?[14]

I disagree with the hypothesis that identity politics is the primary influence and economics is a secondary influence on the mood of America.

These pages drive home the point that capitalism as currently practiced is producing an explosion of economic inequality, and this income and wealth inequality is directly undermining democracy.

Recall two points made in preceding pages. First, as illustrated in chapter 4, two generations of Americans feel that they will not do as well economically as their parents. Second, as noted just above, the cleavage in voting patterns between richer and poorer counties and regions in America is absolutely stunning. Deeper analysis can reveal voting outcomes within counties, but the basic point appears informative.

And a third point: America, while there is still much more to do, has made some progress toward greater equality in race relations, gender balance, age discrimination, religious freedoms, ethnic tolerance, and sexual orientation. Such advances seem to have slowed in recent years; however, the protest movements of the current decade provide evidence that much of the national psyche still leans toward more progress in these areas. It is difficult to argue that the areas in which America has made progress toward equity are the major cause of political divisions and that the areas in which America has not made progress and is in fact going backward is the minor cause of political divisions.

Fair play in access to income, wealth, opportunity, and security can subsume much of the differences seen in political identities. Most people who perceive that they are being treated fairly do not object to fairness extending to others as well. Many people who perceive that they are being treated unfairly will express that unfairness in identity politics. Economic dissatisfaction fosters political discontent. Fair economic outcomes can blunt the strength of social and cultural differences.

A more equal America will be a more stable America. On the other hand, increasing economic inequality in America will accelerate identity politics. Unfair economics engender grievances. Fair economics mitigate grievances. In the absence of real and perceived fair play in economic outcomes, there may quite possibly be no way to soften identity politics. If this reality prevails, the ultimate cost will be democracy itself.

SHARING THE PODIUM

Let others voice their views as well.

Larry Summers: "By almost any measure, U.S. citizens no longer share a common lived experience. Men age 25 to 54 in Arlington,

Va., have a five percent chance of being without work. Men in
Flint, Mich., have a more than 35 percent chance of that. . . . Areas
with high rates of joblessness also have high rates of depression
and pessimism about the future, and low rates of confidence in
U.S. institutions. . . . The areas where distress is greatest and
opportunity is least provide disproportionate support for
candidates advocating populist nationalist policies."[15]

Larry Diamond, known popularly as "Mr. Democracy": "If you
look at the constituency for illiberal, generally right-of-center
populism . . . they feel threatened by international trade,
threatened by immigration, threatened by a world that's changing
very rapidly. . . . And reinforcing income insecurity is the sense
that they're looked down upon, that this cosmopolitan elite looks
upon them as backward."[16]

Ronald Dworkin: "Why have millions of Americans overthrown
their instinctive prudence and embraced radical ideologies on the
left and the right? . . . Many Americans feel capitalism fails to
satisfy their material interests. It violates their sense of security
and justice. . . . [I]f the donor class wants the great mass of
Americans to move back toward the political center, it must
recognize the nightmare that capitalism has become for many
people—*psychologically*—and why it has driven them to embrace
radical ideologies at both ends of the spectrum."[17]

Benjamin Page, Larry Bartels, and Jason Seawright: "The American
political system has done less than other rich democracies to
redress growing inequality in . . . incomes, and may also have done
more to exacerbate that inequality in the first place. Is this
distinctive political response a reflection of the disproportionate
political power of wealthy Americans? Have the preferences of the
wealthy moved rightward, so that they now exert their power in
more anti-egalitarian directions? Has increasing economic inequality itself increased the power of the wealthy, producing even
stronger obstacles to egalitarian policies?"[18]

Pope Francis: "People no longer seem to believe in a happy future;
they no longer have blind trust in a better tomorrow based on the
present state of the world."[19]

ALTERNATIVES?

Democratic capitalism is under strain in the United States, other wealthy nations, and middle- and lower-income countries as well. If the system continues to falter, what are the alternatives? Extraordinarily rich literature offers many answers to this question, and extensive commentary on the breadth of these interrogations is well beyond the scope and intent of this book. Various writers have spoken of the death of democracy, de-democratization, postdemocracy, democracy without rights, illiberalism, postneoliberalism, populism, neopopulism, and even the resurgence of fascism.

Neoliberalism has been a defining movement of the last several decades, summed up as

> the minimal state and maximal market. With due simplification, neoliberalism can be defined as a special kind of social system, popular discourse, and approach of social sciences based on market fundamentalism.[20]

However, perceptions of economic stagnation and repeated financial crises have taken

> a severe toll on middle class groups whose support for the neoliberal project was predicated on promises of upward social mobility. This means that a central element of neoliberal ideology . . . has been discredited in a very fundamental way.[21]

Populism is perhaps the easiest of current developments to recognize:

> Populism is a political and social phenomenon that arises from the common man, typically not well-educated, being fed up with 1) wealth and opportunity gaps, 2) perceived cultural threats from those with different values in the country and from outsiders, 3) the "establishment elites" in positions of power, and 4) government not working effectively for them. In other words, populism is a rebellion of the common man against the elites and, to some extent, against the system. These sentiments lead that constituency to put strong leaders in power.[22]

> Throughout the world, populist parties on both the right and left are gaining ground. . . . Fanning widespread hostility to immigrants, distrusts of free trade, and xenophobia plays on people's fears. . . . [A]nxieties about . . .

employment, the financial crises, the slowdown in economic growth, rising debt, and increasing inequality seem to be universal factors.[23]

Shortcomings within global neoliberalism and a clear rise of nationalist populism suggest that alternatives to democratic capitalism are very much on the table and entirely possible. The principal alternatives might be grouped into two broad camps: democratic socialism and authoritarianism. The first is declining as an option, while the second is strengthening.

Socialism, at least that aspect of socialism that calls for greater state ownership of economic assets, is fading. And rightfully so. Government control of the means of production has two insurmountable problems. First, more often than not it leads to poor economic performance as economic entities become extensions of political control, operated for patronage instead of profits. Second, seen all over the world, government control frequently enables corruption, as elected and unelected officials so often find it easy to steal from public treasuries and accounts. No nation comes to mind that is currently pursuing a determined path toward heightened democratic socialism or markedly increasing state ownership within a democratic society. The Scandinavian countries do a brilliant job of balancing public and private interests, and even there the trend is toward relaxing rather than strengthening government control over free markets.

The realistic—not theoretical but realistic—alternative to democratic capitalism is not democratic socialism but, unfortunately, authoritarianism. In its several iterations, it is now on the rise around the world. Weakening democracy is giving ground in many countries to strengthening authoritarianism.

Scholars identify many variations on the authoritarian theme: non-Western, indigenous, hybrid, imperfect, transitional, plutocratic, autocratic, oligarchic, kleptocratic, and more. In these pages, all are addressed as authoritarian to a greater or lesser degree.

Freedom House's Arch Puddington makes the case for a clear understanding of democracy:

I'm not impressed by the proposition that others have advanced that there are "many paths to democracy." There are clearly different routes to freedom. But to achieve real democracy requires a set of strong institutions that are common throughout the democratic world. Honest elections, a diverse media, an independent judiciary, property rights, a state that tolerates a critical press and an independent civil society, minority protections. . . . [T]here is no such thing as "illiberal democracy."[24]

Puddington also argues that

> Modern authoritarian systems are not simply adversaries of free socie-
> ties. They also represent an alternative model—a nuanced system an-
> chored in regime control of government policy, the political message, the
> economy, and the organs of repression and a steadfast hostility to free ex-
> pression, honest government, and pluralism.[25]

Puddington fears that

> modern authoritarianism is a permanent and increasingly powerful rival to
> liberal democracy as the dominant governing system of the 21st century.[26]

Authoritarianism around the world derives much of its attractiveness and
power from its capacity for self-enrichment, taking full advantage of capitalism's financial secrecy system to amass fortunes in hidden wealth.
Quite simply, authoritarianism provides a path to riches.

> Twenty-first century authoritarianism cannot be dissociated from klep-
> tocracy. They have tied the knot. Where we find one, we find the other.
> Authoritarian kleptocracy has been growing, while freedom and democ-
> racy has been in recession.[27]

Erstwhile authoritarians often come to power and put on a show of na-
tionalism for a year or two while building the structures and installing the
henchmen who will facilitate strong-armed robbery. Money then flows to
the alpha authoritarian and his or her family, cronies, party members,
generals, donors, and supporters. Virtually every authoritarian regime
today steals and sends money into external accounts, assisted by foreign
enablers. A significant reason why democracy is declining and failing in
many countries is just this; democracy's counterpart—capitalism—is undermining democracy by providing the means for theft. The shadow financial system easily moves trillions of dollars of stolen and illegally
generated money into outside coffers.

Simply put, authoritarianism is a profit-generating scheme, one of the
best ever devised. Capitalism's financial secrecy system incentivizes kleptocracy and authoritarianism, creating and marketing a feedback loop
that can easily destroy democracy. With financial secrecy mechanisms
in place and readily accessible, global political movements are not in the

direction of democratic socialism but rather toward authoritarianism. Put aside any idea that we can successfully counter authoritarians while at the same time enabling and welcoming the riches they steal. As long as the financial secrecy system exists, authoritarianism will exist. Promoting democracy and abetting robbery is unworkable.

Authoritarian regimes are often supported by wealthy members of their societies. The route to wealth runs through the national treasury, state-owned enterprises, and government contracts. Authoritarianism resolutely weakens democracy for the specific purpose of focusing power onto the business of generating and preserving wealth for the few. Undermining Western institutions and social norms can be a useful part of the playbook.

Authoritarian leaders often use electoral processes to gain power and then weaken checks and balances, aiding political entrenchment for years. Hungary's prime minister Viktor Orbán rips off the state while declaring that "Christian democracy is, by definition, not liberal: it is, if you like, illiberal."[28] Poland has moved backward since the days of Lech Wałęsa as regime members profit from theft. Turkey, implicated in money laundering scandals involving the United States and Iran, has an entrenched strongman bolstered by flawed elections. Egypt's generals run suspect businesses in many sectors of the economy, making it virtually impossible to move toward popular government.

Democracy does not eliminate corruption, but authoritarianism virtually guarantees corruption. I have watched democracy overthrown in many countries and deeply compromised in scores more. In nearly every situation, emerging political elites soon take advantage of or accelerate their use of the available financial secrecy system for personal enrichment. Exceptions to this observation are extremely rare.

All democracies are imperfect, always in process, never complete. But what is evident today in many countries is an abandonment of democracy or a weakening of its ideals.

The Pew Research Center analyzed data from more than two dozen countries—rich, middle income, and poor—to

better understand what was driving dissatisfaction with the way democracy is working. We found that the strongest predicator of being dissatisfied was being unhappy with the current state of the national economy.[29]

IDEA's Global State of Democracy 2021 report, lamenting "grotesque levels of economic inequality," finds that the number of countries moving towards authoritarianism is approximately three times as high as the number moving towards democracy. The monumental human victory achieved when democracy became the predominant form of governance now hangs in the balance like never before.[30]

Fair economic outcomes could alter this reality, but fair economic outcomes are not possible within an economic system specifically designed to move money—making the point again—from bottom to top, poor to rich, criminal to legitimate, and corrupt to respectable. This has become a major function within capitalism as it is practiced today, and if this motivation and practice continues, democracy itself will be the victim.

At the beginning of this chapter a causal sequence was laid out, summarized from previous pages, briefly as follows:

Capitalism has adopted a secrecy motivation.

This new motivation has led to the creation of an overarching and multifaceted financial secrecy system invisibly handling and hoarding trillions of dollars.

Secrecy and its trillions contribute to crime and corruption and, most importantly, to widening economic inequality.[31]

To this sequence, this chapter adds the most damaging product of these realities: their combined impact on democracy itself. There is no known way to effectively and consistently enhance democracy in the midst of widening economic inequality, whether experienced or perceived by major portions of a nation's citizens or by the bulk of humanity.

The bottom line is that rogue capitalism, lacking transparency and accountability, is undermining democracy. Rogue capitalism actively · seeks to limit the encroachments of equitable democracy. For many of the rich, weakening democracy is a price well worth paying in order to garner and hide wealth. Transparent democracy and secret capitalism cannot coexist. If the democratic-capitalist system is to survive and prosper, the capitalist component must be rebuilt.

PART II

Corroding the Commons

OVER THE LAST HALF CENTURY, capitalism has adopted a culture of secrecy and deception, now permeating the operations of banks, corporations, lawyers, and accountants and fully supported by governments. This culture differs substantially from what prevailed in earlier years in both complexity and scope. In many situations, as the chapters in part II emphasize, democracy itself is the ultimate victim.

The level of dishonesty and subterfuge evident in the affairs of many banks is absolutely staggering, as the next chapter illustrates. Multinational corporations have invented the tax evading and avoiding and money laundering strategies later associated with criminal enterprises. Banks and corporations alike utilize lawyers and accountants to accomplish some of their most compromised dealings, not only in foreign countries but at home as well. Governments across the globe—the United States also—are fully complicit in either legalizing or ignoring mechanisms that undermine the integrity of capitalism and therefore the sustenance of democracy. International institutions can contribute to putting capitalism and democracy back on sound footing, but unfortunately, too often they are dominated by the same governments that are supporting rogue capitalism and watching while democracy depreciates.

Banking, corporate, professional, government, and institutional interests have enabled the secrecy structure now embedded within capitalism and turned a blind eye to the outcomes it produces. The following six chapters provide a window into a selection of activities within these interests that are harmful to capitalism and therefore to the broader democratic-capitalist system.

Some of the examples offered and realities discussed have been ad-judged as criminal or illegal, and many more have not been subjected to court decisions. Short of a legal ruling, no one is accused of illegal be-havior. Having said this, the larger question is, do some of these activi-ties now, or might such activities in the future, constitute crimes against humanity?

6

Broken Banks

THE HEAVIEST RESPONSIBILITY for capitalism's failure to curb illegality and spread prosperity rests with its banking sector. After operating for well over a century with only occasional scandals, the last two decades have revealed more illicit and unethical dealings within the banking and financial sectors than have occurred across any other similar period in history. Readers of the financial pages know many of these scandals, yet what is not adequately grasped is how devastating these practices are to the democratic-capitalist system as a whole, driving a wedge between these two fundamental pillars.

Competing for deposits, almost every bank in the world will take in suspect money. No bank says to its potential customers that it will handle only money that is legally earned, transferred, or utilized. Competing for profits, the biggest banks bend trading rules, often adopting positions contrary to the interests of their own customers. This is passed off as games played between sophisticated parties, simply taking advantage of one another's ignorance. Driven by the new motivation within capitalism—secrecy—miscreants are virtually assured that they can get away with their ill intents. Despite complaints about too much regulation, the fact is the gap between scandal and reform is widening, not narrowing. In the history of banking misdeeds, there has never been a period like the past two decades.

Common opinion holds that the global financial community is aggressively fighting money laundering, the process of converting dirty money into funds that cannot be traced back to a source. Anti–money laundering efforts have been under way for 30 years, yet money laundering has been growing for 30 years.

In 2015, the IMF estimated that money laundering is about 2–5 percent of the world's GDP, perhaps as high as $4 trillion a year today. The UN Office of Drugs and Crime in Vienna estimates that criminal proceeds may be 3.6 percent of global GDP, perhaps $3 trillion a year.

In 1989, the G7 countries agreed to establish the Financial Action Task Force (FATF) to fight money laundering. Housed at the OECD in Paris, the FATF functions as an intergovernmental association of 37 countries that agree to adopt common AML standards and periodically permit evaluations of compliance and effectiveness within each country. An additional 100 countries are now linked to the original group. No country, however, has achieved full compliance. The United States, for example, has been repeatedly downgraded in part because every state in the union for years permitted the formation of anonymous entities with unknown owners.

The Bank Secrecy Act of 1970 requires US banks to report suspect financial activity and allows the secretary of the Treasury to specify procedures that banks are to follow in submitting Suspicious Activity Reports (SARs) and Currency Transaction Reports (CTRs). Initially, banks were expected to prevent receipt of suspect money. However, in the wake of the 9/11 terrorist attack, US policy veered from preventing to tracking. Rather than trying to block incoming dirty money, the Treasury Department encouraged banks to receive dirty money and then file SARs and CTRs so that depositors and their sources of funds could be traced, thus pursuing terrorist financing back to the perpetrators. The rationale was that turning money away at the door would only serve to push it into underground channels that are harder to trace and investigate.

Banks responded, weakening oversight before the deposit and relying on FinCEN to check the provenance of funds after the deposit. Today, US banks and other financial institutions file close to 80,000 SARs and CTRs each business day. Annually, only about 2,500 of these SARs and CTRs lead to money laundering charges brought against legal entities or persons.

Filing 80,000 reports a day is not evidence of US anti–money laundering efforts working; it is evidence of US anti–money laundering efforts failing. Banks simply throw money defensively at compliance programs, leaving the investigative process to the government. Some years ago a FinCEN director estimated that 99.9 percent of laundered money presented for deposit in the United States successfully enters the legitimate financial system. Total failure is just a decimal point away.

For years, the US Treasury Department has been of two minds. One side of the bureaucracy holds sacred the importance of funding US bud-

get and trade deficits and favors attracting incoming money almost regardless of its provenance. The other side wants to fight drugs, crime,
and terrorism by every means possible and favors much more aggressive
efforts to block dirty money in its various manifestations. This two-track
policy is contradictory, contributing to the United States becoming the
largest recipient of ill-gotten gains of any nation.

> The U.S. is still the venue of choice for money launderers, cartels, and cor-
> rupt politicians the world over. Our anti–money laundering framework
> is filled not with cracks or crevices but rather is replete with open doors,
> windows, and arms.[1]

The United Kingdom is no better. With 22 supervisory agencies responsible for addressing AML issues in various sectors of the banking
and business communities, a recent study found that 20 were inadequate
in their standards of enforcement, "hampered by an institutional tendency towards secrecy."[2] Much the same can be said of France, Germany, Italy, Belgium, the Netherlands, and other countries. The Basel
Institute of Governance finds "consistently poor results" in anti–money
laundering endeavors because bank compliance programs are "ineffective in practice."[3] As one expert put it, "Anti–money laundering legislation is the least effective of any anti-crime measure, anywhere."[4]

The key fallacy in US and global anti–money laundering efforts is the
idea that we in the wealthier countries can hold on to our use of every facet
of capitalism's secrecy structure to move our tax evading and tax avoiding
money to enrich ourselves and, at the same time, make the criminals, the
corrupt government officials, and the terrorist financiers give up their use
of exactly the same secrecy structure to move their money. This is not possible. We have to be willing to give up our use of the structure if we are
going to prevent their use of the structure. There is no other option.

In 1999, the US Senate's Permanent Subcommittee on Investigations
held hearings critical of Citibank taking in deposits from assorted thieves
in other countries. Two days of hearings excoriated Citibank for money
laundering, whether legally provable or not, ultimately contributing to
the resignation of the bank's president five months later. Riggs National
Bank in Washington, D.C., was similarly hauled before the Permanent
Subcommittee. Riggs was accused of handling the stolen money of Au-
gusto Pinochet of Chile and Teodoro Obiang of Equatorial Guinea, even
accepting suitcases of cash carried through the front door. HSBC, originally the Hongkong and Shanghai Banking Corporation, accepted

transfers of $7 billion from its Mexico branch without adequate anti–
money laundering oversight and was fined $1.9 billion in 2012. Then
again in 2019 HSBC's private bank in Switzerland entered into a deferred
prosecution agreement with the US Department of Justice (DOJ) confirming its conspiracy in tax fraud and paid $192 million in settlement.[5]

GREAT RECESSION

The subprime mortgage crisis, which nearly brought down the global
economy in 2007–2008, showed that bankers had been overstating assets and gouging customers. They bundled weak and strong mortgages
together to create securitized packages that were rated highly and sold
to unsuspecting buyers, often with purely fraudulent intent. Fine print
in lien documents led to higher interest rates, which homeowners could
not afford, and foreclosures exploded. The story is well known: Lehman
Brothers collapsed, American International Group (AIG) teetered, and
Wall Street went running to Washington for a bailout, arguing that the
government had to accept private finance as "too big to fail," bolstering
arguments with nearly $350 million in lobbying distributions in the first
three quarters of 2009. The George W. Bush administration provided
$787 billion in emergency extensions to banks through the Troubled As-
sets Relief Program, with the final bailout price tag reaching $1.8 tril-
lion. In the following years the middle class paid the price, with families
losing homes, median annual income dropping $4,000, unemployment
moving close to 10 percent, and youth unemployment above 20 percent.

The US government did extract some settlements from the financial
industry:

Bank of America	$17 billion
JPMorgan Chase	$13 billion
Deutsche Bank	$ 7 billion
Credit Suisse	$ 5 billion
Goldman Sachs	$ 5 billion

Altogether, fines and penalties imposed on the financial industry for the
subprime mortgage crisis and other malpractices in the decade following were more than $320 billion, most by the US government.[6] But these
charges and the billions in legal fees spent to fight such charges are tax
deductible. Bank profits scarcely suffered, share prices held, and execu-

tive compensation rose. Citigroup, as an example, which received $45 billion in the bailout, reduced its consumer banking business by a third, laid off 40 percent of its staff, and closed 62 percent of its branches in middle America.

In its essence, corrupt banking outplayed social responsibility, even democratic government. The banks effectively saddled the citizenry with their losses. Stiffer regulatory proposals via the Dodd-Frank Wall Street Reform and Consumer Protection Act of 2010 and other legislations were fought not just from the beginning but even after being passed as banks worked to overturn constraints on future dealings. Quite simply, in emerging from the subprime mortgage crisis, the banks won.

Along the way, there have been additional outrages facilitated by motivations driving and mechanisms offering secrecy.

LIBOR

LIBOR, the London interbank offered rate, was supposedly an average of the short-term borrowing costs of banks. The benchmark influenced rates applied to some $350 trillion in loans and securities across the globe. Overseen by the British Bankers Association, some 150 rates reflecting different currencies and different borrowing terms were reported daily based on submissions from 18 of the world's largest banks. As the 2007 financial meltdown gathered momentum, some banks found it to their advantage to misreport their borrowing costs in order to deflect attention from their liquidity concerns. Sensing that LIBOR was not accurately reflecting borrowing costs, the Commodity Futures Trading Commission in the United States launched an investigation, followed later by the Serious Fraud Office in the United Kingdom. Deutsche Bank admitted colluding with other banks in rate submissions and paid $2.5 billion to US and European regulators. Barclays paid $435 million plus another $100 million to 44 US states. UBS admitted to wire fraud in its Japan subsidiary and settled with the US Department of Justice for $1.5 billion. Also implicated were Bank of America, Citigroup, JPMorgan Chase, HSBC, Bank of Tokyo, Mitsubishi, Credit Suisse, Lloyds, Rabobank, WestLB, the Royal Bank of Scotland, and Société Générale, with fines totaling around $10 billion. Additional claims are being sought through private suits. Having lost its credibility, LIBOR was discontinued in 2022, a victim of massive dishonesty now replaced by a panoply of specialized indices.

FOREX

Immediately on the heels of the LIBOR case came the forex case, which involved the manipulation of foreign currency exchange rates. Exchanging currencies is roughly a $6 trillion business daily, so the smallest possible margins can produce enormous gains. Manipulating exchange rates is done in a variety of ways. For example, if you know that a large trade is about to take place, you can buy a position on one side or the other of the impending transaction and then profit when the market is moved slightly by the big transaction. This is called "front running." Or you can advise a customer for whom you are about to handle a currency swap that the best possible exchange rate is assured, when in fact the transaction can have hidden fees or margins or can be timed based on knowledge of other trades about to occur. Or you can finalize a transaction at the most profitable rate available the day of the trade rather than the rate in place when the trade is booked. Or you can simply create fake trades on your computer terminal, giving the illusion that the market is moving one way or the other, a practice known as "painting the screen."

Beginning in 2007, a group of traders working for major banks in London began communicating among themselves through emails, instant messages, and chat rooms, exchanging information on currency positions and customer orders and eventually identifying themselves as "The Cartel," "The Mafia," and "The Bandits' Club." They manipulated trades by corporations, pension funds, nonprofits, and even other financial institutions, hugely profiting their banks and themselves.

Collusion in the forex market was suspected for years before the Financial Conduct Authority in the United Kingdom and the Commodity Futures Trading Commission in the United States finally launched successful investigations. In 2015, Citigroup and JPMorgan Chase pleaded guilty to criminal charges for colluding to manipulate prices in currency markets, the first criminal admissions by major US banks in decades. Barclays and the Royal Bank of Scotland pleaded guilty to criminal offenses also, and UBS pleaded guilty to a lesser charge of wire fraud. US attorney general Loretta Lynch blasted the banks for inflating profits "while harming countless consumers, investors and institutions around the globe, from pension funds to major corporations, and including the banks' own customers." The scandal soon engulfed Bank of America, Goldman Sachs, Morgan Stanley, State Street, Standard Chartered, Société Générale, HSBC, BNP Paribas, Deutsche Bank, and more. Fines and penalties topped $10 billion.

If you ain't cheating, you ain't trying.[7]

So said one of Barclay's traders, encapsulating the motivations of the individual miscreants and, unfortunately, some of their vaunted institutions.

LONDON WHALE

Simultaneously with the LIBOR and forex scandals, JPMorgan Chase created its own $65 billion problem. This was the amount of its short position in 2012 in a credit default swap known as the "CDX NA.IG9 10 year index." Originally intended as a hedge against risks, the position gravitated into proprietary trading within the bank's portfolio, partially supported by federally insured deposits.

A bank trader who came to be known as the "London Whale" had massive exposure to possible losses and dumped $7 billion of the index fund in a short period, most of it in three hours. The market price for the index dropped, and the bank's short position benefited from the decline. The manipulation led to a 17-month investigation by the Commodity Futures Trading Commission, resulting in fines of $1 billion paid by the bank to US and foreign authorities. This was the commission's first case asserting violations of Dodd-Frank, which established regulations against conduct aimed at market manipulations. In a scathing rebuke, the CFTC's director of enforcement criticized the practice of "dumping a gargantuan, record-setting volume of swaps virtually all at once, recklessly ignoring the obvious dangers."[8]

SPOOFING

Early in the electronic age, commodities and futures traders learned how to mislead others about price movements. Traders can place fake orders indicating an intention to buy or sell—thus, markets can be affected up or down by these declared intentions—and then traders can cancel the orders and capitalize on price movements they cause.

Although illegal, such "spoofing" is not uncommon especially in efforts to fool high-frequency algometric trading. Deutsche Bank, HSBC,
Merrill Lynch, and UBS have paid penalties for such actions. The
biggest penalty was assessed in 2019 against JPMorgan Chase for
"tens of thousands" of deceptive gold, silver, platinum, and palladium
futures orders "in an attempt to profit by deceiving other market participants through injecting false and misleading information concerning the existence of genuine supply and demand for precious metals."[9]
A "total criminal monetary" assessment of $920 million resulted,
along with guilty pleas by two officers and four others awaiting trial.[10]
Brian Benczkowski, head of the DOJ's criminal division, referring to
the Racketeer Influenced and Corrupt Organizations Act, said that
"this is precisely the kind of conduct the RICO statute is meant to
punish."[11]

CUM-EX

Another scandal rocking financial institutions and governments centers
around tax rebates on dividend payments. Often in trading practice
when corporate dividends are paid to stockholders, the financial institution handling the transaction withholds appropriate tax. Several European governments then permit stockholders to apply for refunds of this
tax, with stockholders expected to account for the refund in their own tax
filings. Shares traded before dividends are paid out are "cum" dividend,
and shares then traded again after dividends have been paid out are
"ex" dividend.

If two parties appear to own the same shares at the same time, then
the government will make two refunds. This can be accomplished by
one party lending its shares to another party just before the dividend
payment date so both parties appear on the record date to be owners of
the same investment. Therefore, both appear entitled to receive the dividend and therefore both appear entitled to receive the dividend tax refund. To accomplish this in a disguised fashion, banks, brokers, dealers,
and accountants plus lawyers blessing the schemes obscure the trail of
ownership through short sales and rapid trades, going through a dozen
or more quick steps that are nearly untraceable.

Examining the matter in 2020, the European Securities and Markets
Authority, referring to a court ruling in Germany, noted that

parallel multiple ownership of the same shares for tax purposes and therefore multiple refunds of capital income tax that has only been withheld and paid to the tax authorities once is logically impossible.[12]

As one commentator noted,

Cum-Ex deals illustrate perfectly how easily complexity is used as a tool in finance to misdirect, obfuscate and perplex. The complexity also plays a key role in clouding public understanding of these alleged crimes.[13]

Perpetrators of the Cum-Ex scam operated principally out of London, with American financial institutions playing central roles. European governments including Germany, Denmark, France, Spain, Austria, and more lost upward of $60 billion. Reportedly, some 100 banks and almost 1,500 individuals and financial operators are under investigation, with convictions mounting. This stunning example of turpitude is likely to roll on through the courts for years to come.

TRADING WITH THE ENEMY

A different type of scandal ensnared BNP Paribas, violating US sanctions against trading with the enemy. Iran, Sudan, Cuba, and Burma were on the list of countries barred from dealings through the US financial system. The Treasury Department's Office of Foreign Assets Control found that beginning in 2002, 3,897 transactions totaling some $30 billion had been routinely stripped of information identifying these countries as the origins of the funds, which were then routed through correspondent bank accounts in New York. The US attorney in Manhattan denounced BNP for "perpetrating what was truly a tour de fraud." President Françoise Hollande of France personally appealed to President Barack Obama for lenience and was wholly rebuffed, leaving the matter entirely in the hands of US authorities. And BNP Paribas was not alone; also fined for breaking sanctions with these countries were Lloyds, Credit Suisse, Barclays, ABN AMRO, Standard Chartered, ING Bank, HSBC, Crédit Agricole, and RBS, racking up collectively some $5.4 billion in penalties. BNP Paribas apparently did not get the message; in 2018 it was charged with manipulating prices for currencies of countries in central and Eastern Europe, the Middle East, and Africa and fined another $90 million.

WELLS FARGO

> When a megabank has engaged in a pattern of extensive violations of
> law that harms millions of consumers, like Wells Fargo has, it should not
> be allowed to continue to operate within our nation's banking system.[14]

Thus, did Democratic members of the Financial Services Committee
of the U.S. House of Representatives make their opinions clear in 2018.
They were reacting to revelations of a culture of crimes and abuses cultivated in one of the nation's oldest banks, which had for years aggressively promoted an image of courtesy and service.

A succession of CEOs at Wells Fargo concentrated on "selling money,"
that is, selling to customers multiple financial products that earned fees
and interest for the bank. "Going for Gr-Eight" was the mantra from management, meaning employees were driven under enormous pressures coupled with compensation incentives to sell to each customer eight accounts,
services, or protections that raked in profits.[15] With their jobs on the line,
thousands of the bank's staff, as subsequently admitted, revealed, or alleged, indulged in just about every imaginable way to cheat depositors and
borrowers. Deposit and credit card accounts were created without authorization. Overdraft fees were charged on unauthorized accounts. Customers
were enrolled in services they did not request and then charged fees. El-
derly and immigrant customers were targeted for unneeded services. Even
serving military personnel were run out of their homes for missing mortgage payment dates when the bank itself was fully complicitous.

These were not occasional lapses. An estimated 3.5 million fraudulent
accounts were opened. Some 800,000 customers were charged for unneeded auto insurance. More than half a million customers were put into
unauthorized online bill paying services.

Years ago, inside whistleblowers called attention to Wells Fargo's illegal activities. Complaints streamed into human resources departments
and ethics hotlines all over the country.

> Everyone knew there was fraud going on, and the people trying to flag it
> were the ones who got in trouble.[16]

The utterer of these words was fired. In fact, blame for the whole of Wells
Fargo's illegal practices was shifted by upper management onto lower levels, as 5,300 employees were terminated over a five-year period.[17]

Between 2000 and 2021, federal and state authorities cited Wells Fargo and its subsidiaries 220 times for assorted banking violations, mortgage abuses, consumer protection lapses, money laundering deficiencies, and more, assessing a whopping $21.77 billion in fines and penalties.[18] All 50 states and the District of Colombia filed an action against the bank, citing laws prohibiting identity theft, computer data breaches, and unfair competition, settled in 2019 for $575 million.[19] Los Angeles, Sacramento, Seattle, Chicago, Philadelphia, and other jurisdictions ceased or curtailed doing business with the bank. Even the Navajo Nation Department of Justice sued and won its case against Wells Fargo for "egregious and predatory misconduct." Shareholders filed class action lawsuits, still being heard.

Chairman and CEO John Stumpf, recipient of numerous industry awards, resigned in 2016. In 2018, the Federal Reserve subjected him to a withering appraisal of his tenure as the head of Wells Fargo:

> Your performance in addressing these problems is an example of ineffective oversight that is not consistent with the Federal Reserve's expectations for a firm of WFC's size and scope of operations.[20]

More than $135 million was forfeited or clawed back from Stumpf and the former head of retail banking.[21]

Stumpf's successor, Timothy Sloan, was lambasted on Capitol Hill in late 2018 and again on March 14, 2019. The next day he received an "annual incentive award" of $2 million from his board. Two weeks later he resigned, eliciting a tweet from Senator Elizabeth Warren:

> About damn time. He enabled Wells Fargo's massive fake accounts scam, got rich off it, & then helped cover it up.[22]

Most of the board has since been changed. The Fed took the extraordinary step in 2018, never done before, of mandating that Wells Fargo cannot grow its asset base until it cleans up its executive, managerial, and operational deficiencies.

Even this did not end the bank's problems. In 2020, the Office of the Comptroller of the Currency forced former CEO Stumpf into a monetary penalty of $17.5 million and a ban on participating in the banking industry.[23] The OCC likewise initiated action against five other former executives, seeking $37.5 million. The Department of Justice slapped a

$3 billion criminal penalty on Wells Fargo in a deferred prosecution agreement, noting that the bank's

> onerous sales goals and accompanying management pressure led thousands of its employees to engage in: (1) unlawful conduct to attain sales through fraud, identity theft, and falsification of bank records, and (2) unethical practices to sell products of no or low value to the customer, while believing that the customer did not actually need the account and was not going to use the account.[24]

Then the majority staff of the Committee on Financial Services in the US House of Representatives produced an extensive analysis of the bank, the Fed, and the OCC, criticizing not only the bank's board and management but also inadequate compliance oversight by the two regulators.[25] The Congressional Research Service noted calls by critics aimed at "breaking up the bank."[26]

The saga of Wells Fargo illustrates the degree to which a culture of financial secrecy, a lack of transparency and integrity, an almost unfathomable degeneration of principles gravitated right down to the consumer banking level in the American economy. Banks should not be in the business of selling money. Their business should be about empowerment and progress for depositors and borrowers, conducted within a culture that builds trust and confidence, steeped in the highest ethics.

But high ethics are certainly not evident in many more dealings by officers of major banks creating and advancing schemes of bribery and corruption, utilizing elements of the financial secrecy system with which they were thoroughly familiar. A few more examples will illustrate the degree of depravity seen in recent years.

GOLDMAN SACHS AND 1MDB

Former Goldman Sachs regional chairman Timothy Leissner is guilty of bribery, another coconspirator is convicted, chairman Lloyd Blankfein stepped down, the US Department of Justice went after stolen money, a Trump fundraiser pleaded guilty, and ten more countries plunged into one of the biggest financial scandals of all time. The former chairman of Goldman Sachs, John Whitehead, a D-Day veteran, exemplar of leadership with integrity, former chairman of the Brookings Institution, and former deputy secretary of state, would be simply appalled.

Najib Razak, scion of Malaysia's ruling coalition in power since 1957, became prime minister in 2009. He immediately took control of a sovereign wealth fund established in the oil-rich state of Terengganu and renamed it 1Malaysia Development Berhad (1MDB). As its chairman and also as finance minister and prime minister, Najib gained total control of a golden vehicle for kleptocracy.

Wasting no time, in September 2009 1MDB approved an investment of $1 billion in a Saudi Arabian company with bloated promotional rhetoric and near-zero assets, PetroSaudi International Group, not to be confused with other entities similarly named. Initiating the transaction, Deutsche Bank's branch in Kuala Lumpur was instructed to transfer $700 million to an account at RBS Coutts in Switzerland.[27] It later became known that instead of belonging to PetroSaudi, the account was for the benefit of Jho Low, Harrow- and Wharton-educated Malaysian playboy and friend of Najib.

Deutsche Bank proceeded with additional loans of $1.2 billion to 1MDB for an investment in Aabar Investments, a subsidiary of the state-owned International Petroleum Investment Company in Abu Dhabi.[28] To receive the money instead, Low created two lookalike entities, Aabar Investments PJS Ltd. in the British Virgin Islands and Aabar Investments PJS Ltd. in the Seychelles, neither with any relation to the Abu Dhabi business. Some $875 million was transferred into these two accounts. With $250 million of the supposed investment, he bought a yacht called *Equanimity*. Low went on to use additional entities with names suggestive of legitimate businesses, such as Blackrock Commodities (Global) Ltd., Blackstone Asia Real Estate Partners, and Affinity Equity International Partners.[29] Among his extravagances he funded the production of *The Wolf of Wall Street*, which earned a best actor Golden Globes award for Leonardo DiCaprio. This along with high-end properties in New York and California, a jet, and multimillion-dollar artworks.

In 2009 Timothy Leissner, holding various managing director and chairman positions at Goldman Sachs, initiated relationships with Jho Low, and over the next five years the bank handled dozens of dubious transactions for Low and for Malaysia.[30] Most glaringly, Goldman Sachs undertook three bond sales on behalf of 1MDB totaling $6.5 billion. On this the bank earned nearly $600 million, more than 9 percent, an exorbitant fee for handling transactions for a sovereign wealth fund. Leissner reportedly took $200 million for bribes, and his later guilty plea required him to forfeit $43.7 million that he apparently kept for himself.

It was soon reported that Goldman Sachs chairman Lloyd Blankfein met with Jho Low on three occasions and also with Prime Minister Najib.[31] As news of the scandal spread, Blankfein stepped down in 2018, and Leissner was indicted one month later. His deputy, Roger Ng, has been tried and convicted in the United States, and another of the bank's executives is being investigated.

The Malaysian government lodged criminal charges against Goldman Sachs, seeking $7.5 billion in recompense, and eventually settled for $3.9 billion. The US Department of Justice investigated $4.5 billion allegedly diverted from 1MDB. EY provided tax advice to 1MDB, KPMG and Deloitte agreed that their earlier audits could not be relied upon, and PwC is reviewing accounts covering the last several years.[32] Jho Low launched a lobbying campaign in the United States seeking to divert attention from the 1MDB scandal, resulting in George Higginbotham, former Department of Justice employee and Trump booster, pleading guilty to conspiracy.[33] Low is now on the run and believed to be in China. Besides Malaysia and the United States, investigations into bank transfers, companies, and properties proceeded in Australia, Hong Kong, Indonesia, Luxembourg, Seychelles, Singapore, Switzerland, the UAE, and the United Kingdom.[34]

Goldman Sachs's Leissner said in court that the bank's "culture" included bypassing compliance procedures.[35] Earlier alleged examples of the bank's "culture" included the construction of derivatives to help Greece obscure the true condition of its finances, another revealed that before the financial crisis the bank configured investment products designed to fail and sold them to unsuspecting clients, and yet another involved flawed derivatives trades made on behalf of the Libyan Investment Authority.

In a 2020 deferred prosecution agreement, the US Department of Justice was blunt:

> Goldman, through certain of its agents and employees, together with others, knowingly and willfully conspired and agreed with others to corruptly provide payments and things of value to . . . foreign officials and their relatives. . . . In total, . . . approximately $1.6077 billion.[36]

Goldman agreed to pay more than $2.9 billion in fines and disgorgements, the largest ever under the U.S. Foreign Corrupt Practices Act, and accepted that its Malaysian subsidiary was guilty of criminal conspiracy. In addition, Goldman agreed to a $3.9 billion settlement with the

Malaysian government. Twelve current and former executives, including the chairman, reportedly must forfeit or return some $174 million in compensation.[37] An investor class action lawsuit has been initiated in New York against Goldman and former executives. By mid-2021 Malaysian authorities had filed 22 civil suits for damages, with JPMorgan Chase and Deutsche Bank among the defendants.[38] Ambank Group settled claims for $689 million. Deloitte agreed to hand over $80 million for purportedly flawed audits.[39] KPMG is denying allegations of negligence.[40]

Najib lost his bid for reelection in 2017 and was indicted under suspicion of having received $700 million of stolen 1MDB funds. Raids on his properties produced 12,000 items of jewelry, 423 watches, and 567 handbags. Najib returned to parliament in 2020 but was finally convicted of corruption in 2022.

1MDB is a hugely destructive scandal that took advantage of every particle of opacity available within financial secrecy structures. This included connivance with and use of the stature and expertise of one of the world's most prestigious banks. John Whitehead is rolling over in his grave. Goldman Sachs has some rethinking to do about its proper function in the capitalist system.

CREDIT SUISSE AND MOZAMBIQUE

Tales of corruption seldom get more sordid than this. Three Credit Suisse executives, while working for the bank, conspired with the most senior intelligence and finance officials in the government of Mozambique to load the country with $2 billion of debt and rake off hundreds of millions of dollars in kickbacks and bribes. This case will be ongoing for years to come.

The Privinvest Group bills itself as a shipbuilding, logistics, and maritime security organization, headquartered in Abu Dhabi and Lebanon, with facilities and partnerships in the Middle East and Europe.[41] In 2011, the company initiated discussions allegedly with the president of Mozambique that led to the creation of three entities. The first was to provide materials and training to protect Mozambique's coastal waters, the second to establish a tuna fishing venture, and the third to set up a shipyard to service the vessels of the other two companies. To get things moving, Privinvest's representative approved $50 million in bribe and kickback payments, referred to in communications as "50 million chickens," plus an additional $12 million for coconspirators.

Simultaneously, Privinvest negotiated with Credit Suisse to provide funding for the project. Andrew Pearse, the bank's managing director who led the global financing group operating from London, met with Privinvest in late 2012 and, together with two other senior officers of the bank, "conspired to circumvent [Credit Suisse] internal controls to enrich themselves and win the . . . business for [Credit Suisse]."[42] In 2013 Credit Suisse made three loans to the first of the newly established companies in amounts of $372 million, $132 million, and $118 million. Manuel Chang, Mozambique's minister of finance, duly signed the loan documents without consultations, despite the fact that the country's constitution requires parliamentary oversight for transactions carrying sovereign guarantees.

For the second company, Credit Suisse, as directed by Pearse and his cohorts, loaned $500 million to Mozambique, and the Russian bank VTB Capital loaned an additional $350 million. Much of the money never went to Mozambique but instead to Privinvest, obscuring the paper trail of the bribes and kickbacks.

For the third company, Pearse and his fellow conspirators arranged a loan of $535 million from VTB Capital, again sent directly to Privinvest, not to Mozambique.

That same year Pearse and another of the trio left Credit Suisse and went to work for Privinvest, helping to oversee the continued bribery and theft. Privinvest wire-transferred more than $45 million into Pearse's account by mid-2014.

By 2015, the three entities could not service their debts. The IMF inquired about the country's use of the loan proceeds and received only deflecting responses. Pearse proposed to the Mozambique government that some of the debt be exchanged for eurobonds, hopefully indicating greater creditworthiness. In a remarkable example of chutzpah, Privinvest had another of its stable of companies, Palomar, provide advice in return for a "running fee" on financial restructuring of the very entities defrauded, with Pearse functioning as chairman.[43]

The bottom fell out when S&P Global Ratings downgraded Mozambique's credit rating to a negative outlook status. The IMF, the World Bank, and bilateral donors then suspended support for the government.

In 2017 the American firm Kroll Inc. was brought in to try to trace some of the assets. Twenty-four fishing boats were located sitting idle in Maputo harbor, purchased from Privinvest at some $22 million each and worth perhaps a tenth of that.[44] A tight veil of secrecy meant that few other assets could be found. During the investigations, Kroll learned that

Credit Suisse and VTB had charged $92 million in up-front fees on their loans to offset a requested low interest rate on the borrowings.

The government charged Chang, the finance minister, and 17 others with various crimes in the matter.[45] But because the ruling party Frelimo and its political control of the country are so intertwined in the scandal, aggressive actions within the state against the accused may not result in just punishments.

With wire transfers sent through New York correspondent bank accounts, the United States charged Pearse, his two coconspirators, two officers of Privinvest, Chang, and two other Mozambique officials variously with money laundering, violations of the Foreign Corrupt Practices Act, and conspiracy to commit wire fraud.[46] Credit Suisse entered into a deferred prosecution agreement with US and UK authorities, agreeing to some $557 million in penalties, fines, and disgorgements plus $200 million of debt relief to Mozambique.[47]

Credit Suisse senior officers and Mozambique senior officials conspired together to pull off one of the most brazen frauds of the century. While acting on behalf of the bank, Pearse and his coconspirators negotiated the loan documents, directed kickbacks to themselves and to government officials, falsified documents, obscured compliance oversight and due diligence procedures, avoided noting that the loans they were arranging were contrary to the constitution of the country, and then went to work for the principal instigator in the scheme to ensure that the massive con progressed to everyone's advantage. Mozambique government officials created the entities to perpetrate the scam, directed the distribution of kickbacks, hid proper accounting for years, lied to the IMF, and effectively bankrupted their country.

The London-based and highly respected *Africa Report* lamented that the Mozambique case

> highlights the crucial elements that are needed to make corrupt schemes like this work. . . . The billions of dollars in loans in Mozambique could not have been accessed without greedy politicians in positions of authority, weak government institutions, ineffectual international financial bodies, banks willing to turn a blind eye in return for big profits and contractors crafting projects that focus more on commissions than creating functional companies.[48]

An excellent analysis, "Costs and Consequences of the Hidden Debt Scandal of Mozambique," estimates that in just the first four years after

this example of transnational venality became known Mozambique lost
$11 billion of GDP, plunging 2,000,000 into poverty.[49] Imagine, 2,000,000
plunged into poverty while Credit Suisse, aspiring to be a $1,000,000,000
bank, gets off with a slap on the wrist.

THE PAST IS PROLOGUE FOR THE FUTURE

While earlier years exposed the scale through which banks benefit from
illegal and illicit dealings, proceedings from 2018 onward confirm how
large financial institutions continue to act as key enablers of dirty money
worldwide. A selected list of particularly egregious deficiencies coming
to light illustrates these trends.

NatWest
The renamed RBS Group pleaded guilty in 2021 to three criminal
charges for inadequate anti–money laundering enforcement and was fined
£265 million, the first time a UK financial institution has been prosecuted for such violations.

Danske Bank
Unbelievably, $235 billion reportedly gushed out of the small Estonia
branch of Danske Bank between 2007 and 2015, much of it originating
from dubious clients in Russia, Ukraine, Azerbaijan, and Moldova.

Deutsche Bank
Continuing its decades-long string of scandals and penalties, Deutsche
Bank was fined $150 million in 2020 for failing to monitor client activity
and then another $130 million in 2021 for FCPA violations and com-
modities frauds.

Swedbank
Not to be left out of the riches flowing from Russia and other former Soviet Socialist Republics, Swedbank handled billions of dollars of high-
risk nonresident money, variously estimated at $10 billion to $150 billion,
still under investigation as the former CEO faces charges.

UBS
In 2019 UBS, one of the world's most prolific acquisitors of financial sanctions, was charged €4.5 billion in fines and civil damages by a French

court for soliciting and laundering money and helping clients evade French taxes.

ING
The Netherlands' largest financial services provider, having paid a fine of $619 million in 2012 for handling transactions for Cuba, Iran, and other sanctioned countries, was again fined €775 million in 2018 for allegedly laundering money for a Uzbekistan client.

ABN AMRO
Despite its three centuries of storied history, the Netherlands' third-largest bank was hit in 2021 with €300 million in fines and €180 million in disgorgement of profits for serious violations of compliance regulations, activities constituting culpable money laundering.

Rabobank
Yet another bank in the Netherlands, Rabobank pleaded guilty in 2018 to impairing, impeding, and obstructing regulators examining weaknesses in anti–money laundering procedures in its California branches and agreed to pay a fine of $369 million.

Commonwealth Bank of Australia
In 2018, civil proceedings surrounding more than 50,000 breaches of anti–money laundering and counterterrorism financing regulations by Australia's biggest bank resulted in a fine totaling AUD700 million, about $534 million.

Westpac Bank
In 2020, Westpac was assessed by AUSTRAC, Australia's anti–money laundering agency, with a fine of AUD1.3 billion, about $900 million, for 23 million occasions of contravening AML laws and due diligence requirements.

Bank Hapoalim
Israel's largest bank and its Swiss subsidiary admitted in 2020 to conspiring with US taxpayers to 1) open and maintain accounts with pseudonyms and code names, 2) enable US account holders to evade reporting requirements, 3) provide "hold mail" services to limit account information from reaching prying eyes, 4) process wire transfers in amounts below $10,000 to avoid scrutiny, and 5) offer back-to-back loans facilitating

use of funds held in offshore accounts,[50] ultimately assessed $874 million in penalties, fines, and restitutions.

US Bancorp
Joining ranks with Rabobank, ING, UBS, and more, US Bancorp was fined $613 million in 2018 in settlement of two criminal charges surrounding failed AML procedures.

This brief recitation could go on across dozens of additional banks. How does this happen? How do major financial institutions in the United States, Europe, and around the world so easily, knowingly, and carelessly participate in illicit dealings harming the citizens, companies, and countries they are supposed to serve? The financial secrecy system has become so pervasive that most banks will find a reason to accept deposits and facilitate transactions involving commercial, criminal, and corrupt dirty money, provided that the flimsiest possible excuse can be conjured to justify the interests and fees to be earned. Compliance regulation and law enforcement are inadequate instruments because regulation and enforcement do not work when applied against a secret system. As said repeatedly, you cannot regulate secrecy. The idea is a contradiction in terms. For banks, billions of dollars in fines and penalties for occasional breaches discovered are simply a cost of doing business on the way to hundreds of billions of dollars in profits.

This is a harsh judgment for a profession that in earlier years I found to be universally respectable. The pervasive financial secrecy system with its many components and tentacles, developed over the last half century, dominates much of the operations of capitalism.

While banks are the grand facilitators of illicit dealings, corporations are the grand generators of illicit dealings. So, it is to them, the corporations, that we now turn.

7

Covetous Corporations

ORPORATIONS TOGETHER WITH BANKS are driving the financial secrecy system.

Corporations are determined to hold on to abusive transfer pricing. This—falsified trade—is the principal mechanism enabling tax evasion and tax avoidance between wealthy countries and likewise facilitates the movement of revenues from soft currencies in developing countries into hard currencies. Apple, Google, Starbucks, Amazon, Facebook, GE, and other firms are often in the news for paying little or no taxes in countries where they generate billions in revenues. The global financial secrecy system, with trade misinvoicing as its most frequently used component, facilitates tax dodging at every turn. This has become completely normalized in global business.

Corporations are the loudest complainers about corruption in foreign governments and cross-border crime that affects their distant operations. Yet the financial secrecy system that corporations use every day is exactly the same system that the corrupt and the criminal use to move their money into overseas accounts. As stated in the last chapter, global anti–money laundering efforts fail because we in the wealthier countries are the biggest users of disguised corporations, anonymous trusts, hybrid entities, tax havens, and mechanisms for falsifying trade, and therefore the idea that we can stop the criminal and the corrupt from using identical mechanisms is fundamentally flawed at the outset. As long as the system exists to move corporate money, it will be used to move corrupt and criminal money. For corporations, it seems that this is an acceptable risk in return for massive profits arising through their own financial misdealings. For the health of the democratic-capitalist system, it is not.

Corporate executives and counsels argue that they are not doing anything illegal. In scores of countries around the world from which profits are extracted with no or minimum taxes paid, assertions of innocence are most certainly not correct. Many countries have satisfactory statutes in place making clear that in related party transactions, manipulating trade prices in violation of arm's-length principles is illegal. The problem is that most countries lack the capacity in customs departments and revenue agencies to enforce such laws. Corporations take advantage of these weaknesses thousands of times every day, structuring transfer prices to shift profits out and minimize taxes in foreign countries. Not only are foreign countries disadvantaged, but small companies also very often find that they cannot compete with larger entities able to buy secrecy and shift revenue at will. Fair trade is not possible when rules of trade are so badly abused.

Dozens of stories of ill dealings within the corporate world can be related. The following only begin to illustrate how secrecy in financial affairs drives corporate crime, corruption, and other misbehavior.

SHELL IN NIGERIA

The history of Shell Oil in Nigeria is fraught with poor business decisions, environmental degradation, corruption, and criminality. Current legal proceedings will determine whether senior executives at the very top of Shell and others acting for or on their behalf go to jail.

Risks of sabotage and violence affecting its onshore oil operations led Shell in 2011 to dispose of two concessions. One block, Oil Mining Lease (OML) 42, was sold to Neconde Energy Ltd. for $385 million. Overseeing this and other transactions was Shell's vice president of commercial operations in sub-Saharan Africa, Peter Robinson, an Australian. With suspicions arising from another sale, his home in Perth was raided in 2018. Documents recovered there confirmed that Robinson had created a secret Seychelles company, Energy Venture Partners Ltd., believed to be a conduit for bribes in connection with the OML 42 sale.[1] Swiss bank accounts were linked to Robinson that reportedly contained several hundred million Swiss francs.[2] Shell reported its former senior executive to Dutch authorities, saying "we suspect a crime may have been committed."[3]

Which leads to Shell's bigger problem, the second concession, Oil Prospecting License (OPL) 245, a sordid tale already stretching over two decades involving an alleged billion-dollar bribe. OPL 245 may contain the largest oil reserves in Africa, possibly nine billion barrels, offshore in the Gulf of Guinea more than a mile deep.

In 1998 Nigerian minister of petroleum Dan Etete awarded the massive oil block to Malabu Oil and Gas Ltd., a company created days earlier and secretly owned by the minister himself and the son of the dictator Sani Abacha. Abacha's death forced Malabu to seek foreign participation in or sale of the block. Shell offered to buy 40 percent of the block, but the new government under President Olusegun Obasanjo revoked Malabu's license. In 2002 the government awarded full ownership in the block to Shell for $210 million, which Malabu legally contested. In 2006 the government reversed itself and awarded full ownership back to Malabu for the same amount of $210 million, which Shell legally contested.

While Shell and Malabu were fighting it out in court, two former British intelligence officers maintained communications between the two parties. Meanwhile, Etete was convicted in absentia in France for money laundering. Still aggressively pursuing purchase of the block from Malabu, by 2009 Shell's CEO was informed by his intelligence sources that as negotiations progressed,

> Etete can smell the money. If at nearly 70 years old he does turn his nose up at nearly $1.2 bill he is completely certifiable. But I think he knows it's his for the taking.[4]

The president of Nigeria, Umaru Yar'Adua, passed away in 2010, succeeded by Etete's friend, Vice President Goodluck Jonathan from the Niger Delta. Elections were coming the next year, and the Jonathan campaign needed money. His attorney general was tasked with bringing the OPL 245 negotiations to a successful conclusion, containing the prospect of huge bribe payments. Shell, Malabu, government officials, and a new partner in the deal, Eni, owned largely by the government of Italy, gathered repeatedly around the table in the attorney general's office to hammer out a deal. The Nigerian government agreed to act as a middleman between the contesting parties. A price for OPL 245 set at $1.1 billion would be paid to the government via an account with JPMorgan Chase in London. The government would then distribute proceeds secretly to Etete and others, presumably including those running for election. Shell could claim that it was simply making payment to the government. Peter Robinson, the same individual involved in the OML 42 deal, offered "compliments to our legal team who have done a brilliant job."[5]

Part of the money flowed in May 2011, with $801 million transferred quietly to five accounts.[6] But the secret deal came unstuck. Dutch and Italian police raided Shell and Eni offices in the Hague and Milan, collecting enough evidence to charge both companies with bribery as well as Shell's former executive director of exploration and production, Eni's then CEO, the two ex-intelligence officers employed by Shell, and nine others. In 2021 the case in Italy was dismissed, infuriating activists, while Netherlands prosecutors consider separate proceedings. The government of Nigeria filed suit in the United Kingdom against JPMorgan Chase for negligence in handling the massive transfers but lost in the initial round of hearings. These legal actions and doubtless appeals will continue for years.

So lumbers forward one of the largest bribery and corruption cases in history, with major corporations operating in the shadows yet actually holding the very center. And this afflicting Nigeria, home to some 200 million people, with 100 million living in absolute poverty, and 10 million children not even in school.[7]

GLENCORE

The world's largest mining and commodities trading organization grew out of the illicit dealings of Marc Rich, an American fugitive financier. After a 20-year career at Phibro LLC dealing in minerals and agricultural products with fragile states in Africa and Latin America, Rich with partner Pincus Green set up Marc Rich & Co. AG, incorporated in 1974. In less than a decade the two were indicted in New York by US attorney Rudy Giuliani on 65 counts of mail and wire fraud, tax evasion, racketeering, and trading with the enemy, Iran.

Rich and Green fled to Switzerland in 1983 and through bribery, kickbacks, money laundering, and offshore companies built a multibillion-dollar metals, oil, and commodities trading business. Rich renounced his US citizenship and subsequently held passports from Belgium, Bolivia, Spain, and Israel. A failed attempt to corner the world market for zinc led Rich to sell his interests to his partners, who in 1994 renamed the business Glencore. Rich and Green were pardoned in 2001 by Bill Clinton in the last hours of his presidency, a move that led to a criminal investigation and remains resoundingly criticized to this day.

Thus, Glencore took off with a well-established history of corrupt dealings across the globe. What better place to apply these skills than the

Democratic Republic of the Congo (once the personal possession of King Leopold II of Belgium), staggeringly rich in resources and for well over a century the most exploited country on Earth.

Expanding from trading activities into mine ownership and operation, Glencore, already active in Africa, set its sights on copper and cobalt deposits in the Congo. Needing an introduction to the newly ensconced young president Joseph Kabila, Glencore sought out Dan Gertler, an Israeli diamond merchant implicated in arms trading and close to the head of state. Gertler had secured mining rights and subsequently ownership interests in two valuable properties, Mutanda and Katanga, both producing copper and high-content cobalt. Glencore invested in the projects, depending on Gertler to shepherd the company's interactions with the government. Later in negotiations to increase its investment in Katanga, the government's asking price of $585 million was, through suspected intercessions by Gertler, reduced to $140 million.[8]

Complicating the relationship between Gertler and Glencore was an American company, Och-Ziff Capital Management Group. This New York investment company and hedge fund manager was accused by the US Securities and Exchange Commission (SEC) in 2016 of bribery and corruption in Libya, South Africa, Guinea, and the Congo. Och-Ziff had given investor funds to an "Israeli businessman, Dan Gertler," who "used a substantial amount of the money to bribe high-ranking DRC officials with the aim of securing mining assets for both himself and Och-Ziff."[9] Gertler, the accused, was now a serious problem for Glencore. Gertler agreed to sell his stake in Mutanda and Katanga to Glencore for $572 million in share purchases and $388 million in loan forgiveness. But he insisted on continuing to receive 2.5 percent in royalty payments on the value of production from the mines. Glencore, anticipating US sanctions if it paid Gertler in dollars while he was under Treasury Department sanctions, agreed to pay royalties in euros, hoping that this might be acceptable to US regulators.[10] Once again, the corrupt middleman generated huge problems for the corrupt multinational.

Much of this information emerged through revelations in the *Panama Papers* and the *Paradise Papers*, released in 2016 and 2017 by the International Consortium of Investigative Journalists. Gertler and Glencore, taken together, are mentioned more than 320 times, with numerous anonymous companies hiding their transactions in the Cayman Islands, the British Virgin Islands, and other tax havens.[11] In fact, Glencore, adept at backdating documents, had a room dedicated to its nefarious activities at the Appleby law firm in Bermuda, containing confidential emails, board minutes, tax restructuring diagrams, billion-dollar loan contracts, sales agreements and frank conversations about what rules could and could not be bent. . . . The records shed light on how a global colossus, aided by a trusted offshore law firm, uses financial havens to cloak its lucrative dealings.[12]

In 2019, International Rights Advocates filed in the Washington, D.C., District Court a searingly critical complaint and demand for injunctive relief on behalf of 13 Congolese "Doe" plaintiffs against defendants Apple, Alphabet, Microsoft, Dell, and Tesla. Though not itself a defendant, Glencore appears 79 times in the complaint in connection with ownership, operation, and supply of cobalt mined in the DRC. The complaint alleges that the defendants are

knowingly benefiting from and aiding and abetting the cruel and brutal use of young children . . . to mine cobalt, a key component of every rechargeable lithium-ion battery used in the electronic devices these companies manufacture.

The supply chain is, by design, hidden and secretive to allow all participants to profit from cheap cobalt mined . . . by desperate children forced to perform extremely hazardous labor without safety equipment of any kind.[13]

This case bears following closely. Like coal before it, cobalt cannot be allowed to advantage some at the cost of life and limb to others.

During the early part of this century the DRC experienced the most war-related deaths of any country since World War II. In this environment of violence, poverty, and corruption, Glencore utilized virtually every mechanism available within the financial secrecy system to mine and export at the lowest costs possible the minerals needed for electrical power and digital communication. What recompense is appropriately owed to the 90 million people of the Congo?

ODEBRECHT AND OPERAÇÃO LAVA JATO

Brazil, a nation of proud, optimistic people, is the second richest and most populous country in the Western Hemisphere. Endowed with natural resources and a boisterous democracy, the twenty-first century promised a rise to upper-income status. That is, until Operação Lava Jato (Operation Car Wash) shattered its self-confidence and forced a rude awakening. The global financial secrecy system proved just how damaging it can be to the economic and political ambitions of 200 million people.

In 2013, a routine money laundering investigation in the capital, Brasilia, focused on a currency exchange house connected to a gas station, which also had a car wash. A known *doleiro* (black market currency dealer), Alberto Youssef, had given a Range Rover to a senior officer, Paulo Roberto Costa, at the state-controlled oil company Petroleo Brasileiro S.A., known as Petrobras. After their arrest, the two men agreed to talk in return for Brazil's new policy of "collaboration leniency." Costa admitted to receiving $31 million in bribes paid into a Swiss bank account. This triggered an investigation that led to the indictment of hundreds of executives, legislators, and bagmen.

Petrobras produces 90 percent of Brazil's oil, owns all the refineries, manages more than 20,000 miles of pipelines, and operates the largest chain of service stations. In 2006, enormous oil deposits were discovered 125 miles offshore from Rio de Janeiro under more than a mile of water and another mile-thick presalt layer. Petrobras planned a huge capital expenditure program, some $220 billion over five years, to meet the technical challenges and access the potential revenue stream. Three local engineering companies had formed a cartel in the late 1990s to divide up Petrobras contracts among themselves, giving illegal kickbacks to these and other officials and both legal and illegal donations to political parties. In 2008 they were joined by two more companies, adopting the names "G-5" or "Tatu Tênis Clube," and eventually additional firms were invited to cooperate. With this structure in place, they rigged winning bids, parceled out contracts, loaded costs, arranged kickbacks to awarding officials, and kept political parties and politicians happy.

An alleged leader of the cartel was the construction company Odebrecht S.A., founded in the 1940s by an engineer whose family had emigrated from Germany a century earlier. Odebrecht held a controlling interest in Braskem S.A., a petrochemical company in which Petrobras was a minority owner. With connections reaching the top of Petrobras and the political elite of Brazil, Odebrecht built and bribed its way into a multibillion-dollar business handling the largest construction projects, operating in 27 other countries as well, with a reported total of 250,000 employees at its peak.

Bribes were so numerous that Odebrecht created a special Division of Structured Operations to function off the balance sheet, funded through unrecorded revenue streams and operating with code names, passwords, and secure computer systems. Two shell companies were established in the British Virgin Islands, and another in Belize to manage the activity.

With the original leads provided by Youssef, the money launderer, and Costa, the Petrobras official, a determined federal judge, Sérgio Moro, took command of "car wash" cases in 2014, ably assisted by his chief legal prosecutor, Harvard-trained Deltan Dallagnol. Over the next two years they and a small team of federal police investigated 429 individuals, including Petrobras officers, elected senators and deputies, construction industry executives, other corporate titans, and assorted money launderers and other criminals. At last count, more than 200 convictions had been adjudicated.

The toll was particularly steep on Odebrecht. Because American depository shares were traded on the New York Stock Exchange and US bank accounts were used for some bribery disbursements, the Department of Justice investigated. Calculating that it could reasonably fine the company as much as $12 billion, DOJ then settled on a criminal penalty of $2.6 billion, at that time the largest fine ever exacted for violations of the Foreign Corrupt Practices Act. Partial payment was allocated to the United States and Switzerland, with 80 percent of the penalty payable to the Brazilian treasury. In addition, Odebrecht's subsidiary Braskem acknowledged that $250 million went offshore into shell companies to facilitate bribe payments in connection with price concessions on chemical purchases from Petrobras and tax exemption strategies with Brazilian states. Braskem entered into its own plea agreement with DOJ for an additional fine and disgorgement of profits totaling $957 million, also mostly payable to the Brazilian treasury.

In its pleadings Odebrecht outlined its bribe payments in 11 other countries: Angola, Argentina, Colombia, the Dominican Republic, Ecuador, Guatemala, Mexico, Mozambique, Panama, Peru, and Venezuela. In Peru three former presidents faced accusations of accepting bribes, and one, Alain García, committed suicide. Two former presidents of Panama have been accused. The vice president of Ecuador allegedly received bribes from Odebrecht and was sentenced to six years in prison. Nicholas Madura in Venezuela reportedly asked for $50 million but got only $35 million. Argentina's intelligence chief was accused of receiving a bribe through a Hong Kong account. Mexico has been slow to pursue its participation in the scandal.

Marcelo Odebrecht, CEO of his namesake company, was sentenced in Brazil to 19 years in prison but soon gained early release to house confinement. As contracts dried up and the staff dwindled to one-sixth of its earlier peak, Odebrecht declared bankruptcy in June 2019.

Petrobras itself was hardly an innocent victim. For its violations of the Foreign Corrupt Practices Act, DOJ extracted a criminal penalty from the corporation of $853 million, and the Securities and Exchange Commission entered into a cease-and-desist order for another $933 million, with 80 percent of each penalty payable to the Brazilian treasury. Petrobras settled class action pension fund and investor lawsuits filed by 19 claimants, including the Bill and Melinda Gates Foundation, for $2.95 billion, with part of this amount offsetting the DOJ and SEC claims. Numerous executives of Petrobras resigned, and a new CEO ensconced in 2015 to clean up the company was himself jailed in 2018. One company official got off by agreeing to return the $100 million in bribes he had received. Further shareholder suits and actions in multiple countries continue. Switzerland acknowledged having more than 300 depositors' accounts that could be related to the schemes and froze some $400 million in its banks.[14] Meanwhile, Petrobras's market value dropped by some $250 billion.

The scandal decimated the political elite of Brazil. Luiz Inácio Lula da Silva, a former president, was alleged to have taken favors from the construction company OAS and was sentenced to 12 years in prison. His successor as president, Dilma Rousseff, who had been chairperson of Petrobras from 2003 to 2010, was impeached and removed from office. Her successor, Michel Temer, has been accused of agreeing to payments of hush money for a former speaker of the lower house, Eduardo Cunha, who was himself accused of laundering $40 million into Swiss bank accounts and was sentenced to 15 years in prison. The former governor of Rio de Janeiro state, Sérgio Cabral, was accused of accepting $64 million in bribes and sentenced to 14 years in prison.

Deltan Dallagnol, the prosecutor, summed it up well:

> With money we lose here, we could spend three times as much on public health. We could multiply the amount spent on education. We could lift ten million Brazilians out of poverty.[15]

Their democracy in shambles, Brazilians in 2019 voted into the presidency a right-wing ex-military officer, Jair Bolsonaro. "Car wash" judge Sérgio Moro was minister of justice in the new government for 15 months and sought to strengthen laws against bribery and corruption until resigning after clashes with Bolsonaro. By the end of 2020, the president and his family members were being investigated for corruption at the same time that COVID-19 was absolutely devastating the country and fires threatened to permanently devitalize the Amazon. Lula was soon out of jail and running again for the presidency.

The path to political and economic recovery for the largest Latin American nation will be arduous. Structures of the financial secrecy system remain available, enabling theft and subterfuge to continue.

WALMART

Startling news emerged in 2005 from Bentonville, Arkansas, the headquarters of what was then named Wal-Mart Stores Inc. The corporation's former vice chairman, Thomas Coughlin, friend of Sam Walton, the founder, was under investigation by the Department of Justice and the subject of a grand jury probe. Despite his seven-figure salary and tens of millions in stock, Coughlin ultimately pleaded guilty to multiple counts of wire fraud for using company gift cards intended for employees for his own personal enrichment, giving himself an all-terrain vehicle, shotguns, a computer, a dog kennel, wine, beer, and more, in other words ripping off his own employer. Facing possibly decades in prison, he agreed to 27 months of home detention and then sued his company for payment of his retirement benefits, agreed at $6.75 million. Perhaps this episode reflected a corporate culture that was soon to get Walmart into much more serious trouble.

An explosive string of stories appeared in the *New York Times* beginning in April 2012 detailing Wal-Mart's bribery in Mexico; the series later won a Pulitzer Prize.[16] These reports revealed that Wal-Mart had for years greased its rapid expansion in Mexico with bribes to local officials for property easements and building permits, utilizing third-party intermediaries called "gestores" to distribute handouts. A former company executive, Sergio Cicero Zapata, apparently angry at being passed over for promotion, described

> personally dispatching . . . outside lawyers to deliver envelopes of cash to government officials. They targeted mayors and city council members, obscure urban planners, low-level bureaucrats who issued permits— anyone with the power to thwart Wal-Mart's growth. The bribes . . . bought zoning approvals, reductions in environmental impact fees, and the allegiance of neighborhood leaders.[17]

A second piece in the *New York Times* the same year described how

> Wal-Mart de Mexico was not the reluctant victim of a corrupt culture
> that insisted on bribes as the cost of doing business. . . . Rather, [the com-
> pany] was an aggressive and creative corrupter, offering large payoffs to
> get what the law otherwise prohibited. It used bribes to subvert demo-
> cratic governance—public votes, open debates, transparent procedures.
> It used bribes to circumvent regulatory safeguards that protect Mexican
> citizens from unsafe construction. It used bribes to outflank rivals.[18]

Troubles in Wal-Mart de Mexico were not new. In 2003, the investigating firm Kroll Inc. reported that high-volume customers were aided in
evading sales taxes, later resulting in $34 million paid by the company
in retributions.[19] A second investigation found that the Mexico subsidiary's internal audit and antifraud division was "ineffective," with employees promoted "after the suspicions of fraudulent activities had
surfaced."[20] Within this environment, when bribery problems could no
longer be ignored, lawyers in the United States recommended a major
external investigation, but executives in Bentonville shut down this idea
and instead "referred the matter back to the . . . general counsel in
Mexico—the very lawyer who was allegedly at the center of the bribery
scheme."[21]

None of this tarnished the rise of Wal-Mart de Mexico CEO Eduardo Castro-Wright, fully aware of what was powering rapid growth in
his country and soon summoned to Bentonville and promoted to vice
chairman of the whole company in 2008. And none of this prevented
Wal-Mart from crowing in its 2011 Global Responsibility Report that
"we believe transparency and accountability are part of being a good
and responsible company."[22]

The Department of Justice apparently disagreed and launched a
widespread investigation, which soon spiraled beyond Mexico:

> In India, because of Walmart's failure to implement sufficient internal ac-
> counting controls related to anti-corruption, . . . Walmart's operations
> there were able to retain TPIs [third-party intermediaries] that made im-
> proper payments to government officials in order to obtain store operating
> permits and licenses. These improper payments were then falsely recorded
> in Walmart's joint venture's books and records with vague descriptions
> like . . . "miscellaneous," "professional fees," "incidental" and "govern-
> ment fee."

. . . Walmart Brazil continued to retain and renew contracts with
TPIs . . . , including a construction company that made improper payments
to government officials. . . . [One TPI] whose ability to obtain licenses and
permits quickly earned her the nickname "sorceress" or "genie." . . .

In China, Walmart's local subsidiary's internal audit team flagged
numerous weaknesses in internal accounting controls[,] . . . and the subsidiary failed to address nearly all of the anti-corruption–related internal
controls audit findings.[23]

By the time all these investigations were finished, the statute of limitations had run out on the worst of Walmart's problems, and US authorities essentially limited charges to books and records violations
under the Foreign Corrupt Practices Act. In 2019, Walmart settled Securities and Exchange Commission charges for $144 million and De-
partment of Justice charges for $138 million and in the same year settled
a class-action lawsuit by unhappy investors for $160 million.[24]

Enter the opioid crisis, which has killed more than half a million
Americans. The biggest penalties thus far have appropriately been assessed against producers, with Purdue Pharma and others pushed into
bankruptcy but continuing operations and paying for their misdeeds.
One brave judge threw out an $8.3 billion settlement agreement with
Purdue, infuriated that the Sackler family controlling the company up-
streamed "some $10.4 billion out of the company, . . . over half . . .
either invested in offshore companies . . . or deposited into spendthrift
trusts that could not be reached in bankruptcy."[25] He forced the Sacklers to agree to contributing up to $6 billion to the final settlement.

Another brave judge, Dan Polster in Cleveland, Ohio, has been tasked
with finding appropriate penalties for opioid distributors—pharmacy
chains profiting from the sale of millions of pills in just two counties. The
outcome has huge consequences for thousands of other lawsuits around
the country, as other states, local governments, and even Native American tribes are following the proceedings and the outcome. Sensing the
scope of the problem, Rite Aid and Giant Eagle settled for undisclosed
amounts. Walmart, Walgreens, and CVS agreed to a jury trial.

After six weeks of evidence presentation and a week of jury delibera-
tions, it was found in mid-2022 that

1. oversupply of legal prescription opioids, and diversion of those
   opioids into the illicit market outside of appropriate medical
   channels, is a public nuisance and

2. each of the three defendants (CVS, Walmart, and Walgreens) engaged in intentional and/or illegal conduct which was a substantial factor in producing the public nuisance.[26]

Judge Polster, referring to his earlier position that "if the jury finds defendants liable for public nuisance . . . ,"

then it is *for the court* to decide all matters connected to abatement, including: (a) whether and how the nuisance can be abated; (b) if abatement is possible, whether the costs of abatement can be apportioned to the defendants on some logical or reasonable basis, or instead those costs must be borne by defendants jointly and severally; and (c) if the costs can be apportioned what the apportionment should be."[27]

Thus fortified in his views, Polster in August 2022 awarded $650 million to the two counties, with the three defendants jointly and severally liable. Appeals may go on for years.

Walmart said it had been sued "in search of deep pockets."[28] Perhaps the Sacklers felt the same way. Or perhaps Walmart got off easy. A ProPublica piece in 2020 reported that the company came close to being criminally indicted over opioids. Federal prosecutors in Texas spent two years compiling a case on Walmart's practices, arriving in Washington in 2018 to present their findings to the Drug Enforcement Administration. They

laid out the evidence. Opioids dispensed by Walmart pharmacies in Texas had killed customers who had overdosed. The pharmacists who dispensed those opioids had told the company they didn't want to fill the prescriptions because they were coming from doctors who were running pill mills. . . . Investigators had obtained records of similar cries for help from Walmart pharmacists all over the country: from Maine, North Carolina, Kansas and Washington, and other states. They reported hundreds of thousands of suspicious or inappropriate opioid prescriptions.[29]

Traipsing over to the Department of Justice, they made their pitch to Rod Rosenstein, deputy attorney general, arguing that "dispensing opioids without a legitimate medical purpose is legally akin to dealing heroin." The DEA's director pushed for a criminal case, since a fine would be ineffective because Walmart "has more money that it knows what to do with." Rosenstein reportedly answered in return, "Not that there's anything wrong with that. We are all capitalists here." Further attempts to pursue the case got nowhere, as the Texas prosecutors found their efforts repeatedly blocked by Washington officials.[30]

Now comes the money transfer case. Walmart has for years transferred money for its customers, utilizing services such as Western Union, MoneyGram, and Ria. The range of Walmart's financial services includes money orders, transfers, credit cards, debit cards, bill paying, and check cashing, all helping to drive customers into its places of business. In 2014 Walmart initiated Walmart2Walmart, enabling low-cost transfers from one company store to another company store. Transactions are facilitated even when no user identification is provided or fake IDs are suspected. As a result, Walmart is responsible for high percentages of fraudulent transactions that flow through MoneyGram, Ria, and Western Union. MoneyGram even suspended doing business with Walmart in some high-traffic locations.

Noting that Walmart "has not taken adequate and timely steps to address the deficiencies and inconsistencies in its own anti-fraud program, policies, and procedures and to address consumer fraud at its locations,"[31] the Federal Trade Commission finally had enough and sued Walmart in 2022:

> For over a decade, fraudsters around the world have used money transfers to obtain money from victims, especially U.S. consumers, and Walmart has long been aware that its locations have been used to perpetrate these frauds, . . . including person-in-need scams, government agent impersonator scams, and lottery, sweepstakes, and price scams, among others. . . . Walmart's decision not to train or instruct its employees to deny or reject payouts of money transfers that were suspicious and potentially due to fraud allowed fraudsters to more easily receive payouts of fraud-induced money transfers at Walmart locations.[32]

> Consumers have lost hundreds of millions, and the Commission is holding Walmart accountable for letting fraudsters fleece its customers.[33]

This is another case that will likely go on for years.

Walmart has more than 10,000 stores in 24 countries and 2.3 million employees, some 1.6 million in the United States. Good Jobs First's Violation Tracker lists 463 records of penalty assessments by US authorities against Walmart since 2000 totaling $2 billion. Wage and hour issues and employment discrimination total 82 of these violations of record.[34]

The earlier section on wealth inequality in chapter 4 notes that the Walton family is increasing its net worth by about $100 million a day, and newly hired Walmart employees make about $100 a day . . . and at that point I ask a question, "Is this capitalism performing at its best?" You be the judge.

APPLE INC.

Earlier pages have laid out the structure of the financial secrecy system, the centrality of trade manipulation, and the repricing of intangibles by multinational corporations as a principal means of evading and avoiding taxes. The technology giant Apple Inc. represents the perfection of opacity, operating through entities that existed literally nowhere.

Taking advantage of tax avoidance opportunities afforded under Irish law, Apple began establishing entities in Ireland in the early 1980s, soon including Apple Operations International (AOI) as a holding company for other overseas activities and Apple Sales International (ASI) buying finished products from manufacturers and reselling to additional Apple offshore distribution subsidiaries. Observing the enormous accumulation of untaxed profits, the Permanent Subcommittee on Investigations of the US Senate launched an examination of Apple's tax-dodging strategies. Questionnaires sent to the firm requested basic corporate data, producing for the committee staff, led by the indefatigable Elise Bean, a shocking revelation:

> One Irish subsidiary . . . had left a blank when asked to name the country where that subsidiary was a tax resident. The missing data caught the eye of one of our tax experts. Apple's representatives [were asked] to fill in the blank. They tried ducking the question, but . . . after some hemming and hawing, looking up at the ceiling, down at their shoes, and then at each other, Apple's tax team finally admitted they'd left the question blank, because the Irish subsidiary wasn't a tax resident of any country.[35]

As the subcommittee investigators pressed on, when asked where AOI was in fact managed and controlled Apple's lawyers went through the following verbal gymnastics:

> Apple has determined that AOI is not managed and controlled in Ireland based on the application of the central management and control test under

Irish law. The conclusion that AOI is not managed and controlled in Ireland does not require a determination where AOI is managed and controlled.[36]

The Permanent Subcommittee held hearings focusing on Apple in May 2013. Senator Carl Levin, committee chair, summarized as follows:

> Sending valuable intellectual property rights offshore together with the profits that follow those rights is at the heart of Apple's tax-avoidance strategy. More and more, intellectual property is the dominant source of value in the global economy. It is also highly mobile—unlike more tangible, physical assets, its value can be transferred around the globe, often with just a few keystrokes. The secret to Apple's business success isn't in the aluminum and steel and glass of my iPhone and other Apple products. Its profits depend on the ideas that bring those elements together in such an elegant package. That intangible genius is intellectual property that is nurtured and developed here in the United States. The key to offshore tax avoidance is transferring the profit-generating potential of that valuable intellectual property offshore so that the profits are directed not to the United States, but to an offshore tax haven. . . .
>
> . . . Apple says that although AOI is incorporated in Ireland, the company is not managed and controlled in Ireland and therefore not tax resident in Ireland. U.S. tax law, on the other hand, generally turns on where a company is incorporated, not on where it is managed and controlled. Apple says since AOI isn't incorporated in the United States, it is also not present in the U.S. for tax purposes. Magically, it's neither here nor there. . . . Apple has performed the same alchemy with ASI as with AOI—it's incorporated in Ireland, operated from the United States, but, Apple says, is tax resident in neither country. . . .
>
> . . . Apple is exploiting an absurdity.[37]

The 2013 Permanent Subcommittee hearing on Apple spawned further activity by the European Commission in 2016. When expanding its subsidiaries abroad, Apple twice negotiated with Ireland for what appeared to be concessionary tax rates, agreed at 2 percent, well below the country's standard 12 percent. Giving this advantage to Apple led the commission, guided by its aggressive competition advocate Margrethe Vestager, to charge Ireland with according illegal tax benefits and thus state aid to the multinational valued at €13 billion. The commission asserted that "the tax treatment in Ireland enabled Apple to avoid taxation on almost all profits generated by sales of Apple products in the entire

EU Single Market."[38] Echoing the Permanent Subcommittee in the United States, the European Commission laid out its case:

> Following an in-depth state aid investigation launched in June 2014, the European Commission has concluded that two tax rulings issued by Ireland to Apple have substantially and artificially lowered the tax paid by Apple in Ireland since 1991. As a result of the allocation method . . . Apple only paid an effective corporate tax rate that declined from 1% in 2013 to 0.005% in 2014 on the profits of Apple Sales International.[39]

Ireland, objecting to an intrusion into its domestic affairs, declined to collect the €13 billion tax penalty from Apple. Apple and Ireland sued the European Commission, a case heard before the General Court of the European Union. Pending the court's judgment, Apple in 2018 paid the tax and interest into an escrow account. In 2020 the court decided against the European Commission, asserting that Ireland had provided no state aid to Apple and therefore Apple did not owe the purported tax to Ireland. The European Commission promptly appealed the decision to the European Court of Justice, the ultimate arbiter. When finally decided, this hugely important case will have considerable influence worldwide on the relationship of corporations to governments, indeed the relationship of capitalism to democracy.

In 2017, the Institute on Taxation and Economic Policy reported that "Apple has booked $252.3 billion in profits offshore on which it has not paid a dime in U.S. taxes."[40] And Apple is certainly not alone in taking advantage of available measures to feather its own coffers. Structures that in various ways accomplish similar outcomes have allegedly been put in place by Google, Amazon, Microsoft, Facebook, McDonalds, Starbucks, Ikea, eBay, Mastercard, Nike, Uber, Allergen, Qualcomm, BASF, Fiat, Gazprom, and many, many others.

No one should be under the impression that US corporations are merely taking advantage of loopholes left in tax laws by unsuspecting legislators. On the contrary, tens of billions of dollars have been spent across decades fiercely lobbying to encode into law preferable treatments enabling deferral of taxes on profits accumulating abroad and not returned to the United States, "check the box" options that allow profit shifting between subsidiaries to go untaxed, look-through provisions that ignore subsidiary structures, avoidance of arm's-length pricing requirements in intracompany transactions, and more. The truth is, corporations have bought the laws securing, maintaining, and maximizing their own income and wealth.

A commentator writing at the time wondered whether

> corporate sovereignty has replaced nation-state sovereignty as the most important source of sovereign power in the international regime.[41]

Note carefully a key point: Dozens of American corporations, operating behind layers upon layers of secrecy, exploited complex tax schemes for more than 25 years before US legislators arrived at a limited understanding of what was going on. Industry giants all over the world, utilizing and expanding every component of the financial secrecy system, continue to avoid accountability for their activities. Business titans dominate elected representatives. Capitalism subordinates democracy.

NOT TO BE LEFT OUT: FIFA

The biggest sports scandal in history, now spanning three decades, centers around the Fédération Internationale de Football Association, with ongoing money laundering investigations and criminal sentencing. In a 2002 news conference at FIFA headquarters in Zürich a dogged Scottish journalist, Andrew Jennings, provided impetus to the story. "I'm surrounded by all these terribly posh reporters in suits and silk ties and buttoned up shirts for God's sake. And here's me in me hiking gear. I get the mike and I said 'Herr Blatter. Have you ever taken a bribe?'"[42] Herr Joseph "Sepp" Blatter had recently been reelected president of the body as hints of corruption began popping up around the world.

May 27, 2015, was a pivotal moment. The FBI and the Internal Revenue Service, acting on information and secret recordings provided by an American confidential informant beginning in 2010, indicted 14 FIFA officials and associates for wire fraud, racketeering, and money laundering. Simultaneously, guilty pleas were unsealed on four more football officials and two firms. And on the same day seven current FIFA officials were arrested at a hotel in Zürich. And the Miami office of the North American regional football confederation was raided. Before the end of 2015, nine additional officials of FIFA and two of its regional confederations were indicted, along with five corporate executives. US action ultimately accelerated investigations in Switzerland, Germany, the United Kingdom, Australia, Brazil, Argentina, Colombia, and Costa Rica, apparently making FIFA the most widespread corruption case of all time.

FIFA, composed of 209 national and territorial members and six continental confederations, had become utterly corrupted, with officials raking off hundreds of millions through several schemes. First, there was a widespread pattern of soliciting and receiving bribes from sports marketing companies for commercial and media rights, including broadcasting, advertising, sponsorship, licensing, hospitality, and ticketing. Second, FIFA officials took bribes to award games to competing nations. Third, FIFA officials even paid bribes to seek their election or reelection to governing world and regional bodies.

As the US Department of Justice summarized,

> The conduct engaged in by various members of the conspiracy included . . . trusted intermediaries, bankers, financial advisors, and currency dealers, to make and facilitate the making of illicit payments; the creation and use of shell companies, nominees, and numbered bank accounts in tax havens, and other secretive banking jurisdictions; the active concealment of foreign bank accounts; the structuring of financial transactions to avoid currency reporting requirements; bulk cash smuggling; the purchase of real property and other physical assets; the use of safe deposit boxes; income tax evasion; and obstruction of justice.[43]

Investigations into financial institutions handling the proceeds of FIFA corruption are still ongoing. In 2017, a former managing director of Julius Baer pleaded guilty to laundering more than $25 million to secure FIFA broadcast rights for a client.[44] The Swiss Financial Market Supervisory Authority, called Finma, has taken mild enforcement actions against Credit Suisse for serious lapses in handling the money of FIFA entities and officials.[45] The two US indictments handed down in 2015 list many other banks handling funds emanating from the FIFA scandal. At a minimum, adequate due diligence was not performed on more than $50 million in dubious transfers.

Journalist Jennings, who passed away in 2022, lived just long enough to be proven absolutely correct:

> These scum have stolen the people's sport.[46]

Whether FIFA, Apple, Walmart, Odebrecht, Glencore, Shell, Credit Suisse, Goldman Sachs, Wells Fargo, or any of scores of other corporations and banks, none are going it alone. All need professional help. Enter the enablers.

8

Enablers

BANKS AND CORPORATIONS OPERATING on or over the edges of legality need lawyers and accountants to sanctify their furtive schemes. To service these needs, many attorneys and auditors readily sell their services and their imprimaturs, providing counsel and cover to malefactors operating within the broad latitudes of the financial secrecy system. Hundreds of billions of dollars paid to these facilitators buy knowledge, experience, and, in many cases, the artful dodge. A culture of secrecy and deception has permeated deeply into operating mechanisms of the capitalist system.

LAWYERS

In 2015, the nongovernmental organization Global Witness undertook a stunning piece of work after carefully analyzing potential risks and courageously moving ahead. A well-dressed undercover investigator posing as a representative of a foreign official and equipped with a hidden camera in a briefcase called upon 13 law firms in New York seeking advice on how to secrete abroad and utilize funds obviously stolen from an African country. Playing his role well, he suggested that his client, not identified by name or nationality, was a government minister and the money was acquired through bribery. Secrecy was needed to facilitate purchases of a jet, a yacht, and real estate. Twelve of the 13 firms, likely recognizing that the purported funds were stolen, nevertheless engaged in discussions concerning mechanisms to handle the millions proffered:

All but one of the lawyers provided suggestions on how one could move suspect funds into the U.S. This is important: If you have suspect funds to move, you need access to the legal and financial system to hide money, and move it around without detection from law enforcement.[1]

Global Witness, quoting the investigator and naming several lawyers interviewed, reported as follows:

INVESTIGATOR: One crucial point: because the minister is a politician, and there is more and more pressure as well on those countries in Africa to be more transparent and do something against corruption. It's corruption, but we name it differently, as I told you. So, he is giving lots of speeches about all the measures the government has put into force against corruption and so on. So if his name is in or is out . . .

LAWYER: He would set up this Swiss bank account. If it's not in his name, then he needs what is known as a straw man.

LAWYER: [You] probably want to set up a trust. I'm a trustee of a trust with a client. The trust would, might even be offshore. Probably should be. That would fund the airplane deal. You basically want a couple of layers.

LAWYER: So we have to scrub it at the beginning, if we can, or scrub it at the intermediary location.

LAWYER: I'm the trustee of various family trusts. So we deal with a lot of trustees and money managers. And I would suggest three or four to you. Some are bigger, some are smaller. The smaller ones are often more flexible and understanding and less concerned about their reputation, because they fly to a great extent below the radar screen.

INVESTIGATOR: And you don't have to declare to bank authorities where the money comes from, because you said you even don't know who they are?

LAWYER: [Referring to existing relationships with a bank] They've asked me 'so you have a lot of money coming in.' I said yes, it's real estate deals. 'Oh thank you very much.'

INVESTIGATOR: No other questions asked? Even if it's foreign money?

LAWYER: The money came in; they can tell it's from an offshore bank. I said: 'I did a real estate deal.' The money came in day one, it went out on day five, that's the way it works. . . . That's how I do, that's my normal real estate pattern no matter who the client is. So it's totally normal, nothing unusual about what I just described. Nothing at all.

INVESTIGATOR: Presumably we would set up a little bit of a series of owners to try and protect privacy as much as anything else.

LAWYER: So Company A is owned by Company B, who is owned jointly by Company C and D and your party owns all of or the majority of the shares of C and D.[2]

Among the lawyers interviewed, Mark Koplik, managing partner at Henderson & Koplik and, according to his website, previously with at least two other major firms, was recorded saying that lawyers are a "privileged class" in America. He then offered the perfect coda to the investigation:

We make the laws, and when we do so, we make them in the way that's advantageous to the lawyers.[3]

Global Witness's findings, aired on the CBS program *60 Minutes*, do not appear to have caused major ripples among named attorneys because discussions with the potential client were exploratory and the lawyers broke no laws. It did, however, move US legislators closer to requiring beneficial ownership information on companies in the United States.

Lawyers and Malaysia
Chapters 6 and 7 relate a selection of examples of financial shenanigans carried out by banks and corporations. Most of these activities, of course, were facilitated by attorneys. Take just one example, Malaysia's 1MDB scandal described earlier, and consider the white-shoe law firms involved in handling hundreds of millions of stolen dollars through their accounts, as detailed in a complaint filed by the Department of Justice:

- Shearman & Sterling received from Switzerland an estimated $368 million in 11 wire transfers into its Sherman Interest on Lawyer Account (IOLA). These funds were then transferred from the IOLA to buy a Beverly Hills hotel, several luxury properties including a Time Warner penthouse in New York, and a Bombardier jet and to pay for interior decorators, yacht rentals, and $25 million in what appear to be gambling debts owed to Caesars Palace and the Venetian in Las Vegas.

- DLA Piper received $205,900,000 into its IOLA and subsequently transferred $202,206,876 to Commonwealth Land and Title Insurance Company, facilitating the purchase of the Helmsley Park Lane Hotel in New York. In a later transaction, DLA Piper received $13,000,000, sent onward to Chicago Title to handle the purchase of a condominium.
- Greenberg Traurig received into its account two transfers totaling $51,596,281, which then were onward transferred for purchase of the Walker Tower penthouse on West 18th Street in New York.
- Sullivan & Cromwell, serving as counsel to Great Delight Limited, incorporated in Seychelles and linked to the 1MDB scoundrels, received into its IOLA approximately $12,000,000 from the Shearman IOLA account and subsequently transferred $10,786,706 to Singapore to facilitate Great Delight's purchase of a Beverly Hills property.[4]

None of these firms is accused in the DOJ complaint of breaking any US laws.

College for Sale?

Other examples of attorneys acting badly, operating within the protections of the financial secrecy system, could be cited at length, but hopefully the point is reasonably established with the stories above. How such activities can go so far as to undermine another pillar of democracy does, however, merit a few paragraphs. The assault on fair access to education in the United States, with lawyers playing an integral role, has shocked the nation, as nearly 60 people have been charged by the FBI.

Gordon Caplan, then cochairman of Willkie Farr & Gallagher LLP, with 700 attorneys in New York, Washington, London, Paris, Brussels, Rome, and more, was lauded in 2018 as a "dealmaker of the year" by the *American Lawyer*.[5] Eleven months later he was indicted by federal prosecutors for his role in a massive college admissions scam called the "Varsity Blues."

The FBI's 2018 criminal complaint identifies Edge College & Career Network and Key Worldwide Foundation as perpetrators of college admission schemes for the children of wealthy parents, in the process raking in some $25 million. The complaint outlined the conspirators' several approaches to cheating on college entrance exams and falsely claiming athletic skills. To boost ACT or SAT scores, for example, Edge and Key advised clients to request extended time for their children to take the exams, often claiming a learning disability, and then change the location of the exam to a test center in Texas or California controlled by the conspirators. In a wiretapped telephone conversation with Caplan concerning his daughter, it was explained as follows:

> So here's the first thing we need to do. . . . We need to get your daughter tested for a learning difference. . . . I can have her [academic] test at one of my schools, and I can guarantee her a score. If it's ACT, I can guarantee a score . . . in the 30s. And if it's the SAT, I can guarantee her a score in the 1400s. . . . I can make scores happen.[6]

Responding later the same day, Caplan said,

> I'm particularly interested in working with you guys. . . . [T]his notion of . . . flying out to L.A., sitting with your proctor, and taking the exam is pretty interesting. . . . So, how do I get this done with you? What do I need to do?[7]

Quoted a price of $75,000, Caplan in a later conversation said, "Done, done, not a problem. . . . We are in for that, at 75. . . . I'm not worried about the moral issue here."[8]

Attorney Caplan, charged with conspiracy to commit fraud, pleaded guilty, served one month in prison, paid a fine of $50,000, and committed to 250 hours of community service. Disgraced, he is no longer co-chairman of his firm and is disbarred from practicing law again in the State of New York. Nearly 50 others among the wealthiest people in America, some the biggest names in entertainment, have pleaded guilty, most serving short sentences in prison, while others are defending their actions in court. One commentator summarized nicely:

> Just an astonishing display of elitism and rule breaking. It's like every hard-working poor kid's worst dream—not only do they have to beat an educational system that is slanted against them, but rich parents are able to throw money at illegal schemes to get their kids in the best colleges.[9]

Previous chapters have addressed the economic divide in America undermining democracy itself. Yet, so many practitioners of the law seem to be "not worried about the moral issue," as Caplan said. This unfortunately has become common among far too many attorneys in America and abroad. If we cannot depend on high or even reasonable standards of integrity in the legal profession, then the democratic-capitalist system is in worse shape than we thought.

AUDITORS

The auditing profession may be the most conflicted of all. Literally conflicted, because there is a built-in conflict of interest in the largest and most prestigious firms: selling financial and tax services and simultaneously reviewing management performance. There is no way to undertake both responsibly.

Consulting services have in fact become larger revenue generators than auditing services for each of the Big Four firms (figure 8.1).

Auditors can advise companies on executive compensation, which can certainly help in retaining clients. Advice on tax avoidance schemes have been sold even if there is only a 25 percent chance that a scheme will be acceptable to authorities. Advice on setting up opaque offshore entities can help minimize taxes. Bribe payments can be overlooked. Advice on depreciation and amortization can influence how revenues are recorded. The larger firms can rotate in and out of corporate clients so that consulting and auditing appear as separate functions but carry over from

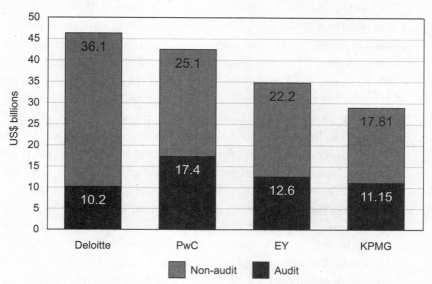

FIGURE 8.1 Revenue of the Big Four accounting firms, 2018
Source: Chart from Adam Leaver et al. Used with permission.[10]

one cycle to another. Sarbanes-Oxley legislation passed in 2002 said to US firms that consulting and auditing could not be offered by the same firm at the same time, but this has not been strictly enforced, and similar requirements have not been adopted in the United Kingdom and in most other countries.

The first decade of the new century was littered with corporate shenanigans that went unchallenged by auditors. In the United States, Enron, with purported asset values of $65 billion, filed for bankruptcy in 2001, shortly followed by WorldCom in 2002 at $104 billion. Arthur Anderson audited both and subsequently ceased operations, putting its 88,000 employees out of work. Logically this should have been warning enough to the auditing profession, assuring that a combination of absence of diligence and presence of duplicity never happens again. Not so. The financial scandals of 2008–2009, for which auditing firms have a substantial measure of responsibility, nearly brought down the global economy. Even after government bailouts, financial institutions and their auditors continued to take incalculable risks:

- Bear Stearns, warned by the SEC in 2005, continued to overextend in mortgage-backed securities and finally collapsed in 2008. A class action lawsuit caustically criticized Deloitte, asserting that audits were "so deficient that the audit amounted to no audit at all, were an egregious refusal to see the obvious or investigate the doubtful, and/or disregarded specific 'red flags' that would have placed a reasonable auditor on notice that the Company was engaged in wrongdoing."[11] Deloitte paid $19.5 million to settle claims.

- EY for seven years approved Lehman Brothers' "Repo 105" tactic whereby mortgages valued at, say, $105 million were ostensibly "sold" to various offshore banks for $100 million to get them temporarily off Lehman's balance sheet and then repurchased days later at $105 million. Lehman, with debts of $768 billion, also collapsed in 2008. New York state attorney general Andrew Cuomo filed suit against EY, asserting that "Repo 105 transactions . . . served no purpose other than to artificially reduce the leverage ratio. Aware that the public was being misled, EY never questioned the practice or sought to have it disclosed to the investing public."[12] EY settled this suit for $10 million and an investor suit for $99 million.

- Washington Mutual, headquartered in Seattle, tired of being a stodgy lender, ramped up its home loan business in 2005. Adjustable rate mortgages quickly became the majority of its portfolio, and when borrowers fell behind according to a sweeping complaint filed in Western District Court, the bank treated these "negative amortizations" as "non-cash income created solely from a borrower's failure to pay full interest."[13] "Non-cash income rose from $76 million . . . to $1.7 billion" in five months. Deloitte issued unqualified audit opinions, and after the bank was forced into receivership the auditors contributed $18.5 million to a $208 million settlement.[14] Washington Mutual thus became the biggest bank failure in US history.

- AIG had already been fined $1.6 billion in 2005 for misstating its accounts, and PwC likewise paid $97.5 million for auditing those misstated accounts, when they found themselves in extremely serious trouble again in 2008. AIG had entered into credit default obligations insuring more than $400 billion of AAA-rated mortgage securities held by major US and foreign banks. As the mortgage market collapsed, AIG's possible failure threatened to shatter the global economy. The US government stepped in with, finally, $182 billion for AIG to forestall a meltdown. Meanwhile, PwC was valuing obligations at one price for AIG and the same obligations at a different price for, say, Goldman Sachs.[15] These and other questionable audit practices led to class action suits, with AIG paying out $960 million in one consolidated case, while PwC settled for $10.5 million.[16]

- MF Global hired Jon Corzine, ex-CEO of Goldman Sachs, ex-governor of New Jersey, ex-U.S. senator, in 2010 to lead the futures trader into investment banking. MF Global promptly entered into massive purchases of risky European sovereign bonds at discount prices, then through a complex two-layered deal resold the bonds to the London Clearing House for delivery at a later date. As prices on the bonds weakened, MF Global had to make up the difference, which it did in part by taking money out of its brokerage customers' accounts. Collapsing in 2011, the bankruptcy plan administrator sued PwC charging that

> professional malpractice and negligence caused the Company massive damages in connection with its investment in billions of dollars in European sovereign debt instruments. PwC incorrectly and negligently advised the Company to account for these . . . transactions as if they were "sales" by immediately booking revenues from these purported "sales" up to 21 months before the Company actually received those revenues and using off-balance-sheet accounting for those investments.[17]

Facing a claim of between $1 billion and $3 billion, PwC settled in 2017 for an undisclosed amount. The firm also settled shareholder suits for $65 million. Corzine and colleagues settled suits for another $64.5 million.[18]

- PwC's troubles accelerated. In 2017, the Federal Deposit Insurance Corporation brought an action against the firm ordering it to pay $625 million for "professional negligence" in connection with the 2009 collapse of Colonial Bank in Alabama. The judgment was later settled for $335 million.[19] Colonial Bank officers had conspired with mortgage originator Taylor Bean & Whitaker, buying fake securities. Taylor Bean's liquidator sued PwC for $5.6 billion, which PwC settled for an undisclosed amount in midtrial.[20] The US Department of Justice extracted a fine of $149.5 million from Deloitte for years of faulty audits of Taylor Bean.[21]

These are only a few examples of staggering audit and ethical failures in the United States. But such failures are seen across the ocean as well.

Modern-day auditing developed in England in the mid-1800s, and today PwC, Deloitte, and EY have their global branding and coordinating offices situated in England, while KPMG is in Switzerland. All four operate as cooperatives in one form or another—collections of legally distinct local firms—purposefully to avoid global repercussions when any one office is charged or sued. The Big Four are amply criticized in rising tones particularly in the United Kingdom since the financial crisis of 2007–2008. A widely respected authority for three decades, Prem Sikka, professor at the University of Essex, and coauthor Austin Mitchell argue cogently as follows:

> The state has been rolled-back and hollowed-out to serve multinational corporations. . . . A popular myth is that accountancy firms are in the front-line of the war against white-collar crime, but too many have become key players in white-collar crime. Their values are summed-up by a partner who declared, "No matter what legislation is in place, the accountants and lawyers will find a way around it. Rules are rules, but rules are meant to be broken."[22]

The financial crisis brought down two UK banks. Northern Rock was creating home mortgages and bundling them into securities for sale, underwritten by Lehman Brothers. As liquidity dried up Northern Rock sought support from the Bank of England, which led to panicked depositors rushing to withdraw their savings, the first such run in the country in

150 years. Taken over by the government, Northern Rock's auditor, PwC, faced immediate criticism for lack of warnings about rapid growth and lack of liquidity.

The Royal Bank of Scotland, for a brief time the biggest bank in the world, aggressively bought interests in banks in Spain, Belgium, the Netherlands, and the United States. The financial crisis led steadily to departures by RBS's corporate customers and, having avoided the problem too long, finally required the chairman to call the chancellor of the exchequer on October 7, 2008, to report that he would be out of cash by the afternoon. Parliamentary investigations into the RBS affair and its auditor, Deloitte, were hard-hitting:

> Either they were culpably unaware of the mounting dangers, or, if they were aware of them, they equally culpably failed to alert the supervisory authority of their concerns.[23]

While this passes for blunt language in England, it did not stop a continuing string of audit lapses and investigations, a small number summarized as follows:

- KPMG is being probed by the Financial Reporting Council for its audits of Rolls-Royce after the technology company admitted in 2016 to bribes paid to government officials in Thailand, Brazil, Kazakhstan, Azerbaijan, Iraq, and Angola. Fines paid by Rolls-Royce in a global resolution totaled more than $800 million.[24]
- Carillion plc, a construction and facilities management company with 43,000 employees in several countries, grew rapidly through acquisitions and increased its dividend payout every year, with executive bonuses rising apace. That is, until 2017 when it simply ran out of money and promptly went into liquidation, leaving employees, pensioners, and suppliers out of luck. Each of the Big Four—PwC, KPMG, Deloitte, and EY—provided auditing and consulting services to Carillion. A parliamentary select committee led by Rachel Reeves from Leeds West was scathing in its criticisms:

> There are conflicts of interest at every turn. KPMG were Carillion's external auditors. Deloitte were internal auditors and EY were tasked with turning the company around. PwC had variously advised the company, its pension schemes, and the government on Carillion contracts. . . .

. . . The panoply of auditors and other advisors who looked the other way or who were offered an opportunity for consultancy fees from a floundering company have been richly compensated. . . . Carillion was not just a failure of a company; it was a failure of a system of corporate accountability which too often leaves those responsible at the top—and the ever-present firms that surround them—as winners, while everyone else loses out.[25]

Reeves offered her personal views:

KPMG, PwC, Deloitte, and EY pocket millions of pounds for their lucrative audit work—even when they fail to warn about corporate disasters like Carillion. It is a parasitical relationship which sees the auditors prosper, regardless of what happens to the companies, employees and investors who rely on their scrutiny.[26]

Grilling a KPMG partner, one member of Parliament said that

I would not hire you to do an audit of the contents of my fridge.[27]

- In 2019 PwC and EY were both criticized in connection with the failure of the tour company Thomas Cook, which abruptly stopped flying in October, leaving 600,000 customers stranded all over the world. Rachel Reeves, ramping up her push for tougher regulation, slammed the two firms: "How many more company failures, how many more egregious examples of accounting do we need before your industry opens its eyes and recognizes you're complicit in this and that you need to reform?"[28]

Prem Sikka summarized his long-held views and, following a career focused on financial and accounting integrity, was made a member of the House of Lords in 2020:

Big accounting firms have a history of using financial/political resources to dilute reforms. They have been delivering dud audits, engaged in tax avoidance and insolvency abuses for decades and governments have done nothing. Ordinary people pay the price of this corrupt indulgence.[29]

The record of audit failings continues to grow in the United States, the United Kingdom, Brazil, South Africa, Malaysia, and many other countries despite literally dozens of government regulators supposedly watching the till. The inability of regulators to ensure high-quality audits is further evidence of a key point made throughout these pages. No one can regulate a secrecy system, this system of financial secrecy that has arisen in the last half century and is now used the world over to move and hide revenues and profits.

Furthermore, firms offering both auditing and consulting services have built-in conflicts of interest. There is no way to sell tax and accounting services with one hand and then objectively audit management performance with the other hand. This is simply unworkable. Previewing conclusions in chapter 14, these two functions must be separated.

Banks, corporations, lawyers, and accountants are the four principal legs on which the capitalist system rests. This chapter and the two preceding are highly critical of failings within each of these components of our chosen economic arrangement. But the failings are not all of the same import. There is one part of this system that has little of redeeming quality, that is so compromised as to require prompt and profound change: auditing, concentrated in power, conflicted to the core, and unrepresentative of the public good, demands purposeful resolution.

Having said all this, there is an additional component of the broader democratic-capitalist system that is deeply complicitous in the global realities undermining equity and freedom in the twenty-first century. And that is the role of governments themselves, so often supportive of the subterfuges emerging in recent decades in our national and global economic and political affairs. It is to governments and their deficiencies that we now turn.

9

Complicit Governments

THE SECRECY STRUCTURE NOW EMBEDDED into the motivations and operations of capitalism was laid out in chapter 1. Crucial to an understanding of this structure and its impact on the world are two points.

First, every element of the structure has the support of governments, particularly Western governments. Capitalism has bought and paid for the laws enabling the hidden accumulation of income and wealth, driving inequality and undermining democracy. No part of the secrecy structure benefits poor and middle-income classes in any country; every part of the shadowy system is designed to benefit the rich across the world.

Second, access to the secrecy structure is driving authoritarianism. Despots, dictators, the mildly corrupted, and the wannabes know that they can steal with abandon and find ready venues to hold and hide their swag. Authoritarianism comes with the opportunity for self-enrichment of governing cliques, enabled by capitalism's financial secrecy system.

Capitalism and democracy should be equal partners, contributing to prosperity and freedom. Instead, capitalism is buying governments, buying off democracy, and relegating democracy to a lesser status in the partnership. If this continues, it will ultimately defeat the democratic-capitalist system.

This chapter proceeds with a look into debilitating realities prevailing in Russia, China, Guatemala, Venezuela, South Africa, Myanmar, and Iran as unambiguous examples of how malpractices within capitalism undermine liberty and prosperity for billions of people. It concludes with the United States, demonstrating the manifest complicity of the greatest power in the mechanisms supporting rogue capitalism and, in the process, weakening democracy, both for Americans and others around the world.

RUSSIA

Vladimir Putin is almost certainly the richest crime boss of all time, skill-fully using the financial secrecy system to procure and shelter a stagger-ing accumulation of wealth. Brazen robbery of assets within Russia by him and by successive and obeisant oligarchs is absolutely breathtaking in its dimensions. Adding to this is his utter disdain for the supposed moral superiority of the West, which readily welcomed all that could be stolen and shifted out of his country. Rising from poverty and obscurity, Putin seems now to have become thoroughly maniacal and absolutely paranoid. Convinced of his superiority and the West's depravity, in Feb-ruary 2022 he launched a killing spree in Ukraine aimed at validating his own long-held grievances and suspicions.

Richard Nixon, writing a memo in 1992 titled "How to Lose the Cold War," nailed it, excerpted here:

> Will the United States and the West snatch defeat from the jaws of vic-tory in the Cold War? We are told time and again that the Cold War is over and that the West has won it. This is only half true. The commu-nists have lost the Cold War but the West has not yet won it. Commu-nism collapsed because it failed. Freedom is now on trial. If it fails to produce a better life, we shall witness not a return to communism but the rise of a new despotism in which people will give up freedom for security and entrust their future to old hands with new faces.
>
> . . . What happens in Russia will affect the next century. If freedom succeeds in Russia this will be a powerful example for others to follow. . . . If it fails in Russia we will see the tide of freedom which is sweeping over the world begin to ebb and the Cold War will be succeeded by a Cold Peace with devastating consequences for those who must endure it.
>
> We must remember that while Russia is no longer communist it is still Russian with a centuries-old tradition of expansionism and a people who during times of trouble tend to turn to a strong hand—even dictatorship for leadership.[1]

Vladimir Putin is worse than the "dictatorship for leadership" foretold by Richard Nixon. He is a skilled and ruthless criminal, head of a net-work bent on plundering the cowed people of Russia.

The KGB assigned Putin, a fresh law graduate from Leningrad State University, to Dresden in the 1980s, where he seems to have observed high-level crime by Russian diplomats and East German intelligence officers. Returning to St. Petersburg in 1990, Putin soon gravitated from the KGB into local administration, watching Mikhail Gorbachev and Boris Yeltsin preside over the chaos of perestroika and collapse of the Soviet Union. Handing out opportunities and contracts to a select circle of friends and likely enriching himself in the process, Putin formed the alliances that would serve him well over the next 30 years. Rising through positions and party ranks and relocating to Moscow, he became director of Federal Security Services and then prime minister in 1999 and president in 2000.

Determined to avoid the mistakes of his immediate predecessors, Putin promptly initiated "The Reform of the Administration of the President of the Russian Federation," giving himself and his office extraordinary control over the country:

> The new President of the R.F. will orient himself to realizing his presidential powers and conclude the final stage of allocating positions within the government to people he trusts.

> To ensure and promote the activity of the President of the Russian Federation, the Administration realizes the following functions:
> - Draft plans for laws.
> - Draft conclusions on bills passed.
> - Draft plans of decrees, assignments, and appeals.
> - Control and supervision of the realization of federal laws, decrees, and directives.
> - Collection, processing, and analysis of information about socioeconomic, political, and legal processes in the state and abroad.
> - Guaranteeing the unity of the information and legal space.[2]

In addition, a secret section of the document lays out plans to "*tangibly* and *concretely* influence all political processes," encompassing parties and movements, public leaders, heads of regions, legislative powers, electoral associations, candidates, mass media, and journalists.[3] With this in hand, Putin's control was planned to be and remains essentially unlimited.

Wealthy oligarchs became fabulously rich, taking over banks and companies during the Yeltsin years, but they were not all part of Putin's inner circle. Several, after transferring much of their wealth abroad, departed to Israel, the United Kingdom, and the United States. Mikhail Khodorkovsky, who owned 78 percent of the oil company Yukos, proved troublesome and was jailed in Siberia for 10 years, losing much of his wealth. Boris Berezovsky, another oil and media titan, was found hanged in his London abode. Through these and similar actions leading to exile and death for perceived opponents, Putin made it unmistakably clear that submission and tribute were owed to him. The first round of billionaires lost favor and were replaced by a second round of trusted and opportunistic cronies as companies were renationalized so they could be more easily ransacked.

And these favored few, working with security services and organized crime, are aggressively robbing the state, using capital transactions and trade transactions alike to shift stolen money abroad. Based on entirely fictitious dealings in shares, assets, and debts, hundreds of billions of dollars in capital move through willing banks, mostly in Europe as chapter 6 detailed. Again, based on entirely fictitious trade pricings, imports and exports are misinvoiced, shifting hundreds of billions of dollars into subsidiaries abroad then into the pockets of the anointed accomplices. Across a decade, underinvoicing of exports from Russia plus overinvoicing of imports into Russia, researched through gaps appearing in data with trading partner countries, is put at nearly $637 billion.[4]

Bloomberg Economics estimated that basic mechanisms for robbery accounted for some $750 billion extracted from Russia.[5] Atlantic Council scholar Anders Åsland puts the figure at $1 trillion or more of wealth shifted out of Russia. Oliver Bullough, author of *Moneyland*, agrees and makes clear just how much this really is:

> If you had a trillion U.S. dollars in bills, and you settle down to count them, you know, one dollar at a time, one a second until you'd finished, that would take you about 30,000 years; it's an incredible amount of money. And once that amount of money has been put on the sort of balance against democracy . . . it is a profound threat to any kind of democratic order.[6]

While bemoaning "the general lack of international financial transparency," the US-based National Bureau of Economic Research says

> what we know for sure is that the magnitude of cumulated Russian trade surpluses and total missing wealth over the 1990–2015 [period] is extremely large (at least 200% of Russia's national income).[7]

Gazprom, the national oil and gas company, has been plundered for decades, as Putin's confidants outright steal from the entity, underprice exports out of the country, and overprice equipment and material brought into the country. Gazprom's market value on international stock exchanges has fallen over recent years from a high of $369 billion to less than $100 billion.

Various estimates of Putin's wealth run from tens of billions to hundreds of billions of dollars. Every transaction of $1 billion or more is said to require his personal approval. One exile suggested that "typically half of any crony business went to Putin."[8] An observation that his wealth abroad might be on the order of $40 billion elicited a laugh from a US intelligence official.

Roman Borisovich, a Russian-born, foreign-educated, anticorruption activist living in London and occasional tour guide to crooks' properties around the city, puts it clearly:

> You have to understand that Russia is an absolute kleptocracy. That means that the political elite is plundering the country—robbing their fellow taxpayers blind—but the money doesn't stay in Russia. As soon as it is stolen it comes out immediately, and after a quick spin in the laundromat of British offshore territories, it comes here. . . . It is totally emboldened by the fact that, unlike in the time of the cold war—in the Soviet era—people who are perceived to be new enemies are allowed to access banks and all financial instruments of the west. Their money is hidden somewhere in plain sight, somewhere here, and nothing is being done to them.[9]

Though their country is endowed with enormous natural resources, Russians have lower median incomes than most of their ex-communist neighbors, including those in Poland, Hungary, Belarus, Lithuania, Estonia, Croatia, Slovakia, Slovenia, and the Czech Republic.[10] In what has been called the "Putin Exodus," nearly two million have emigrated out of Russia since he assumed power, mostly the young and educated opting for freedom and opportunity.

> So long as authoritarianism and politically connected economic privilege continue in Russia, talented people will continue to leave.[11]

After stealing the first billion dollars, what is the point of further theft, a question that was puzzling to me for years. The fact is that continued theft is a necessary instrument of power. It can be shared, but it cannot be ended. The alpha kleptocrat must retain the position of "thief in chief."

Putin's crony capitalism condemns Russia to near stagnation for as long as he stays in power. No political or economic reform is on his agenda, since reform would undermine his political power.[12]

In 2020 Putin rammed through his compliant legislature, then confirmed with a foregone public referendum, an amendment to the constitution allowing him to remain in power until 2036. Coupled with this, he is immune from prosecution for life, and details of his financial and personal affairs and that of thousands of coconspirators are classified.

Putin is accused of weaponizing kleptocracy. In a study by this name, the Hudson Institute reported that

the Kremlin hopes to infect Western countries with its own kleptocratic virus, refashioning them in Russia's image. The Kremlin uses its kleptocratic networks . . . to fuel the subversive "active measures" of hybrid warfare.[13]

Catherine Belton, in her book *Putin's People*, connotes that Putin holds a

long-standing cynical view that anyone in the West could be bought and that commercial imperatives would always outweigh any moral or other concerns.[14]

This "cynical view" may very well have contributed to Putin's idea that he could invade Ukraine and get away with it. After all, Europe is dependent on his oil and gas, and both Europe and America bask in their holdings of a trillion-plus dollars of Russian state funds and private capital. If so, he miscalculated the latent strength of the North Atlantic Treaty Organization, the courage and intransigence of the Ukrainian people, and even the degree to which corruption had undermined his own military and intelligence services.

While America and Europe rather weakly threatened economic retaliation against Russia before the attack on Ukraine, no dissuading measures were put in place until after the attack was initiated. Then, some foreign currency holdings were frozen, access to the global banking system was restricted, financial transactions through SWIFT were partially blocked, purchases of Russian resources and products were limited, and sanctions were heaped upon the assets of Russian oligarchs and government officials. The ruble plunged in value, the Moscow stock exchange closed, and bank withdrawals were limited as the Russian economy veered into decline.

Unable to get at Putin's wealth directly, the US Treasury Department and a number of other countries launched the Russian Elites, Proxies and Oligarchs (REPO) Task Force aimed at investigating and prosecuting the billionaires aligned with Putin. For its part, the Department of Justice launched KleptoCapture, putting oligarchs' assets and properties in the crosshairs. The problem is, most such holdings and their ownership are purposefully and deeply concealed.

> You can't just walk up and grab somebody's yacht. You have to walk through the facts that link the property to a crime.
>
> That's going to be the challenge and it will take months or years—not days.[15]

In other words, the financial secrecy system has done a superb job of hiding and protecting these stolen hoards, and sanctions against Russian banks, companies, and individuals will be ineffective in the short term and perhaps undecisive even in the long term. Putin and his band of thieves have enormous reserves to fall back on.

Gordon Brown, former UK prime minister, got it right:

> The crimes of Vladimir Putin are so heinous, outrageous and extensive that we should now consider how to bring him to justice not only for his crimes of aggression against Ukraine and his continuing reign of terror, but for his three decades of deceit and corruption: his looting of Russia's resources and his and his collaborators' fraud, expropriation, extortion, bribery, and their subsequent money laundering and exploitation of offshore tax havens to hide the scale of their crimes. . . . [H]e has also been able to act with impunity because in the world's financial centres . . . bankers, accountants, lawyers, estate agents and PR advisors, who, knowing perfectly well they are covering up crimes, have been willing to use every loophole in domestic and international law to offer his cabal safe havens.[16]

For half a century Western officials, analysts, and commentators have drawn attention to corruption in Africa, Latin America, and Asia, often expressed with contempt for foreign ethnicities perceived to be of lesser character. What we have with Putin, his crony kleptocrats, and their European and American facilitators should, quite honestly, put an end to such Western arrogance. Who is more guilty, the one stealing or, fully aware of its provenance, the one receiving stolen property?

Theft and secrecy lie at the very heart of the Kremlin's modus operandi. How the West could have so fully and cooperatively supported this process is beyond comprehension.

Putin is the greatest example in current times of the whopping returns on investments gained through authoritarianism. He serves as a model for aspiring autocrats, demonstrating that adhering to lofty democracy is far less profitable than exploiting flawed capitalism.

What Putin has done in Ukraine may have geopolitical implications as significant as 9/11, the terrorist attack on the United States. Hopefully, among these implications will be a determination to shut down the financial secrecy system, the instrument of a significant part of his arrogance and depravity and that of his henchmen.

Let there be no doubt; invisible trillions and authoritarian rule threaten humanity.

CHINA

Russia, the second-biggest heist in history, is vastly exceeded by China, number one with trillions of dollars shifted abroad, utilizing basic opportunities provided by the financial secrecy system. The process is unusually simple due to the attachment of Hong Kong, one of the world's great tax havens and clandestine jurisdictions.

The two usual mechanisms—foreign trade and foreign investment—have been carried to extremes in shifting money out of China, particularly from the enormous state-owned enterprise sector. During the last decade of available data, trade misinvoicing alone shifted a whopping $4.5 trillion across China's borders.[17] A *New York Times* analysis put outflows at $1 trillion over just an 18-month period.[18] A Bloomberg analysis reports a "cash exodus" from China 56 out of 60 months through early 2019.[19]

Investment flows show tens of billions of dollars moving, at least temporarily, into tens of thousands of offshore companies in the British Virgin Islands, the Cayman Islands, Singapore, and other havens that provide incorporation services behind a cloak of anonymity. Much of that Chinese money, having acquired a foreign identity, is roundtripped back through Hong Kong, which accounts for some 70 percent of foreign direct investment into China. In other words, Chinese money that moves abroad and incorporates as a foreign company and is then reinvested via Hong Kong into China. thus gains permanent channels through which further trade, dividends, and interest payments can legally continue to shift money out of China. While the Chinese government buys US Treasury bills, Chinese businesspeople buy foreign real estate and luxury goods and "golden visas" enabling transfers of residence and citizenship out of their home country. Stagnating foreign exchange reserves and a likely current account deficit begin to complicate China's fiscal dilemmas going forward. Moody's and Standard & Poor's have downgraded Chinese sovereign debt.

Not only are citizens sending their wealth out, but Chinese money launderers are also taking over from Mexicans and Colombians who for decades dominated the business of moving drug proceeds. Utilizing Chinese flying money mechanisms, dollar transactions are routed through China, where banking oversight is lax, on their way to the Sinaloa Cartel and at least three other drug trafficking organizations as well.[20]

Credit has to be given to China for lifting 800 million people out of severe poverty. Government investment through state-owned companies, infrastructure development, and controlled entrepreneurship combined to accomplish in a few decades the greatest improvement in living standards ever seen. Accompanying this, however, has been the fastest separation between rich and poor ever seen, with China now having more billionaires than any country except the United States and, as the IMF reports, a Gini coefficient making China "among the most unequal countries in the world." This record of achievement, appealing to both poor and rich, gives China a persuasive argument against democracy and aids in marketing its brand of authoritarianism.

Why, then, with a booming domestic economy and living standards improving for virtually the whole of its citizenry, does so much money exit China? Because, like other authoritarian states, many Chinese, particularly those billionaires and multimillionaire aspirants, do not trust the long-term stability of their wealth in their own country and seek instead Western alternatives.

In 2012, Xi Jinping was elected secretary-general of the Chinese Communist Party (CCP) and chairman of the Central Military Commission and then in 2013 added the ceremonial positions of president and head of state. Xi promptly launched a campaign to fight corruption which, if unchecked, could "doom the party and the state."[21] Soon, three tigers were ensnared—a member of the Politburo, an advisor to the preceding party secretary, and a provincial leader. Within the powerful Central Committee, 35 members and alternates have been disciplined, overcrowding the upscale prison on the outskirts of Beijing.[22] As of 2018, 2.7 million officials had been investigated, 1.5 million punished, and literally tons of cash recovered. A Bank of China report "revealed that public officials—including executives at state-owned companies—had embezzled more than $120 billion out of China since the mid-1980s."[23]

Western scholars and observers have long wondered whether China's anticorruption drive is aimed primarily at the reality of corruption or at cleansing the regime of political rivals. A 2018 analysis concludes that "individuals with personal ties to Xi Jinping appear to be exempt from investigation while, individuals with ties to . . . other . . . members of the Politburo Standing Committee had no special protection."[24] For years multiple agencies have been tasked with fighting corruption, including the National Anti-Corruption Bureau, the Office Against Dereliction of Duty, the Ministry of Supervision, local Commissions for Discipline Inspection, the anticorruption department of the Supreme People's Procuratorate, and the overarching Central Commission for Discipline Inspection. Through a 2018 constitutional amendment, all of these were subsumed by a new National Supervisory Commission, virtually equal to if not above the Supreme People's Court and the State Council, with unchecked powers of detention and prosecution over party and nonparty personnel. Interpretations of the enabling legislation indicate that decisions of the National Supervisory Commission cannot be appealed, a clear indication of the party absorbing the state.

Since 2012 Xi has steadily consolidated his power and, in addition to his other titles at the pinnacle, now also serves as chairman or head of the following bodies:

National Security Committee
Foreign Affairs and National Security
Taiwan Affairs
Financial and Economic Work
Network Security and Information Technology
Deepening Reforms of National Defense and the Military
Joint Operations Command Center of the People's Liberation Army
Military and Civilian Integration Development Committee
Group for Comprehensively Deepening Reforms[25]

In 2017 Xi's guidance, redolent of Mao Zedong, was added to the party constitution as "Thought for the New Era of Socialism with Chinese Special Characteristics." In 2018 the People's Congress scrapped presidential term limits, potentially securing Xi's reign for a third term to 2027 or a fourth to 2032. With his thought enshrined, time in office perpetuated, and control of every lever of power, Xi's brand of authoritarianism will long dominate the world's most populous country, "securing the longevity of a CCP led by red aristocracy."[26]

And even these powers are buttressed by a massive digital monitoring system that requires state control over websites, forums, and online blogs and then watches 800 million citizens using smartphones and the internet. Add to this some 200 million surveillance cameras and exploding facial recognition technology able to check on people's movements and pick out individuals in a crowd.

> The goal is for this system to provide "100 percent" coverage in specified types of areas—including public spaces in residential communities—by 2020. With assistance from an associated database, officials will be able to cross-check data from cameras all over China.[27]

Add to this again a social credit rating system—an algorithmic scorecard—that tracks individuals, corporations, and government entities on school performance, jobs, travels, financial accounts, loan payments, complaints, bankruptcies, and more, with privileges or punishments meted out accordingly. All of these measures, sometimes called "digital totalitarianism," and the unchecked powers of the National Supervisory Commission are aimed at maintaining control by the CCP over the Chinese state forever.

How long is forever? One school of thought points to political unrest in Hong Kong and predicts that the current regime will fall within 10 years. Another school of thought predicts that nothing will shake party control for the next 50 years. Michael Pillsbury writes of the "hundred-year marathon,"

> a plan that has been implemented by the Communist Party leadership from the beginning of its relationship with the United States. The goal is to avenge or "wipe clean" (*xi xue*) past foreign humiliations. Then China will set up a world order that will be fair to China, a world without American global supremacy, and revise the U.S.-dominated economic and

geopolitical world order founded at Bretton Woods and San Francisco at the end of World War II.[28]

Nor is China content to apply its authoritarian control mechanisms only internally. The Belt and Road Initiative, intending to link Chinese commerce across 144 or more countries in Asia, the Middle East, Africa, and into Europe, is already being promoted not only with highways, railroads, port construction, loans, investments, and other inducements but also with accompanying arguments lauding the benefits of political authoritarianism, aided with surveillance technologies that China is pleased to provide. Within the Chinese example of economic progress linked to surveillance capitalism, democracy faces a severe and daunting challenge likely to influence political and economic affairs for the rest of this century.

Relations with the West are complicated by multiple factors. COVID-19 may have originated in China in either a wet market or a Wuhan lab. The Chinese government is widely accused of repressing internal and external information about the pandemic and its spread as Xi struggles to maintain control of the narrative and deflect party criticism.

Next, the plight of the Uyghurs, a mostly Muslim Turkic group of some 11 million people, has grabbed world attention, with Amnesty International calling the repression "crimes against humanity" and a joint Newslines/Raoul Wallenberg report calling it "genocide."[29] In 2020 the Australian Strategic Policy Institute estimated that 1 million Uyghurs have been forced into reeducation facilities and work camps and identified 82 foreign and Chinese companies "potentially directly or indirectly benefiting from the use of Uyghur workers outside Xinjiang through abusive labour transfer programs" and "54 companies . . . implicated in what could be forced labour schemes within Xinjiang itself."[30] Technology and textile products, produced under coercive conditions, are flowing from these installations to many of the biggest names in global manufacturing and commerce.

Then the West watched in 2020 as Beijing broke its guarantee to Great Britain of measured autonomy for Hong Kong, used its military to crush democracy protesters, and subjected the city's chief executive and legislature to CCP approval. The United States and some allies responded with weak sanctions against the emboldened regime. Now Taiwan quivers as Xi, speaking to the CCP's 100th anniversary gathering, guaranteed that "resolving the Taiwan question and realizing China's complete reunification is a historic mission and an unshakable commitment of the

Communist Party of China."[31] Claudia Rosett, of the Hudson Institute, lamented that

> for Hong Kong, it is a colossal tragedy. For all of us, it is a harbinger of the 21st century world order that China's ruler, Xi Jinping, is already heavily influencing and proposes to dominate under his vision of a "shared future for mankind."[32]

The US-based International Republican Institute issues clear warnings

> As China's global influence continues to grow, so too does the threat to democracies worldwide.[33]
>
> The CCP—which systematically suppresses political pluralism and free expression in China—is increasingly attempting to use similar practices abroad to manipulate internal political and information environments to its own benefit. China's preference for opaque, corrupt economic deals corrodes democratic institutions and leaves countries increasingly beholden to their Chinese creditors.
>
> These actions, in conjunction with China's support for likeminded, illiberal partners, and growing advocacy for its authoritarian model, have the potential to draw fragile democracies into China's orbit and away from the United States and the democratic West.[34]

Some analysts and commentators posit democratic socialism as the alternative to democratic capitalism. This may be true in theory, as said earlier, but it is not true in the real world of today. Authoritarianism is the alternative to democratic capitalism and is becoming an increasingly attractive alternative for scores of countries.

As an ideology, authoritarianism will likely widen and then eventually fail, but as it widens and fails it has the potential to take democracy and the democratic-capitalist system down with it. The essence of this potential failure—the point of this book—is that the capitalist component within democratic capitalism is inadequately spreading fair shares of wealth and prosperity and failing to hold up its end of the grand bargain between these two ideologies and therefore is primarily responsible for risking the whole of the democratic-capitalist system, including and most especially its democracy component.

Is China's example of authoritarianism a likely or possible fate of democratic capitalism? The answer to this lies primarily within our system's capitalist component.

GUATEMALA

Ninety percent of cocaine coming into the United States transits through Guatemala, and one of the world's highest murder rates threatens its citizens. Of the estimated 1.5 million Guatemalan-born residents in the United States, two-thirds may be in the country illegally. More family units come to the border seeking entry or asylum than from any other country. Four out of five Guatemalan presidents in this century have been imprisoned or are accused of corruption. Democracy is under assault. And the financial secrecy system lies at the heart of the country's decline.

Alfonso Portillo was inaugurated president of Guatemala in 2000. One of his first actions changed central bank rules. Until then, dollar currency to be repatriated to the United States had to be brought to the central bank, recorded, and then returned by the central bank to the United States, all legal under Guatemalan and US law. Portillo said no; now commercial banks can take their dollar currencies directly to the United States for deposit into their accounts, again legal under both countries' laws. The effect of bypassing the central bank, enabling commercial banks to gather dollars from branches all around the country and fly them for deposit into US banks with no reckoning of where the money came from, instantly made Guatemala the preferred receiving, marshaling, transiting, paying, and recycling center of the North American drug world. In short order, nearly 500 clandestine landing strips were reportedly carved out to handle drugs and money, and opium poppy production expanded in rural areas.

Freeing local banks of constraints on money laundering threw open the doors to wider political corruption. Portillo accepted a bribe of $2.5 million from Taiwan to retain Guatemala's diplomatic recognition. He "embezzled tens of millions of dollars in public funds."[35] Proceeds flowed to banks in the United States, France, Switzerland, and Luxembourg, finally producing indictments of him and ten of his officials. Portillo was extradited to New York in 2014 and served nine months in a US prison.

Sinking under the weight of decades of civil war that killed an estimated 200,000 people and ongoing violence and thievery at the highest levels, Guatemalans next selected the reform-minded Óscar Berger as president and the able Eduardo Stein as vice president. The team soon welcomed a United Nations Comisión Internacional contra la Impunidad en Guatemala, an anti-impunity body—CICIG—charged with investigating, dismantling, and prosecuting networks and individuals involved in murder, bribery, and money laundering, in cooperation with the attorney general. Berger's presidency was marred when his top drug enforcer was lured to the United States by the Drug Enforcement Administration and arrested for facilitating trafficking.

With CICIG at the center of widespread investigations, the next three presidents all faced charges of corruption and money laundering. The loser to Berger in 2004, Álvaro Colom, was inaugurated in 2008, and rumors soon circulated that money from the Zetas drug gang financed his campaign. A radio announcement was broadcast in 2010 saying, "This is a message to the President of Guatemala. We are the Zetas group, and we just wanted the country to know that President Álvaro Colom received $11,500,000 before election ended."[36] Colom was arrested in 2018 along with nine of his former cabinet members for possible embezzlement in connection with the purchase of hundreds of buses for public transportation. After six months in jail, he was released and may face further prosecution.

The loser to Colom in 2008, Otto Pérez Molina, a former general and director of military intelligence, was inaugurated president in 2012, and he and his vice president, Roxana Baldetti, promptly launched multiple opportunities to rip off the state. The most brazen earned the nickname "La Línea" (telephone line) and comprised an estimated 60 or more individuals heard on 60,000 wiretapped calls colluding to reduce customs duties on imports for more than 1,000 companies in return for bribes, likely generating in excess of $1 million a month.[37] Another scheme involved plans to build a $255 million container port, with the Spanish contractor allegedly agreeing to $30 million in bribes. Yet another scheme involved kickbacks on some 70 state contracts, producing an estimated $38 million.[38] The Guatemalan attorney general working closely with CICIG forced the resignations of both publicly disgraced politicians, the vice president then receiving a 15-year jail sentence, while Pérez remains on trial.

Guatemalans needed relief, so the next president taking office in 2016 was a TV comedian, Jimmy Morales, who ran on a campaign of "Ni corrupto, ni ladron" (Neither corrupt, nor a thief). His evangelical Christian faith and PhD in security studies seemed right for the times. Within a year, however, his brother and son were arrested on charges of corruption and money laundering.[39] And shortly thereafter, CICIG accused Morales of election financing violations—"illegal donations, including from drug-traffickers"—estimated at more than $800,000.[40] An attempt to strip Morales of immunity resulted in protracted conflict among the congress, constitutional court, attorney general, and ministry of foreign affairs. On his last day in office, the disgraced president barely escaped a public lynching.

CICIG was the first external body ever created by the United Nations to pursue a country's internal corruption. An intrepid prosecutor and judge from Colombia, Iván Velásquez, provided leadership during the organization's last six years, ending its run in 2019 after amassing charges against nearly 700 individuals and obtaining convictions of more than 300 murderers, money launderers, traffickers, and corrupt officials.[41] CIGIG's effectiveness was the main reason for its eventual demise in the country still riven by drugs, bribery, and theft.

The United States brought the full scope of its financial secrecy system to the service of Guatemala as well as Honduras, El Salvador, the rest of Central America, and Mexico. Wachovia Bank was charged with receiving into private accounts $378 billion—that's billion with a "b"—from transferrers south of the border, done without adequate money laundering oversight. Some of the funds were traced to *casas de cambio* (exchange houses) handling illicit money, even directly to the purchase of aircraft used in transporting drugs. Wachovia paid a $160 million fine and was absorbed into Wells Fargo.

Under its next president, Alejandro Giammattei, himself formerly imprisoned, the flow of drugs through Guatemala making their way north into the United States has not diminished. Extreme violence continues, but hunger is now the main driving force for migration north toward and into the United States. The World Food Programme projected that 3.7 million Guatemalans would be in a state of "acute food insecurity" in 2021, with 428,000 in "emergency" conditions.[42] Yet, dollars continue to flow almost unimpeded out of Guatemala and into the US economy.

VENEZUELA

Once an example of strengthening democracy and growing prosperity, Venezuela has been reduced to penury. Every component of the financial secrecy system found use in transferring wealth from the hands of the poor to the lands of the rich.

Small-scale production had been going on for years when Royal Dutch Shell struck oil in the Maracaibo basin in 1922, hitting a reserve that blew out at the rate of 100,000 barrels a day with output peaking to 3.7 million B/D by 1970. Petroleos de Venezuela, S.A. (PDVSA), was formed in 1976, effectively nationalizing the industry, with foreign companies permitted to hold minority participations. The resource curse hit Venezuela hard as corruption exploded and inequality widened. Hugo Chavez, a charismatic populist, was elected president in 1998. With the world's largest oil reserves still to this day, Chavez redirected PDVSA into political projects, along the way firing 19,000 skilled employees, nationalizing farming and manufacturing companies to give to his friends and supporters, and establishing multiple exchange rates so that the favored could convert bolivars to dollars at handsome profits. After Chavez's death in 2013 Nicholas Maduro, trained in Cuba, came to power with neither popularity nor oil profits and promptly drove his country off a cliff.

Vast corruption schemes overlapped both the Chavez and Maduro regimes, often with roots in earlier administrations. Drug trafficking netted billions of dollars for cooperating government officials and cronies. Chavez broke relations with the US Drug Enforcement Administration in 2005. Then he allegedly met personally with senior commanders of the Colombian rebel group FARC in 2007 to confirm that Venezuela would pay for drugs received across the border, providing cash and weaponry aimed at weakening the president of that country, Alvaro Uribe.[43]

After Maduro came to power in 2013, officials of the Venezuela National Guard loaded 1.3 tons of cocaine onto a Paris-bound flight, stunning French authorities.[44] Three years later the former head of the National Guard, General Nestor Reverol, was indicted in the United States on charges of drug trafficking along with General Edylberto Molina, senior director of the antidrug office.[45] Former vice president Tareck El Aissami and his immediate associates allegedly ran a trafficking network of 40 front companies with properties and accounts spread across Florida and tax havens in the Caribbean valued at perhaps $3 billion.[46] The ex-leader of the elected National Constituent Assembly, Diosdado Cabello, found his bank accounts and properties in the United States estimated at $800 million frozen, as he is accused of leading the "Cartel of the Suns" and still faces charges.[47] Not to be left out, Maduro's own family—two nephews of Maduro's wife—were arrested in Haiti in a sting operation as they plotted to smuggle 800 kilograms of cocaine from the presidential jet hangar at Simón Bolívar International Airport through Honduras to the United States, garnering for themselves 18-year sentences in US prisons.[48] Thus, under Maduro, Venezuela came to define the narco state, with trafficking conducted and protected at the highest levels and widest reaches of government.

An easier way to make money is stealing oil revenues. Local suppliers overcharging PDVSA on construction and supply contracts is routine but suffers the disadvantage of generating payment only in bolivars. By far the more attractive avenue is manipulating international sales and purchases to generate dollars. PDVSA owns Citco, the US-based retailer that has usually been well run and offered only minor opportunities for direct theft. Instead, a Panama-registered company, Helsinge Inc., allegedly arranged with PDVSA officials to rig bids on billions of dollars of oil purchase contracts, ensuring that the trading business went their way at favorable prices.

The multiple exchange rate regime started by Chavez and continued under Maduro generated billions, playing on the difference between the official and unofficial bolivar-to-dollar ratios. For example, a privileged individual with access to, say, $10 million, whether obtained legally or illegally, could go to an unofficial money changer and get 600 million bolivars at the prevailing commercial market exchange rate of 60 to 1. Then, the 600 million bolivars could be taken back to an official money changer and converted to $100 million at the government-fixed exchange rate of 6 to 1. Effectively, $10 million is changed into $100 million just by walking across the street and back but only for those favored few authorized to access the official rate. This scheme may have generated up to $20 billion a year.

Another scheme involved fake mutual funds. Banks handling PDVSA assets in the Caribbean were instructed to use dollar accounts to buy mutual funds that had no financial holdings, no underlying reality at all, owned instead by money launderers. This arrangement stretched across the Cayman Islands, the Bahamas, Uruguay, Puerto Rico, and New Jersey. Fake bonds were handled in similar fashion, sold to cooperating foreign buyers at a low price and bought back at a high price, shifting money offshore.[49]

Gold is another source of dollars. In 2016 Maduro created an Economic Military Zone surrounding an area called the Orinoco Mining Arc, rich also in coltan and other precious metals with an estimated value of perhaps $100 billion. Gold mined here is usually smuggled out through Colombia, profiting the army and its generals.[50] Sensing improper manipulations, the Bank of England has resisted handing over $1.8 billion of Venezuela's reserves.[51] Even the IMF declined to give Maduro access to $400 million in special drawing rights.

Food boxes, desperately needed by most families, have been pilfered and diverted. "This goes beyond corruption. This is literally looting the one social safety-net program left in Venezuela," said US Treasury Department official Marshall Billingslea.[52] Among many shell companies in the food import business, Group Grand Ltd., a Hong Kong–based entity possibly linked to Maduro's stepsons, has participated in gutting an estimated 70 percent of the program with stealing and overpricing of imports the preferred mechanisms.[53]

All those involved in trafficking, exchanging, and thieving need money laundering services. Enter Matthias Krull, a German national, formerly a senior director with the Swiss bank Julius Baer, and already well known to many corrupt officials in Venezuela. As money poured out of PDVSA, Krull segued from his employer and joined a conspiracy of banks, real estate firms, brokerage houses, and money managers stretching across Europe, Asia, Africa, and the Americas to launder $1.2 billion, primarily into assets and properties in Florida and New York.[54] Beginning in 2016 a confidential source approached US authorities, admitted his own involvement in money laundering, and offered his cooperation. Two years and a hundred secret wire recordings later, multiple schemes were brought to light, resulting in indictments of Krull and seven others. The former Swiss banker was sentenced to 10 years in prison in the United States, later reduced to 42 months. This set of actors allegedly included Maduro himself and three children of his wife Cilia Flores.[55]

Experience in banking is not necessary to become a money launderer. Chavez's former bodyguard, Alejandro Andrade, later appointed head of the national treasury and the social development bank, was given control of much of Venezuela's central bank reserves on deposit at HSBC Private Bank (Suisse) in Geneva.[56] Andrade allegedly took $1 billion in bribes from a wealthy media mogul, Raul Gorrin, to direct foreign currency exchange transactions his way, which Gorrin laundered through his personal Banco Peravia in the Dominican Republic.[57] Andrade, sheltering his own money in shell companies, had bank accounts with Julius Baer, Credit Suisse, HSBC, EFG, Compagnie Bancaire Helvétique, and PKB PrivatBank.[58] Moving to Florida, he bought an estate and indulged in private jets, show horses, and Swiss watches until he was caught. He forfeited his money and accepted a ten-year prison sentence, later reduced to three and a half years.[59]

These few examples of crime, corruption, and money laundering barely scratch the surface, as thousands of crooks running scores of schemes plundered the state. The wealth taken illegally out of Venezuela over the past two decades could be as high as $300 billion, perhaps even more. Much if not most of this ended up in the United States, facilitated by secrecy structures throughout the financial system. US drug indictments in 2020 against Maduro and assorted cohorts have not yet

changed the political equation. The UN Human Rights Council excoriated the regime for extrajudicial killings, enforced disappearances, ar-
bitrary detentions, and torture. China and Russia, giving major loans to
Venezuela, have now stepped into the heavily mortgaged nation, impacting geopolitical relations.

By the end of 2021, three-fourths of Venezuelans were reportedly living in extreme poverty.[60] Some five million had fled their country, with
predictions that the figure could rise to six million or more, which if realized would make this refugee crisis, like that in Ukraine, one of the
largest in modern history. Parents have left an estimated one million
children behind with grandparents and relatives as they relocate to surrounding countries seeking earnings to send to their struggling families.
Infants by the thousands are left in shelters, abandoned by destitute
mothers.

The United States, Switzerland, and other countries, still harboring
ill-gotten gains, have failed and continue to fail to apply maximum financial pressure on the Maduro regime. Decades will be needed to get
the country back to a reasonable level of democracy and prosperity as it
once enjoyed.

STATE CAPTURE: THE EXAMPLE OF SOUTH AFRICA

First, we had in the global lexicon the idea of corruption, where a few
government officials falsely enrich themselves. Then we elevated this to
grand corruption, referring to the head of state and supporting henchmen looting the treasury. Now in the early years of this century we have
the concept of state capture, referring to the nearly complete takeover of
the state apparatus for the dual purpose of rampant theft carried out with
political control. South Africa, the continent's sole member of the G20,
has in recent years embodied this emergent concept. It will take decades
to recover from the degradation of its economy and polity.

South Africa's National Party tried to hold on to white rule—
apartheid—through the decades of independence and majority rule
sweeping the world in the 1960s, 1970s, and 1980s. But as civil pressure
rose, particularly during the Reagan years in the United States, governments imposed economic sanctions against South Africa, leading to a re-
alization within the white community that security and well-being were
imperiled. This was a clear demonstration that investment, trade, and
financial penalties do sometimes work. Nelson Mandela, released from

27 years in prison in 1990, took the reins of the African National Congress (ANC) and guided his nation to a peaceful transition in 1994, earning the plaudits of the entire world. Serving only one term, he was succeeded by his deputy president, Thabo Mbeki, who had very ably run the government under Mandela and kept the state's economy moving in the right direction.

Unfortunately, Mbeki's deputy president, Jacob Zuma, whom Mbeki fired in 2005, had other ideas. After winning the ANC presidency in 2007, he engineered the resignation of Mbeki in 2008 and then assumed the presidency of South Africa the next year. Earlier corruption charges had not stuck, so Zuma was receptive to the all-embracing notion of state capture.

Unlike mere corruption, state capture usually exhibits some common components. First, power is concentrated into the hands of elected and senior appointed officials in positions of authority rather than residing with bureaucrats, in other words, those who make policy rather than those who execute policy. Second, the goal goes beyond simple enrichment to encompass also the sustenance of power, retaining the levers of control for an extended period. Third, deception and camouflage are important elements of the strategy, enabling a hands-off appearance while exercising hands-on control. As one analyst noted, "legality becomes a function of illegality."[61] Whether through advance planning or street smarts, Zuma embraced all of these on the way toward state capture.

Bribes and kickbacks started flowing on virtually all government contracts, according to a well-placed observer.[62] While this filled the coffers of many appointees and supporters, the essential purpose was to establish firm control over the state through the ANC party structure, hopefully ensuring a long stay in power and no retributions after leaving power.

For the third essential ingredient in state capture—deception and camouflage—Zuma welcomed the services of American consulting and auditing companies, British public relations talent, a German software giant, and a trio of Indian brothers who could operate in South Africa's polyglot environment with seeming impunity. Providing a veneer of international expertise and propriety, these connections facilitated Zuma's control over much of his country's governing apparatus.

The first Gupta brother emigrated from India to South Africa and started a business in 1994 assembling computers from imported parts. Soon joined by two siblings, the three Guptas quickly expanded into mining ventures and media companies and at various times hired several members of Zuma's family, including a son and daughter and one of Zuma's wives. Kickbacks on government contracts were a favorite scheme.

Transnet, the port and rail entity owned by the state, decided that it should buy 1,064 new locomotives, the biggest government procurement ever. A partnership with a local company linked to the Guptas allegedly led to a $1 billion hike in the agreed price, and one of the winning bidders, a Chinese company, paid another $100 million into shell companies linked to the Guptas.[63]

Eskom, the state-owned power generating firm, earlier had a superb reputation based on modest prices and good management. But this came unglued as rates soared, blackouts rose, maintenance crumbled, spare parts disappeared, and debt exploded, in good part driven by massive corruption at the top ranks of management. Subjected to withering scrutiny,[64] Eskom has become the poster child for ill dealings in the Zuma years, affecting every citizen in the country. But even intense scrutiny did not prevent the Swiss giant Asea Brown Boveri from alleged contract irregularities, resulting in a repayment of more than $100 million, followed by arrest of two directors and their wives in 2022 accused of receiving cars and cash for their facilitations.[65]

KPMG audited the Gupta companies for years, finally admitting that its certifications "fell considerably short" of its own standards and then donated its fees to charities.[66] KPMG also had to acknowledge mistakes in a report compiled on South African Revenue Service, finally refunding the fee earned. The chairman, CEO, COO, and five senior partners resigned as major clients changed to other auditors.

Bell Pottinger, the UK public relations firm, produced a campaign for the Guptas that decried "white monopoly capital" and extolled the Zumas.[67] Resulting from negative publicity for the publicity pros, the British business of the firm collapsed in 2017.

Bain and Company, Boston-based consultants, acknowledged that its work for South African Revenue Service did not deliver "sustainable, positive" results and agreed to set aside its ZAR164 million fee to be used for the benefit of South Africa. The managing partner resigned.[68]

SAP, the tech company, admitted that it paid a kickback of some $6 million to a Gupta company to win contracts. Four executives were suspended, and the company, listed on the New York Stock Exchange, reported its findings to the US Securities and Exchange Commission and Department of Justice.[69]

India's state-owned Bank of Baroda serviced the Guptas' ill dealings for years after Standard Bank, Nedbank, and Absa withdrew. Hundreds of millions of dollars passing through some two dozen shell companies resulted in dozens of suspicious activities reports, which senior managers overruled, finding the flow too lucrative to turn down. After finally coming to light, Baroda closed its South African operations.[70]

With consulting companies, auditors, banks, and state-owned entities willingly cooperating in the far-reaching scheme of state capture, the Guptas, with the active approval of Zuma, extended their reach into the appointment of government ministers. Meeting in their family home, one parliamentarian was reportedly told she could rise to cabinet minister within a week, with Zuma himself emerging from a side room to say "It's okay girl . . . take care of yourself."[71] Another seasoned official was offered a bribe to take the position of treasury secretary—ZAR600,000 in a bag as he walked out the door plus ZAR600,000,000 to be deposited into his bank account.[72] The Guptas were reassuring:

> You must understand that we are in control of everything—the National Prosecuting Authority, the Hawks, the National Intelligence Agency, and the old man will do anything we tell him to do.[73]

Eventually investigations were launched, and death threats flew. Finally ensnared, the Guptas decamped to Dubai. Zuma was forced out of the presidency in 2018. His vice president, Cyril Ramaphosa, took over and instituted a process of culling corrupt government and party officials. Zuma went on trial for earlier bribery charges, which led to violent clashes put down by the military. Acting chief justice Raymond Zondo produced a six-part *Report of the Judicial Commission of Inquiry into State Capture* detailing a "scarcely believable picture of rampant corruption."[74]

This brief story barely touches on the extent of foreign and local companies and institutions deeply embedded in illegal and illicit dealings on the grandest possible scale. The financial secrecy structure within the free market system, facilitated by complicit consultants, banks, and public relations agents, readily aided the process of corruption's ultimate expression: state capture. South Africa, hopefully a beacon of light for democracy on the continent, will spend years recovering from economic and political damage done to its 57 million citizens.

MYANMAR

Perhaps no nation better illustrates how a dishonest, entrenched, and greatly enriched military can exert both the will and the capacity to stifle democracy. Limiting accountability to the civilian government elected in 2015, the constitution of Myanmar gives the military, collectively called the Tatmadaw, "leadership of the state." The military fills 25 percent of the seats in the legislature and 6 out of 11 seats in the overarching National Defense and Security Council while also wielding permanent control of the ministries of defense, home, and border affairs and, for the commander in chief, sweeping powers to declare a state of emergency.

Two state-owned enterprises predominate in retaining the military's power and amassing wealth for its generals, other officers, and service members. The Union of Myanmar Economic Holdings Limited (UMEHL) and the Myanmar Economic Corporation (MEC) were established in the 1990s, each now fortified with their own banks while foreign banks are limited. UMEHL has more than 70 subsidiaries and investments engaged in trading, shipping, transportation, real estate, brewing, and gem and metals mining. MEC has investments in more than 30 subsidiaries and affiliates in steel, cement, telecommunications, ports, and insurance.

Petroleum resources have been important to Myanmar's economy since the mid-1800s, with natural gas now generating more revenue than oil. Exploration blocks are auctioned off to foreign and local producers, with strong pressures to utilize subcontractors designated by the military. The offshore Yadana Gas Project, for example, has been heavily criticized for the level of military involvement. Operated by the French company Total in partnership with the US company Chevron, the onshore portion of the production pipeline runs through 40 miles of Myanmar territory, then exits to Thailand at the border. The Myanmar junta allegedly arranged for pipeline fees to go directly into their accounts, an estimated $4.8 billion during the first 15 years, much of it channeled into two offshore banks in Singapore and later possibly routed on to Dubai, Macau, and China.[75] Two additional parallel pipelines traversing 500 miles across Myanmar transport oil and gas to China, earning fees that could reach $2 billion a year.[76]

Myanmar's exports of jade, mined from the world's largest and highest-quality deposits and nearly all destined for China, are fraught with corruption, tax evasion, and money laundering. A detailed study in 2015 found that in the preceding year official export data totaled $3.7 billion, China's import data showed $12.3 billion, and a reasonable estimate based on tonnages shipped suggested a value of $31 billion. Smuggling likely moves 50–80 percent of the production. Military enterprises and individual military officers and their cronies own jade mining concessions, usually obtained through licensing irregularities. Four military corporations, including UMEHL and MEC, were or still are prominent in the business. The former Supreme General Than Shwe, in power for two decades, amassing a fortune estimated at $4 billion and frequently appearing on "worst dictator" lists, allegedly helped two of his sons, Naing and Kyaing, get into the jade business, with licenses on six mines under their names. The former military commander in Kachin State, Ohn Myint, allegedly put his family into the jade business in an enterprise called Win Gate Gems, named after the famous British commander in the Burma Campaign of World War II, Major General Orde Wingate.

Longtime businessmen in Myanmar's gem trade have said "all good quality jade belongs to the families of generals" and "every . . . company is related to military officers in uniform."[77] Unfortunately, the richest resources in the country, not only jade but also rubies, sapphires, and other gemstones, do little for some of the poorest people in the region.

Drugs are hugely important in the economy. Most of Myanmar's opium output is cooked into morphine base and purified into heroin in local processing facilities, supplying some 25 percent of the world market, second only to Afghanistan. Shan State, with good transportation infrastructure, is the epicenter, bordering China and shipping most of its product eastward. But tastes there are gravitating toward methamphetamines, called "yaba," which scores of labs in Shan and Kachin produce and sell throughout Asia, including Australia. Reportedly, pills are available for as little as 20 cents each.[78] Some drug kingpins have become locally respectable, laundering their money into banks and properties.

Illegal logging, primarily of teak and rosewood, has contributed to a reduction of Myanmar's forest cover from almost half to less than 20 percent of its land area.[79] Wildlife trafficking—ivory, skins, exotic birds, and pangolin scales in particular—is threatening some local species. Women and children are trafficked for sexual exploitation, domestic servitude, and forced labor.[80] Altogether, the government estimates that organized crime accounts for a quarter of the country's GDP of $80 billion.[81]

Myanmar demonstrates the synergy of lawlessness and conflict perhaps more clearly than any other country, most of it linked to the secret machinations of the military. Fifteen combatant and militia groups each have from a few hundred to more than 10,000 armed personnel, frequently attacking the Tatmadaw. Another 15 or so "cease-fire" groups have agreed to cooperate peacefully with the military. What this means is that these groups are permitted to pursue drug production, bride trafficking, illegal logging, wildlife poaching, and other crimes as means of support, in many cases sharing profits with serving military officers provided the cease-fire groups make minimal efforts to keep the peace. With this tenuous and oft-broken pact, civil conflict has remained a reality in Myanmar essentially since the end of World War II.

How frightening this can be erupted into the collective consciousness in 2017 when the Tatmadaw decided to drive Muslim Rohingyas in Rakhine State out of Myanmar. Disparagingly referred to as "Bengali" in a largely Buddhist country, this ethnic group was denied full citizenship rights decades ago then partially exiled in 1978, pushed to resettle abroad in 2012, and violently harassed since.[82] In response to an attack by militant Rohingyas that killed 13 police, the Tatmadaw commander in chief, senior general Min Aung Hlaing, stated that "the Bengali problem was a long-standing one[,] . . . an unfinished job."[83] In a matter of weeks, an estimated 25,000 Rohingya were killed and 700,000 forced into exile in Bangladesh.[84] A UN Human Rights Council investigation in 2018 recommended that named "senior generals of the Myanmar military should be investigated and prosecuted in an international criminal tribunal for genocide, crimes against humanity and war crimes." The report went on to criticize Myanmar's 1991 Nobel Peace Prize winner and leader of the then governing National League for Democracy:

> Nothing indicates that the civilian authorities used their limited powers to influence the situation in Rakhine State where crimes were being perpetrated. The State Counsellor, Daw Aung San Suu Kyi, has not used her de facto position as head of the Government, nor her moral authority, to stem or prevent the unfolding events or seek alternative avenues to meet a responsibility to protect the civilian population.[85]

The International Court of Justice, sited at the Peace Palace in The Hague, received a complaint filed by The Gambia based on the UN report and tried the case against Myanmar in December 2019. Suu Kyi appeared before the court to defend her government's "counterterrorism" program, garnering criticism around the world. Canada and the Netherlands joined The Gambia in the case in 2020.[86] The Court of Justice ruling imposed provisional measures against Myanmar ordering protection of the Rohingya, which the government promptly disputed and dismissed.

The military of Myanmar, for decades obsessed with financial self-enrichment, once again in 2021 removed civilian participation in the

government and retook full control of the country. Some 1,300 protesters have been slaughtered in the streets. Suu Kyi is variously detained or
restrained for purported offenses. Jade, gems, oil, and other resources
continue to pour money into military coffers. Weak Western sanctions
have little effect. Even Chevron and Total finally had enough and in
2022 announced intentions to end their involvements. Yet, Tatmadaw
generals and supporters remain obnoxiously wealthy and completely
untouchable. Democracy is the victim.

IRAN AND THE ISLAMIC REVOLUTIONARY GUARD CORPS

After the 1979 ouster of Shah Mohammad Reza Pahlavi, the returning
cleric Ayatollah Ruhollah Khomeini did not fully trust the country's
army and, upon his ascendance to Supreme Leader, created a separate
entity to ensure the protection of the theocratic regime from domestic
and foreign threats. The Islamic Revolutionary Guard Corps (IRGC)
now embodies the long-feared nexus of crime and terrorism exercised
with the highest levels of state approval, making use of every opportunity provided by the global financial secrecy system. The Basel Institute
on Governance recently ranked Iran number one for risks of money laundering and terrorist financing.[87]

Existing entirely outside regular military command structures, the
IRGC today has ground forces numbering perhaps 100,000, naval forces
of some 20,000 patrolling the Strait of Hormuz, an air force, and the al-
Quds Force performing external, usually clandestine, missions in Syria,
Lebanon, Afghanistan, Mexico, Venezuela, and dozens of other troubled
areas. In addition, in 1981 the IRGC took on oversight of the Basij para-
military force that had been providing hundreds of thousands of young
and poorly armed fighters for the war with Iraq, resulting in massive
slaughter. Then to sort out rivalries, the IRGC absorbed the Basij in
2008, adding perhaps 600,000 more to the organization's ranks. Through
electoral manipulations, the IRGC contributes to a continuing cycle of
conservative leaders, leaving itself economically free to pursue the full
gamut of nefarious activities.

Following the end of the Iran-Iraq War in 1988, the IRGC was given
contracts to repair damaged facilities. This soon led to investments in or
takeovers of businesses in arms manufacturing, aerospace, automotives,
electronics, media, telecommunications, cement, paper, pharmaceuticals,

transportation, importing, oil, mining, smelting, shipping, banking, and even counterfeiting, finally making the IRGC one of the two or three largest conglomerates in the Iranian economy, worth perhaps $100 billion today. Countless entities in the private sector were forced out of business or found themselves competitively disadvantaged.

Constitutionally protected and unaccountable to any judicial or bureaucratic authority, the movement into black market and smuggling pursuits was inevitable. The IRGC controls some 60 jetties for its own use along the 1,500-mile Persian Gulf and Indian Ocean coastlines. These have for years facilitated a robust trade in smuggled goods, even forbidden alcohol, from Dubai and other emirates, producing more billions of dollars in illicit profits. By some estimates, a third of Iran's imports arrive through the IRGC and other black market channels.

Drug trading is a key component of the IRGC's portfolio, taking advantage of high levels of local addiction, a geographic location between Afghanistan and Europe, and close connections with criminal and terrorist groups worldwide. More than 2,000,000 Iranian addicts consume domestically grown opium and imported heroin, while thousands of rehab centers attempt to treat the growing national problem. Obscure labs produce narcotics in powder and rock forms for local consumption and methamphetamines primarily for export. Authorities make a show of executing dealers, which may serve primarily to eliminate the IRGC's competition.

Long-cultivated relations in Afghanistan, particularly with the Taliban, serve to secure Iran's drug supply chain, as more than 100 tons a year of heroin are believed to cross IRGC-controlled points along the more than 500-mile north-south border. Senior ranks in both countries have been sanctioned by the US Treasury Department for drug smuggling. The al-Quds Force, with its extensive external contacts, is active in the so-called Balkan route through Iran, Turkey, and southeastern Europe and in the Caucasus passage from Iran through Armenia, Azerbaijan, and Georgia into southern Europe. Operational linkages endure with Hezbollah, a principal supplier of drugs in Lebanon and other countries in the Middle East and especially active in South America and Mexico.

Paralleling the drug trade is the arms trade. The IRGC supplied weapons to Bosnian combatants in the 1990s, using well-oiled smuggling routes. Small arms, rocket-propelled grenades, mortars, and explosives stream from Iran into Afghanistan for the Taliban, a trade ongoing for decades utilizing drug trafficking connections. The IRGC for years supplied tens of thousands of rockets and other weapons overland to Hezbollah in

Lebanon and Hamas in Gaza, capitalizing on established drug routes. Yemen is receiving drugs and weapons from Iran, mostly smuggled by small vessels operating in the Persian Gulf. Furthermore, the IRGC directs Iran's nuclear and missiles programs and is responsible for procuring needed components through its shadowy channels.

Money laundering facilitates drugs and arms trading, carried out through complicit banks, exchange houses, and shell companies. After serving in the IRGC and working for two years as a driver for Iran's central bank governor, Babak Zanjani became a currency trader and investor, soon setting up credit institutions and banks in the UAE, Georgia, Tajikistan, and Malaysia. Remaining close to the IRGC and rapidly becoming one of Iran's richest and most diversified financiers, he was asked to help repatriate proceeds from oil sales, a task gladly handled through his web of companies. He sold the oil, but with sanctions in place he could not return the money, leaving him owing some $2.7 billion to the Iranian government. Arrested in 2013, he was tried and sentenced to death in 2016, not yet carried out while the oil ministry hunts for its money.

Reza Zarrab owned a string of currency exchange and gold trading companies in the UAE and Turkey. He too was asked to help launder oil proceeds back to Iran. His scheme involved accessing Iranian oil funds stuck in Türkiye Halk Bankasi A.Ş.—Halk Bank—to buy gold in Turkey, ship it to Dubai, and then send either the gold itself or the dollar value to Tehran. This became a problem when gold exports from Turkey showed a massive jump, potentially exposing the scheme and requiring the manipulation of Turkey's financial statistics. So, Zarrab and the bank revised their subterfuge, submitting fake invoices from his UAE offices to Halk Bank ostensibly for food and pharmaceutical purchases, which the sanctions regime permitted. Halk Bank paid against the fake invoices, the money went to Dubai, and from there again gold or cash was sent to Iran.

Halk Bank fully participated in designing and carrying out this scheme, even advising when the fake invoices needed adjustments to appear credible. Zarrab, rolling in money, went to Disney World on vacation, where US authorities arrested him. Zarrab retained Rudy Giuliani as defense counsel. The presiding judge in the case, Richard Berman, noted, "I am still stunned by the fact that Rudy was hired to be—and he very actively pursued—being the 'go between' between President Trump and Turkey's President Erdogan in an unprecedented effort to terminate this federal criminal case in the middle of the case."[88] Recognizing his peril, Zarrab separated from his lawyer, pleaded guilty, turned state's evidence, and went to prison. Among others, he accused Mehmet Hakan Atilla, deputy director of Halk Bank, of complicity in the scheme. Atilla was tried in New York, convicted, and sentenced to 32 months in prison, then released early for good behavior.

These examples only begin to suggest the full range of disguised corporations and cooperating banks facilitating the IRGC's global reach. Central bank officials transfer money to their personal accounts to facilitate prohibited activities. Government-owned commercial banks handle millions of falsified transactions. Iranian front companies by the thousands conduct illicit trades. Fake documentation is normalized. International banks ask few questions or readily process suspect transfers, with nine such banks paying more than $12 billion in fines since 2004.[89] Many sympathetic governments are complicit. As Supreme Leader Ayatollah Ali Khamenei recently said, "We are sanctioned, but there are other ways available for us."[90] This is the point. Within a global structure that is designed to facilitate illicit dealings, no amount of control and oversight is effective.

Following the hostage crisis in 1979 the US government froze Iranian government assets abroad, eventually easing restrictions in 1981. New sanctions were imposed in 1987 aimed at deterring Iran's support of international terrorism. The United Nations adopted resolutions in 2006, and the European Union followed albeit with some reluctance. The Obama administration negotiated the Joint Comprehensive Plan of Action (JCPOA) in 2015, with Iran agreeing to cut the number of operating centrifuges and disable part of a nuclear reactor, while the United States and other nations agreed to ease economic sanctions. In 2018 the Trump administration overturned JCPOA, reimposing restrictions on some 700 entities, which reaccelerated Iran's use of the financial secrecy system to sustain its already weakening economy.

Economic and financial sanctions led by the United States focus on deterring Iran's nuclear ambitions. Some experts argue that a bit of leeway in going after drugs, arms, and money laundering, couched as part of a "realignment" with Tehran, is acceptable while pursuing the more important goal of curtailing weapons of mass destruction. Unfortunately, leeway in criminal pursuits has instead contributed to sustaining Iran's hostile intents and bolstering its nuclear ambitions. Competition for cash drives Iran's ideological factions, all benefiting from "other ways available for us" via the globally accessible financial secrecy system.

UNITED STATES OF AMERICA

In the world's largest economy, the United States, capitalism has promoted and purchased its right to operate and expand the financial secrecy system. As this power has grown, inequality has risen and democracy has declined.

Previous chapters provided examples of how the United States is compromising the legitimate operation of the free market economy in many ways. Anonymous companies have been established in every state of the union, apparently totaling more than in any other country. Multinational corporations are the largest patrons of secrecy jurisdictions. Real estate welcomes inflows of billions of dollars from crooks and tax evaders, driving up property purchase and rental prices in many cities. Banks take in dirty money, filing nearly 80,000 Currency Transaction and Suspicious Activity Reports a day. Lawyers facilitate dirty money through internal accounts. Auditors are deeply conflicted, both creating and approving dubious transactions. Free trade zones, hotbeds of illegal dealings, now number in the hundreds, again more than in any other country.

But these few illustrations barely tell the story. The remainder of this chapter covers more depictions of US duplicity, including failures within the Drug Enforcement Administration, noncompliance with Financial Action Task Force principles, the flawed Golden Visa Program, the QI Program that essentially legalizes money laundering, nearly universal acceptance of falsifying commercial trade, *Citizens United* favoring corporations and undermining democratic processes, the repeal of Glass-Steagall, weakening of the Internal Revenue Service, regulatory capture, and the failed Tax Cuts and Jobs Act passed in 2017.

The Drug Enforcement Administration

In the world's largest economy, the greatest example of failure to fight crime and money laundering centers on the Drug Enforcement Administration headquartered in Washington, D.C. Created in 1973, DEA across its entire existence has never succeeded in curtailing the supply of drugs or raising the price of drugs. Minor fluctuations in some years, but nothing sustained.

This is not a criticism of the brave men and women risking their safety to protect US borders, communities, and citizens. They deserve the fullest measure of respect. It is a criticism of the mandate they are given by DEA management: go after the product. DEA executives thrive on photo ops showing interdicted caches of cocaine and bales of marijuana. They do not thrive on any set of statistics demonstrating sustained success in the fight against narcotics. And now with opioids added to narcotics flowing freely across borders, America's drug problem is as serious as ever.

How do you curtail the supply of something that is in endless supply, a question asked but unanswered in chapter 3? Drugs are in endless supply. The UN Office on Drugs and Crime estimates that globally some 40 percent of hard drugs are interdicted somewhere between production and consumption.[91] The office also estimates that less than 1 percent of drug money is ever recovered. Drug cartels and kingpins can afford to lose 40 percent or 50 or 60 or 70 or 80 percent of their supply if they can keep more than 99 percent of the proceeds.

There is a way to curtail the drug supply: go much harder after the drug money. Drug dealers are in business to make money. Curtail the money, and you curtail the supply.

The DEA assigns only some 10 percent of its agents to anti–money laundering efforts. This is the wrong focus and has proven to be ineffectual ever since the agency was formed.

For years DEA has watched bankers operate funnel accounts, welcoming deposits of less than $10,000 to avoid regulatory reporting requirements, then accumulating funds and wire-transferring to front companies. Wells Fargo, criticized earlier, found one of its California officers arrested and convicted in 2019 for laundering Sinaloa Cartel money.[92]

Bulk cash smuggling of the proceeds of drug sales across the Mexican border succeeds an estimated 99.75 percent of the time, meaning that for every $100, only some 25 cents is recovered by US border agents. Drug cash is used to buy real estate, as described in preceding chapters. Trade-based drug money laundering is soaring through West Coast fashion houses, East Coast gold exchanges, electronics suppliers, and virtually every other form of commerce.

> The U.S. banking system is at the center of these laundering efforts. Once illegal money is deposited in a U.S. bank, it is much easier to transfer and hide behind the smoke screen of an apparently legitimate business enterprise.[93]

And the Treasury Department further undermines US antidrug policy. Treasury encourages the repatriation of drug dollars back into the US economy, explaining that it wants to maintain the US dollar as the major currency in international trade, and presumably this extends as well to illegal trade.

Several years ago, a major Central American figure called on Treasury to ask that banks in his region making direct deposits into US accounts be required instead to deposit their holdings at the central banks of each country so that the central banks could require and record information about sources of the money and then send it on to the United States. This would aid in cooperative efforts in the drug fight. Treasury turned down the request. Free return of US dollars, with few questions asked, was evidently more important than curtailing the impact of drugs on American society.

DEA, the US law enforcement community, and citizens of many countries cheered when the head of the Sinaloa Cartel, Joaquín Archivaldo Guzmán Loera—"El Chapo"—was sentenced to life in prison plus 30 years. Yet, as per an analysis in the *National Interest*,

> El Chapo's downfall hasn't reduced the availability, price, use, or lethality of currently illegal drugs. In 2017, the year of Guzmán's extradition to the U.S., 70,237 people died of drug overdose in the United States. Another 29,168 people were murdered in Mexico.[94]

Anonymous Companies

Failures within DEA highlight a decades-long problem in the US economy, the long-standing role of anonymous companies. Finally, the Financial Crimes Enforcement Network (FinCEN) in 2016 proposed new regulations to press for knowledge of owners of accounts in the US financial system. The 2016 action came at the end of a tortuous five-year period of exchanges by the Treasury Department with the banking industry, which tried to water down the impending due diligence requirements.

Even after an introductory period and finally coming into effect in 2018, the new requirements are "shockingly soft" and "riddled with loopholes," according to some analysts. Beneficial interests need be recorded only for owners of 25 percent or more of the entity opening the account, meaning that five equal owners could avoid revealing their identities. In such an instance, a single individual in control of the account could be identified even if sitting in a tax haven, leaving the real owners unknown. And even more worrisome, banks have to confirm only that the identified individuals are in fact real people, not that they are necessarily related to the account. Concentration accounts, as are often maintained by law firms on behalf of multiple customers, are not covered under beneficial ownership requirements. Trust accounts are also not covered.

At last, in 2020 after years of strenuous efforts in the House and Senate pushed by civil society organizations, legislation passed requiring information on each beneficial owner of 25 percent or more of companies incorporated in any state to be made available to the Treasury Department. Companies with more than 20 employees, more than $5 million in revenues, and operating from a physical office in the United States are exempted. Information filed with the Treasury Department remains primarily for government use, not available to the public and not meeting a requirement for transparency. Hailed as a breakthrough by some but also as a "compromise with integrity,"[95] the legislation may take five years to become fully operational; leaves out several types of entities including trusts, partnerships, some hedge funds and private equity funds, money service businesses, and more; and does not stop foreign shell companies from doing business with the United States.

Thus, a key element in capitalism's secrecy structure, the disguised entity, is still available for use by criminals, kleptocrats, terrorist financiers, and of course, as always, tax evaders.

Golden Visas

In the Immigration Act of 1990, the United States set the numbers of employment visas available to foreigners as follows:

EB-1	Priority Workers	40,000
EB-2	Advanced Degree	40,000
EB-3	Skilled Workers	40,000
EB-4	Special Immigrants	10,000
EB-5	Employment Creation	10,000

The EB-5 employment creation visa program, later increased in number to 10,650, was intended to give foreign entrepreneurs opportunities to invest in US businesses and gain citizenship for themselves and their immediate families in the process. Even before passage it was recognized that the program could become a channel for illicit funds flowing into the United States. Nevertheless, it was pushed through because of a perceived need for economic stimulus in the early 1990s.

Foreigners could invest $1,000,000 in new enterprises or $500,000 in a needy "targeted employment area" that would create at least 10 jobs. The latter category led US entrepreneurs to establish regional centers, now more than 900, and sell access to the EB-5 program to wealthy foreigners with the promise to pool foreign funds for onward investment. The law allows for immediate conditional permanent residence, convertible in two years to permanent residence upon demonstration that the investment has been or shortly will be made and jobs created or shortly expected.

Since its creation, the EB-5 program, bringing in some $20 billion, has been mired in controversy stemming from three failings. First, some regional centers have proven to be frauds, cheating foreign investors out of their funds. Second, investments in regional centers—undocumented but roughly estimated at around $10 billion, half the total EB-5 inflows— have often failed to create jobs or instead counted secondary jobs such as in nearby restaurants as meeting the requirement. Third and even more serious is a nearly complete failing to ensure that incoming funds are legally acquired. China is the world's largest exporter of illicit capital, and not surprisingly, Chinese nationals have received nearly 90 percent of all EB-5 visas. This includes millionaires concerned about economic and political stability at home and fugitives on the most wanted list provided by the Chinese Communist Judicial Prosecution Committee.

In effect, the EB-5 program puts American citizenship up for sale. It essentially legalizes receipt into the United States of funds often stolen from other countries. While not necessarily its original intent, this is now the outcome. American capitalism has made democracy subordinate to its greed. This program, terribly flawed in both its conception and its execution, stands as a rebuke to the message penned by the poet Emma Lazarus and resting at the base of the Statue of Liberty:

> Give me your tired, your poor,
> Your huddled masses yearning to breathe free,
> The wretched refuse of your teeming shore.
> Send these, the homeless, tempest-tost to me,
> I lift my lamp beside the golden door!

And the United States is not alone in selling citizenship. In the United Kingdom, permanent residence became accessible in 2008 on a sliding investment scale:

£2,000,000	5 years
£5,000,000	3 years
£10,000,000	2 years

These golden visas have attracted staggering sums from Russia, China, Nigeria, the United Arab Emirates, and other flight capital locales into the United Kingdom, especially into London real estate. Easy availability of such visas through Portugal, Spain, Greece, Cyprus, and Malta provides access across the entire European Union.

In fact, cash for passports has become big business. As of this writing, some 60 countries have citizenship for sale. This movement is beginning to augment or take the place of tax havens, another stark example of capitalism suborning politics, subverting democracy, and expanding the financial secrecy system with the full cooperation of compromised governments.

Legalizing Money Laundering? The QI Program

Robert Rubin, Treasury secretary in the first Clinton administration, approved the Qualified Intermediary Program in 1999, implemented by the Internal Revenue Service in 2000. Under this program, foreign banks entered into agreements with the IRS promising that their individual American account holders would declare their income earned on such accounts or the banks would withhold the appropriate tax and pay to the IRS. But a huge loophole left out corporations and trusts, so thousands of individuals quickly set up foreign entities and continued to avoid both tax payments and accountability to the IRS.

Oliver Bullough in *Moneyland* makes the obvious point: "It was an elegant plan, but it had one small flaw: it required the banks to be honest. Quite naturally, therefore, it failed."[96]

Today, there are some 7,000 foreign banks with QI agreements. Each, under recent rules, is supposed to undertake periodic certifications to ensure compliance with the terms of the program, but this certification can be performed by a local lawyer or accountant or other seemingly qualified consultant. The bottom line is weak compliance by the institution, perfunctory certification by the external party, and inadequate monitoring by the IRS assure that, via the QI Program and its spinoffs, massive money laundering and tax evasion continue.

Failure to Address Falsified Trade

The widespread practice of manipulating trade transactions, key to operating capitalism's secrecy structure, is explained in chapter 1 and illustrated further in chapter 7. Is it legal?

In the United States, courts have consistently ruled that misinvoicing or misidentifying trade that results in underpayment of US customs duties is illegal. But misinvoicing or misidentifying trade that results in underpayment to another country for its customs duties or taxes has only recently been purposefully addressed.

The False Claims Act, excluding from its scope claims or statements made under the Internal Revenue Code, has been narrowly interpreted by the US Supreme Court and is not useful in addressing cross-border trade misinvoicing. The Customs Chapter of the Criminal Code is applicable to manipulation of imports that may deprive the United States of customs duties, but court decisions have introduced a "test of materiality," which significantly limits its application to cases of trade misinvoicing. The Criminal Code also provides for "mandatory restitution to victims of certain crimes," including offenses against property. The False Statements Act has been cautiously interpreted to include misleading information affecting US trade statistics, a low bar for application of the law.

Much more useful is the 1952 Wire Fraud Statute, which amended the Communications Act of 1934 and stated the following:

> Whoever, having devised or intending to devise any scheme or artifice to defraud, or for obtaining money or property by means of false or fraudulent pretenses, representations, or promises, transmits or causes to be transmitted by means of wire, radio, or television communication in interstate or foreign commerce, any writings, signs, signals, pictures, or sounds for the purpose of executing such scheme or artifice, shall be fined under this title or imprisoned not more than 20 years, or both.[97]

In 2005 the Supreme Court upheld a lower court ruling in *United States v. Pasquantino*, confirming that a criminal gang using US mails and wires in the act of smuggling liquor from the United States into Canada and thereby evading Canadian customs duties was guilty. In so doing, it asserted the United States' "substantial interest in preventing our nation's interstate wire communication systems from being used in furtherance of criminal fraudulent enterprises."[98] The limitation of the decision to "criminal fraudulent enterprises" led some US lawyers to advise their corporate clients that trade misinvoicing could continue, since such activity had not yet been clearly interpreted as "criminal."

In the 2015 case *United States v. Georgiou*, the Third Circuit Court of Appeals specifically addressed the "extraterritoriality of United States wire fraud statute," ruling that "indeed, the explicit statutory language indicates that it punishes frauds executed in 'interstate or foreign commerce'" and is "surely not a statute in which Congress had only domestic concerns in mind."[99]

In another 2015 case, *United States v. Bengis*, the Second Circuit Court of Appeals upheld an earlier ruling that "like the defendants in *Pasquantino*, [defendants'] conspiracy to conceal their illegal trade . . . deprived South Africa of money it was due. . . . The defendants' conduct in depriving South Africa of that revenue is, therefore, an offense against property."[100]

Tens of thousands of executives, managers, and employees in US multinational corporations regularly participate behind closed doors in trade misinvoicing decisions depriving their own and other nations of revenues, qualifying as schemes to defraud or offenses against property under US law. Similar laws exist in the canons of most other wealthy countries, quite commonly criminalizing the use of mails and wires in schemes to defraud. Yet, governments persist in defending their corporations because they bring wealth into their home economies. The question is, at what price to the character of their own citizens and the rule of law around the world?

Repeating again, this is the key, the central-most feature within capitalism's secrecy structure that is depriving capitalism of the opportunity to spread income, wealth, and prosperity and through such transparency to contribute decisively to democracy itself.

Citizens United

Nothing in recent memory so clearly demonstrates capitalism's now towering dominance over democracy within the two-part democratic-capitalist system as the 2010 US Supreme Court's decision in *Citizens United v. Federal Election Commission*. With this decision, corporations can utilize financial resources to support issues, giving them advantages over other components of society and strengthening capitalism's ability to ratify its own secrecy and thereby weaken democracy's transparency.

Citizens United had two hearings before the court. After the first, Chief Justice John Roberts wrote a narrow opinion in favor of *Citizens United*. But four conservative justices wanted a broader ruling that would free corporations, and they prevailed on Roberts to join their position. A second hearing outraged the opposing liberal members of the court. As Justice Stevens later wrote, "Essentially five justices were unhappy with the limited nature of the case before us, so they changed the case to give themselves an opportunity to change the law."[101] As a legal commentator noted,

> The crucial flaw in *Citizens United* was . . . the Court saw caps on spending not as crucial protections of democracy but as efforts to "restrict the speech of some elements of our society in order to enhance the relative voice of others."[102]

Legal scholars criticizing *Citizens United* point out that treating corporations as associations of shareholders entitled to free speech misses the reality that investing institutions such as pension and mutual funds own
some 80 percent of shares in US public companies. Penetrating through
multiple layers of organizational structures to reach individual voices belies credulity.

And the Supreme Court was not finished. In a 2014 case, *McCutcheon
v. Federal Election Commission*, the court struck down limits on contributions an individual can make to candidates for federal office in a two-
year election cycle. Justice Stephen Breyer lamented that *McCutcheon*
along with *Citizens*

> eviscerates our Nation's campaign finance laws, leaving a remnant inca-
> pable of dealing with the grave problems of democratic legitimacy that
> those laws were intended to solve. Where enough money calls the tune,
> the general public will not be heard.[103]

In the wake of these Supreme Court decisions, dark money flooded into
US elections. Foreign corporations through their US subsidiaries could
now contribute to political action committees. Nonprofits such as the
National Rifle Association can receive money from a foreign entity,
contribute to electioneering, and not disclose the foreign source of the
money. US corporations with substantial foreign shareholdings can
contribute to elections, effectively giving foreigners a voice in American
democracy.

Ellen Weintraub, a member of the Federal Election Commission, argued persuasively that

> you cannot have a right collectively that you do not have individually. In-
> dividual foreigners are barred from spending to sway elections; it defies
> logic to allow groups of foreigners, or foreigners in combination with
> American citizens, to fund political spending through corporations.[104]

Former *Washington Post* columnist Steven Pearlstein, always a brilliant
commentator, hits the nail on the head:

> The only difference between the current campaign finance system and a
> governing system based on bribery is merely one of semantics. Those with
> money can—and routinely do—buy votes, buy politicians, buy legislation,
> and buy regulations. Under the guise of protecting free speech, the Court

has now created a constitutional right to bribe elected officials, with the prize going to the highest bidder.[105]

Citizens United and *McCutcheon* confirm that democracy is now subordinate to capitalism. These are the worst Supreme Court decisions since *Plessy v. Ferguson* in 1896, which legalized the racial concept of separate but equal and, like *Plessy*, need to be legislated out of legitimacy or explicitly overturned. Left in place, both democracy and capitalism—the democratic-capitalist system—risk irrevocable damage.

Internal Revenue Service Weakened

Joseph Falcone, in a 2018 letter to the *New York Times*, wrote the following:

> I have been a tax lawyer since 1974, having started my career as an Internal Revenue Service lawyer before moving to private practice. It has been clear to those who work with the I.R.S. that both Republicans and Democrats through the years have been trying to cripple the agency through a "death by a thousand (budget) cuts." The purpose is obvious— to protect the rich from tax audits and collection. Both political parties have their friends and donors to protect.[106]

Testimony presented to the House Ways and Means Committee included the chart presented in figure 9.1 demonstrating the severe cuts in IRS enforcement actions. The presenter, Chye-Ching Huang with the Center on Budget and Policy Priorities, commented further as follows:

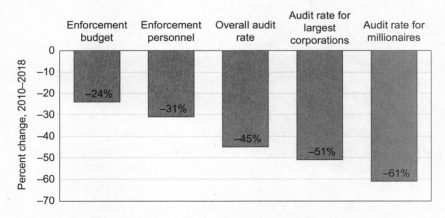

FIGURE 9.1 Severely depleted IRS enforcement
Source: Calculations of IRS data, Center on Budget and Policy Priorities. Used with permission.[107]

Large corporations can use myriad accounting games, entities, and transactions across countries to avoid or evade taxes . . . pour resources into
tax planning, litigation, and lobbying[,] . . . but budget cuts have hampered the IRS's ability to match them.[108]

Larry Summers and Natasha Sarin, in a National Bureau of Economic
Research paper, estimate that between 2020 and 2029 the IRS will fail
to collect $7.5 trillion of taxes due.[109] This means that corporations and
wealthy individuals will pull out of government coffers the greater part
of this uncollected tax, further driving inequality and undermining democracy. Capitalism, operating through the financial secrecy system, is
risking permanent damage to the world's largest economy.

Repeal of Glass-Steagall

Did the repeal of Glass-Steagall contribute to the 2007–2008 financial
crisis? The question is hotly debated. And it is the wrong question. The
much more fundamental concern is did the repeal strengthen the forces
of financial secrecy operating within the capitalist system?

Glass-Steagall, enacted in 1933 after the crash of 1929 and the onset
of the Great Depression, barred commercial banks from having interests in entities "principally engaged" in investment banking. This worked
well for 50 years, as it separated the two types of financial pursuits, but
beginning in the 1980s the Federal Reserve reinterpreted "principally engaged" to allow commercial banks to earn 10 percent of their revenue
from investment banking activities, soon increased to 25 percent. So, even
under Glass-Steagall the separation of the two functions was breaking
down.

New York bankers complained to Congress for years that they faced
stiff competition from European and Asian banks and lobbied hard for
the elimination of the barrier, fiercely arguing that "complementary activities" must be allowed. In 1999 Congress passed the Financial Services
Modernization Act, championed by Treasury Secretary Robert Rubin
in part to legitimize what had already taken place: the $83 billion merger
of Citibank and Travelers Insurance, which also owned the Salomon
Smith Barney stock brokerage firm. With President Bill Clinton's signature, Glass-Steagall was effectively repealed. In 2000 the Commodity
Futures Modernization Act was also passed, largely removing over-the-
counter derivatives from federal and state regulation.

Up until 1999 the Federal Reserve had approved the formation of 40
bank holding companies, authorized to own more than 1 bank. After

Glass-Steagall was repealed most of these 40 became financial holding companies, and by 2006 there were another 550 financial holding companies taking advantage of the now almost unlimited range of permitted economic activities.

So, in less than a decade after the repeal of Glass-Steagall, America experienced a devastating economic meltdown of both commercial and investment banking, both Main Street and Wall Street. The immediate cause centered on the housing market. For years, home financing had been characterized by the chain of speculators, flippers, mortgage originators, lenders who issued mortgages, shadow banks, and mainstream finance firms that bundled mortgages into securities, then created collateralized debt obligations, then sold these securitized bundles to buyers all over the world. Going through this sequence, it often became unclear who held a lien on which property.

As the Financial Crisis Inquiry Commission reported in 2011, "a combination of excessive borrowing, risky investments, and lack of transparency put the financial system on a collision course with crises."[110]

> [O]ver the past 30-plus years, we permitted the growth of a shadow banking system—opaque and laden with short-term debt—that rivaled the size of the traditional banking system. Key components of the market— for example, the multitrillion-dollar repo lending market, off-balance-sheet entities, and the use of over-the-counter derivatives— were hidden from view. . . . [111]

> [T]he dangers of this debt were magnified because transparency was not required or desired. Massive, short-term borrowing, combined with obligations unseen by others in the market, heightened the chances the system could rapidly unravel.[112]

Home prices became overheated, buyers entered into mortgages with little down payment, interest accelerator clauses kicked in, and defaults soared. With subprime mortgages totaling some 43 percent of foreclosures by late 2007, investors, governments, and pension funds in dozens of countries were hit with losses from what should have been a safe bet.

Some analysts argue that the 2007–2008 financial crisis primarily exhibited failings within the shadow banking system, including those mortgage originators, dealers, nonbank lenders, and securitization bundlers. Countrywide Financial Corp., for example, borrowed from banks, originated mortgages, and bundled these mortgages into securities to be

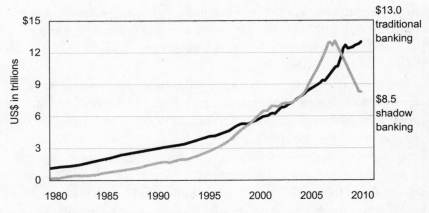

FIGURE 9.2 Traditional and shadow banking systems
Source: Financial Crisis Inquiry Report.[113]

sold. The shadow banking system had in fact been growing along with, even exceeding, traditional banking, as depicted in figure 9.2.

The Federal Reserve seemed unaware that the shadow banking system was generating the majority of consumer credit and in any case lacked the regulatory tools to adequately manage this sector. While this may be true, the largest banks, combining both commercial and investment activities and heavily funding the shadow banking system, were swept up in the crisis. They were highly leveraged, holding mortgages, mortgage-related securities, and derivatives referencing these securities, and any other creditor or banking regulator could force them to liquidate such holdings on notice.

The Financial Crisis Inquiry Commission took the broad view:

> We conclude there was a systemic breakdown in accountability and ethics. The integrity of our financial markets and the public's trust in those markets are essential to the economic well-being of our nation. The soundness and the sustained prosperity of the financial system and our economy rely on the notions of fair dealing, responsibility, and transparency. . . . Unfortunately . . . we witnessed an erosion of standards of responsibility and ethics that exacerbated the financial crisis.[114]

So, in these circumstances, what should be done? Robert Reich, former labor secretary, recommends that financial holding companies be broken up:

Some argue Glass-Steagall wouldn't have prevented the 2008 crisis because the real culprits were non-banks like Lehman Brothers and Bear Stearns. But that's baloney. These non-banks got their funding from the big banks in the form of lines of credit, mortgages, and repurchase agreements. If the big banks hadn't provided them the money, the non-banks wouldn't have got into trouble. And why were the banks able to give them easy credit on bad collateral? Because Glass-Steagall was gone.[115]

Sheila Bair, former chairperson of the Federal Deposit Insurance Corporation, summed up her views:

> Glass-Steagall repeal was part of a broader movement in the late 1990s and early 2000s toward the idea of "self-correcting" markets—that banks knew better than regulators how to manage risk and regulate themselves. To be sure, Glass-Steagall repeal gave birth to larger, more complex institutions which were "too big to fail" given the regulatory tools available during the crisis. So, even if repeal did not drive the crisis, it certainly contributed to the need for bailouts of these behemoths.[116]

The right question to ask is, did the repeal of Glass-Steagall contribute to a more robust and equitable American economy? No, it did the opposite. It confirmed the enormous reach of the shadow financial system. It accelerated the disconnect between the fiduciary duties of commercial and investment banking. And it strengthened the secrecy structures driving inequality and fracturing the social contract.

Capture

For a century academics and investigators have studied the issue of regulatory capture—that is, the industries being regulated dominating the agencies supposedly regulating their activity—without arriving at politically satisfactory means of changing this recurring reality. Three recent examples illustrate capture, each with severe consequences: the Great Recession, the Minerals Management Service (MMS), and the Federal Aviation Administration (FAA).

The Great Recession. The financial crisis of 2007–2008 exposed stunning weaknesses in regulatory oversight. The US federal financial regulatory structure comprised eight major components: the Federal Reserve System, Federal Deposit Insurance Corporation, Office of the Comptroller of the Currency, Securities and Exchange Commission,

Commodity Futures Trading Commission, Office of Thrift Supervision, Federal Housing Finance Agency, and the National Credit Union Administration. None foresaw overleveraging in the finance industry or pending disaster in the housing market, and none had a plan for dealing with the scale of collapse in the banking sector, which required the level of bank bailouts addressed in chapter 6.

Industry chieftains and agency regulators had played musical chairs for decades, particularly with Goldman Sachs and Citibank supplying Treasury secretaries and other commission and bureau officials. There was no question whatsoever that they—the regulators—would prioritize bailing out the banks first, leaving the people to suffer. According to an analysis by the Federal Reserve Bank of San Francisco, the average American lost about $70,000 in lifetime income resulting from the crisis.[117]

Nor is the story of capture complete without emphasizing how powerful the banking industry was and is on Capitol Hill. In Japan it is said that every member of the National Diet knows the head of the Yakuza crime syndicate in their district. In Washington, every member of Congress knows the prominent bankers in their district both for their own wealth and for the money they marshal. With hundreds of millions of dollars in campaign contributions and lobbying expenditures, bankers buy the regulation or the lack thereof that serves their interests. Jonathan Hopkin summarizes nicely:

> The very close connection between the key political actors and financial sector leaders . . . created an indelible impression that the bailout was more about protecting the interests of a close-knit political and business elite, . . . channeling huge quantities of government money directly into the pockets of some of the wealthiest people in America, [and] rewarding them for making spectacularly wrong decisions.[118]

In the wake of the financial crisis, Congress took important steps to improve banking regulation. The Dodd-Frank Wall Street Reform and Consumer Protection Act of 2010, named for its Senate and House cosponsors, attempts across its original 848 pages of text and subsequent 22,000 pages of regulations to legislate away the idea that some banks are too big to fail. Perhaps the single most important provision is the requirement that the largest institutions undergo annual stress tests that analyze their capacity to weather a future crisis, the results of which must be made public. This requirement for transparency is the best protection against excessively risky activities.

Other measures limit banks trading in commercial instruments for their own account, called the Volcker Rule. Capital adequacy ratios were strengthened. A Financial Stability Oversight Council was formed, chaired by the secretary of the Treasury and including the heads of the financial regulatory agencies. An Office of Financial Research was created, tasked with gathering financial information and imbued with the power to standardize data reporting mechanisms. A Consumer Financial Protection Bureau was mandated to promote "fairness and transparency for mortgages, credit cards, and other consumer financial products and services." The Office of Thrift Supervision, deemed ineffective, was closed.

While these steps were laudable, nothing stopped the industry from immediately launching efforts to roll back limitations, and nothing hindered the biggest banks from growing bigger still. Average total assets of the four top-tier banks grew about one-third larger, from $6 trillion to more than $8 trillion, and midtier banks expanded similarly.[119] At the same time, major banks continued expanding their purely corporate activities while reducing loans as a percentage of assets. Publicly reported stress tests, originally required of 50 banks, were later limited to only those with assets of $250 billion or more. The Volcker Rule limiting proprietary trading was weakened. The Consumer Financial Protection Bureau, despite sustained efforts on the part of Senator Elizabeth Warren, saw its legitimacy challenged all the way to the Supreme Court. Even a provision within Dodd-Frank requiring energy companies to report what they pay as royalties and fees to foreign governments was contested.

Plainly speaking, the banking industry won the postcrisis battles, emerging more dominant and powerful than ever. Successful capture of both legislative and regulatory organs of government, paid for in part with bailout money, enabled this achievement.

The Minerals Management Service. Part of the Department of the Interior, the MMS has for years watched a series of disasters in the Gulf of Mexico, now crowded with 3,500 oil-production platforms. In 2010 the half-billion-dollar offshore drilling rig Deepwater Horizon, tethered 5,000 feet above the seabed and drilling another 13,000 feet below the ocean floor, blew out, burned, and sank, taking 11 lives and spewing 200 million gallons of crude oil into the Gulf, damaging shorelines in Texas, Louisiana, Mississippi, Alabama, and further along the coast to Florida.

MMS had for decades been responsible for both overseeing operational safety and collecting royalty revenues, a conflict of interest built into its structure. Vast sums of money payable to the US government were never collected because industry executives cozied up to agency officials. In addition, the agency and the industry regularly exchanged staffs, the revolving door syndrome between industry and government so often lamented.

An Interior Department investigation report released five weeks after the Deepwater Horizon disaster found that MMS employees had indulged in sex and drugs on the job; accepted gifts from oil industry companies; enjoyed hunting, skeet shooting, fishing, golf excursions, and football trips; and even in one instance negotiated for a job with the company being inspected.[120]

Senator Sheldon Whitehouse, addressing both the Wall Street and Gulf of Mexico disasters, said to his colleagues,

> We have known about regulatory capture now for a century. We have seen it in action throughout that period. We have had two of the most catastrophic examples of regulatory capture happen just now on our watch, and in all this time we have never really come up with a mechanism for addressing it, because the pressure on these regulatory agencies is systemic, because it is constant and persistent.[121]

The Federal Aviation Administration. The Federal Aviation Administration may be the organ within the federal government most compromised by corporate capture. For decades industry officials and legislators, particularly from the state of Washington, pressured the FAA to delegate oversight of safety procedures directly to manufacturers. This served to speed up airworthiness certifications to enable US manufacturers, especially the Boeing Company, to turn out new aircraft and compete for global market share with as little interference as possible. Furthering this effort, in 2012 the lofty-sounding Aircraft Certification Process Review and Reform Aviation Rulemaking Committee, comprising one FAA official and eight industry representatives, was tasked with producing "Recommendations on the Assessment of the Certification and Approval Process," with essentially foreordained conclusions submitted a month later.

> Continue to improve the effectiveness of delegation programs . . . . ,
> Expand[] delegation capability to include support for all
>   certification airworthiness standards . . . , and

Leverage the demonstrated capability of top industry performers
and move from detailed oversight of industry operations to more
program-level development and performance analysis.[122]

These recommendations and others led to the FAA Reauthorization Act
of 2018, leading the *New York Times* to comment that

> with a few short paragraphs tucked into 463 pages of legislation, . . . Boe-
> ing scored one of its biggest lobbying wins: a law that undercuts the gov-
> ernment's role in approving the design of new airplanes. . . . [T]hose
> paragraphs cemented the industry's power, allowing manufacturers to
> challenge regulators over safety disputes and making it difficult for the
> government to usurp companies' authority. . . . Now, the agency, at the
> outset of the development process, has to hand over responsibility for cer-
> tifying almost every aspect of new planes. . . . [T]he law allows com-
> panies to make recommendations about the compensation of FAA
> employees.[123]

Near-total regulatory capture is evidenced by powers given to the
industry-heavy Safety Oversight and Certification Advisory Committee,
authorized to

> recommend recruiting, hiring, training, and continuing education objec-
> tives for FAA aviation safety engineers and aviation safety inspectors.[124]

Three weeks after the legislation was adopted, Boeing's newest design
and flagship bearer, the 737 MAX, belonging to Lion Air, crashed into
the Java Sea after taking off from Jakarta. Boeing and the FAA remained
certain that the aircraft was safe. Five months after that crash, another
737 MAX bound for Nairobi (where I had arrived by air a day earlier)
flown by Ethiopian Airlines crashed after taking off from Addis Ababa.
Airlines around the world grounded the MAX, the US president
grounded the MAX, and the Federal Aviation Administration, having
earlier confirmed the plane's safety, then reversed itself and likewise
grounded the MAX.

Boeing had installed a software-driven attitude control system, onto
its newest plane but failed to train pilots on the new system, at first even
avoided mention of it in flight manuals, and circumvented FAA certification. Called the Maneuvering Characteristics Augmentation System

(MCAS), operating in response to external sensors, software would take control of the aircraft. Any malfunction in the sensors or the software effectively disempowered the pilots.

A House of Representatives congressional committee investigation in 2020 was caustic in its final report:

> Boeing failed to appropriately classify MCAS as a safety-critical system, concealed critical information about MCAS from pilots, and sought to diminish focus on MCAS as a "new system" in order to avoid greater FAA scrutiny and increased pilot training requirements. . . .
>
> . . . Boeing sought, and the FAA approved, the removal of references to MCAS from Boeing's Flight Crew Operations Manual. . . . As a result, 737 MAX pilots were precluded from knowing of the existence of MCAS and its potential effect on aircraft handling without pilot command.
>
> . . . Boeing's own test pilot took more than 10 seconds to respond to uncommanded MCAS activation . . . leading to potentially "catastrophic" consequences.[125]

A 2020 Department of Transportation critique reported in a footnote that the "FAA eventually delegated all 91 [flight control and stabilizer] certification plans to Boeing."[126] Regulatory capture does not get any more complete than this.

Retired captain Chesley "Sully" Sullenberger, who famously performed the "Miracle on the Hudson," agreed:

> These crashes are demonstrable evidence that our current system of aircraft design and certification has failed us. . . . We owe it to everyone who flies, passengers and crews alike, to do much better than to design aircraft with inherent flaws that we intend pilots will have to compensate for and overcome.[127]

A former American military and commercial aviation pilot, retired after decades in the air, put it simply:

> How do you certify a plane that the cockpit can't fly?

It took the lives of 346 passengers and crew members to force the question.

In January 2021, the Department of Justice entered into a deferred prosecution agreement with Boeing whereby the company settled for one count of criminal conspiracy to commit fraud with a penalty of $243 million, an additional $1.77 billion in compensation to the company's airline customers, and $500 million into a crash victims' beneficiary fund, totaling a bit more than $2.5 billion.[128]

In a superb piece of writing in the *New York Times* titled "Boeing's Saga of Capitalism Gone Awry," David Gelles, who later wrote a book on the subject, nails it:

> As an avalanche of investigations made clear, the true cause of the crashes wasn't faulty software. It was a corporate culture gone horribly wrong. They started tying executive bonuses to stock performance. It was greedy executives doing short-sighted things to pad their pockets [as they] . . . slashed costs, reduced head count, ramped up outsourcing and increased Boeing's share buyback program and shareholder dividends.[129]

"Capitalism gone awry" directly contributed to lives lost and endangered mine and perhaps yours.

Tax Cuts and Jobs Act

Before COVID-19 devastated the US economy, the Tax Cuts and Jobs Act passed in 2017 produced mixed economic impacts but clear political failings. Billed as a middle-class tax cut and a corporate expansion stimulus, the act produced neither visible income gains for average workers nor sustained indications of business investment. Perhaps more importantly, whatever opportunity may have existed for Americans to perceive movement toward greater fairness has evaporated. Among unmet promises and intended outcomes are the following:

- Average taxpayers received a cut of only some $600 to $800 a year, while the richest 1 percent received average cuts of $50,000 a year.[130]
- Gross national product, lauded to grow at 4–6 percent a year, instead increased by little more than 2 percent a year before falling off the cliff in 2020.
- Corporations, instead of repatriating an overly estimated $4 trillion in accumulated foreign earnings, have brought back less than $1.5 trillion.
- Corporate incentives to shift profits overseas have not been eliminated or significantly curtailed.[131]
- Corporations repurchased more than $1 trillion of their own shares in 2018 and net dividends reached a new high of $1.3 trillion, further

increasing capital gains and incomes for the wealthiest Americans.[132]

- The bill included a $135 billion tax giveaway to real estate developers and hedge fund managers.[133]
- Supposedly morale-building bonuses for workers, according to one study, averaged two cents per hour.[134]
- Tax cuts, instead of paying for themselves through growth, exploded the budget deficit.

William Gale at the Brookings Institution, former senior economist in the administration of President George H. W. Bush, highlighted the economic and political shortcomings of the act:

> It exacerbates preexisting and longstanding trends, rather than aiming to partially compensate for them.[135]

Economist Gabriel Zucman commented that today the American dream is "not doing well," that the US tax system is an "engine of inequality," and then went on to say,

> What's very striking is you see that inequality has been rising since the 1980s. Then in 2017 you have a tax reform which is regressive, which further cuts the rates on the super-rich, and it's hard to interpret that other than by saying it's a form of political capture.[136]

Steve Wamhoff at the Institute on Taxation and Economic Policy said,

> The tax law has made rich people richer, . . . and it hasn't really accomplished very much else. I think this is the exact opposite of what our society needed in this time of greater inequality.[137]

A widely held view among the wealthiest is that rising inequality does not matter so long as the poor and middle class see some upward movement. Evaluating the Tax Cuts and Jobs Act, William Cline commented though not necessarily agreed, as follows:

> In principle a greater concentration of income because of the wealth effect would not mean that lower income groups would be worse off as a consequence to the new tax law. If there are sizable growth effects, the overhaul could make the lower income groups better off than they other-

wise would have been, just not as much better off as would be the outcome for the upper income (and wealth) groups.[138]

This articulates an absolutely fundamental reality in capitalist ideology
as it has come to be viewed and practiced today, a point that is pivotal
within our current dilemmas. For many if not most wealthy Americans,
there is no limit to inequality so long as the poor and middle class have
some upward movement. If the poor are better off by $600 a year, then
it is perfectly agreeable for the rich to be better off by $50,000 a year.
Some minor improvements for the poor and middle class render acceptable massive gains for the upper class. This justification for limitless inequality is what will bring down the democratic-capitalist system unless
addressed purposefully and promptly. The social contract simply cannot hold with endlessly rising economic inequality.

Whether viewed from the perspective of the United States or for that
matter from the perspective of most other countries across the world, the
forces of capitalism are expanding their dominance over the ideals of democracy. Within the two-part democratic-capitalist system, the democracy component is weakening while the capitalist component is
strengthening. Capitalism increasingly operating behind walls of secrecy
undermines democracy endeavoring to guarantee transparency. The resolution of this clash will determine much of the history of the twenty-
first century.

If national governments are compromised, can international institutions soften capitalism's rogue behavior and advance democracy's chance
for justice?

10

International Institutions
to the Rescue?

THE PRECEDING CHAPTER ON NATIONAL GOVERNMENTS, both weak and strong, failing to address the financial secrecy system and its impact on capitalism and democracy leads logically to the question: Can international institutions step up and effectively foster conditions enhancing prosperity for all? The answer is, some can and some cannot. Without attempting to address the full range of work by each major global organization, this chapter focuses on institutional willingness and capacity to deal with striking flaws within capitalism that are undermining democracy.

The United Nations merits high praise. Besides its work through 22 agencies on peace and security, climate change, human rights, gender issues, labor, food, and more, the UN has well embraced the matter of illicit financial flows (IFFs) and how they forestall development for billions of people. In 2010 the UN Economic Commission for Africa, under the leadership of its chief economist, Abdalla Hamdok (later prime minister of Sudan), took up the matter of IFFs impacting Africa; appointed a high-level panel led by Thabo Mbeki, former president of South Africa; and advanced the issue across the continent and into Western capitals. The UN then tasked each of its other four regional economic commissions in Latin America, the Middle East, Europe, and Asia to do the same. Illicit financial flows were secured into the Addis Ababa Action Agenda and the UN Sustainable Development Goals, both adopted in 2015. Now, as said earlier, 193 countries are committed, at least on paper, to curtailing IFFs, the most damaging manifestation of the financial secrecy system.

Not leaving it there, two nations—Nigeria and Norway—have for years aligned in hosting numerous events at the UN and elsewhere to drive home the seriousness of illicit financial flows, leading in 2020 to the appointment of the Panel on International Financial Accountability, Transparency and Integrity. This panel's report has the potential to generate further multilateral commitments addressing the most important changes required in global capitalism. The United States, true to form, aligned with Switzerland and other tax havens and opposed the panel's mandate:

> We are concerned that this body is built upon the faulty premise that the current international architecture to prevent and combat illicit finance is broken or inadequate. We remain concerned about the conflation of tax avoidance and evasion with financial crimes.[1]

Well, tax evasion is a financial crime in the United States, so why do US policy makers have so much difficulty dealing with this reality when the tax-evading money comes from abroad? Fortunately, Norway, Nigeria, and dozens of other countries moved purposefully forward with this important initiative. Under UN auspices, national delegations often— not always but often—demonstrate a willingness to ask hard questions and pursue uncomfortable answers.

US influence is even more evident in the World Bank, more so than in any other global institution, in part because tradition gives the American president the right to name its president. The "Washington Consensus," codified by John Williamson in 1989 while at the Institute for International Economics, laid out 10 economic and policy imperatives for developing countries, and dominated US and World Bank thinking into the next century. Advocating sensible measures needed for stability and growth, the consensus was, however, completely devoid of introspection, failing to include any hint of criticism of financial practices in the West that facilitate billions of dollars illicitly streaming out of developing countries, debasing the lives of generations across the globe. The message to the poor was "be more like us."

The World Bank has been slow and weak for decades in addressing issues that upset the wealthier nations, principal funders of its budget. Beginning in the 1980s, the bank spent 15 years dodging the issue of corruption, arguing that this was political rather than economic and therefore beyond the bank's purview. Finally admitting that illicit activity drains more money out of developing countries than foreign aid brings money into developing countries, the bank now gingerly treats this strictly as a concern surrounding tax collection, and therefore the proper goal should be helping poorer countries strengthen their revenue departments. In other words, the focus of the World Bank is on the victim, not the perpetrator, a common predilection well illustrated by Anand Giridharadas in his book *Winners Take All*.

World Bank analysts studiously avoid the reality, explained earlier, that the primary motivation driving money out of developing countries is the conversion of soft currencies into hard currencies, fully enabled by the financial secrecy system. In millions of international transactions, this is the fundamental point. Tax evasion or avoidance is very much a tertiary concern. But the World Bank cannot go in this direction because the United States in particular and other wealthy countries as well facilitate and welcome illicit money flowing from abroad into the coffers of the already rich. The World Bank will not bite the hand that feeds it, no matter how many people are hurt by its intransigence.

Another reality characterizes the World Bank: an almost universal sense of defensiveness. Both in written materials and public utterances, the bank portrays itself as unfailingly on top of its game, undoubting of its excellence, disseminating necessary wisdom, and solving economic and social problems. The level of self-justification belies a deeper unease. Defensiveness and intransigence go hand and hand, stifling initiative and reducing the bank to a low common denominator. Many extraordinarily capable individuals among the bank's staff of 10,000 are stymied, unable to pursue or suggest fresh thinking. This largely explains the years it took to address corruption and the additional years it will take to address the financial secrecy system and the harm it does to billions of people. Bright voices within the World Bank yearn to speak freely.

Existing within the World Bank Group is the International Finance Corporation, which invests in private-sector ventures across the developing world. Yet, the corporation channels a high percentage of its investments through tax haven entities, which then reinvest in projects. Policing money laundering and tax evasion is left largely to the tax haven parent company, with little oversight from IFC. This puts the World Bank solidly in the business of supporting the financial secrecy system, contradicting its stated principles.

The new mantra in the World Bank is "public-private partnerships," an attempt to marshal accumulating private wealth into development projects. As posited in chapter 2, more than $100 trillion in broad money, much of it earning less than the rate of inflation or even intentionally invested at negative interest rates, is firmly held for security, purposefully avoiding risks, and precious little of it will find its way into joint ventures with foreign governments. Lamenting abdication of its original development mandate, Steven Friedman argues that the World Bank's shift

> places the fate of the global poor largely in the hands of private wealth. It seeks not to find ways in which private money can serve public needs but how public needs can shift to meet the demands of private money.[2]

Among all international institutions, the World Bank most clearly requires redirection and revitalization. Perhaps opening candidatures for the presidency of the bank would be a first step.

Tradition gives Europe primacy in naming the head of the International Monetary Fund. Focusing principally on global financial stability, the IMF nevertheless gets into issues of inequality, corruption, tax evasion, and, of late, illicit financial flows. Engaged in recent years on concerns surrounding inadequate taxation of multinational corporations, the IMF finds itself somewhat constrained on a definitional question: what constitutes an illicit financial flow and therefore contributes to tax evasion? Is tax avoidance, for example, through trade misinvoicing, legal or illegal? Chapters 3 and 9 go to some lengths making the point that trade manipulations done for the purpose of manipulating taxes in nearly all cases constitute schemes to defraud or offenses against property and therefore are illegal. The IMF needs to recognize and treat the financial secrecy system in all its manifestations as threatening to its core mandate: global financial stability.

The Organisation of Economic Co-operation and Development based in Paris, comprising in its core membership 38 higher-income countries, is criticized by civil society organizations as a "rich man's club." Perhaps it is, but the OECD has reached out to more than 60 additional countries to participate actively in its quarter-century effort to reform global taxation far more aggressively than have the World Bank and the IMF, which should be the lead institutions. Recognizing that corporations are not paying their taxes, the OECD launched its "Base Erosion and Profit Shifting" initiative in 2013, focusing on corporate practices that erode tax collections in some countries and shift tax-free profits to other countries. Incomplete as this "BEPS" process is, more than 135 countries are cooperating in the broad effort, providing a starting point for further and more fundamental reform measures. Asked why the OECD, dominated by richer countries, is pursuing this agenda even more than the World

Bank and the IMF, José Ángel Gurría, OECD executive director, said
quietly, "Perhaps because we are not based in Washington."

Five more international organizations are especially important. The
Financial Action Task Force, created in 1989 to set voluntary anti–money
laundering standards, now has 39 member countries and 9 regional
bodies. Noted for its 40 recommendations, which, following 9/11, also encompass terrorist financing, the FATF performs peer group evaluations
of its members on about eight- to ten-year cycles, regularly faulting the
United States for failing to address its millions of anonymous companies.
Curtailing falsified trade, the centerpiece of the financial secrecy system,
is not yet delineated in FATF recommendations.

The Bank for International Settlements, based in Basel, Switzerland,
has for many years compiled confidential data on cross-border bank deposits, that is, how much money citizens of one country have in current
bank accounts in other countries. Recently, with agreements from its
63-member central banks, BIS has begun opening these records. Economists Thomas Piketty, Gabriel Zucman, and others are better able to
estimate the staggering sums stashed outside countries of origin, though
data does not include stocks, real estate, art, and other assets. As covered in chapter 4, James Henry estimates total holdings abroad at well
upward of $30 trillion.

Interpol, now with 195 member countries, includes money laundering,
transnational crimes, and terrorist financing in its coordination and
training agendas, urged particularly by former head Khoo Boon Hui,
Singaporean by nationality and an expert on the subject. Two other past
Interpol leaders, South African and Chinese by nationality, have been
tagged with corruption charges. Interpol is known especially for its "Red
Notices" seeking arrests of wanted persons; other notices include yellow,
blue, black, green, orange, and purple, disseminating information or providing warnings. While Interpol attempts to remain nonpolitical, member governments often use notices against opponents and critics,
complicating the organization's laudable efforts. Through its cooperation with financial intelligence units across the world, linked within what
is called the Egmont Group, Interpol should be an invaluable service in
fighting economic crimes, but its functioning must remain completely
apolitical.

The World Trade Organization based in Geneva and successor to the
General Agreement on Tariffs and Trade, now has 164 member states
that account for 98 percent of global trade. Its stated goal is to "ensure
that trade flows as smoothly, predictably and freely as possible."[3] Note

that this does not include as "legitimately" as possible. While acknowledging that trade should be priced according to authorized valuation standards, the WTO does not get into the business of enforcing legitimacy in pricing. Its operating agreements accept that "the actual price of the goods . . . is generally shown on the invoice." Yet customs agencies in many countries report that 80 percent or more of invoices are falsified. WTO operating agreements also state that there are no "conditions for the valuation of goods for taxation or foreign exchange control."[4] Tens of thousands of trading partners have taken this to mean that one invoice can be used for customs purposes and a different invoice for payment purposes. The WTO's recently named and very capable director-general, Ngozi Okonjo-Iweala, the former minister of finance in Nigeria and thoroughly familiar with the linkage between trade misinvoicing and grinding poverty, will likely push her organization into issues surrounding trade legitimacy.

The World Customs Organization has in recent years taken up the mantel. Growing out of an earlier convention centered in Brussels, the WCO acquired its name in 1994 and today has 183 member countries focusing on best practices in customs administration.

The G20 meeting of world leaders in China in 2016 took the following decision:

> We will continue our work on addressing cross-border financial flows derived from illicit activities, including deliberate trade misinvoicing, which hampers the mobilization of domestic resources for development, and welcome the communication and coordination with the World Customs Organization for a study report in this regard following the Hangzhou Summit.[5]

WCO secretary-general Kunio Mikuriya, from Japan, seized the opportunity to assemble a global conference of experts in 2018, resulting in a 171-page analysis for which he wrote a foreword:

> Over the past decade, the topic of Illicit Financial Flows via Trade Misinvoicing (IFFs/TM) has been debated at length in literature and research publications, with international organizations signaling the dangers of such illicit flows, which enable trade payments and receipts to be exploited for the transfer of capital. . . . During the analytical and compilation process, the Secretariat became increasingly cognizant of the pernicious effects of IFFs/TM, . . . both over-invoicing and under-invoicing, as well as

irregularities in both export declarations and import declarations. . . .
[A]ttention should instead focus on actions to combat IFFs/TM, the existence of which is indisputable.[6]

This is a major breakthrough among international organizations, both
the charge by the G20 and the response by the WCO. Repeatedly within
this book emphasis is laid on the fact that falsifying trade is the primary
means by which the financial secrecy system operates. This is the preferred way to shift illicitly generated money across borders, producing
impoverishment for billions in poorer countries, inequality for hundreds
of millions in richer countries, and enormous wealth for the system's operators in poor and rich countries alike. This is the principal mechanism by which capitalism is undermining the democratic-capitalist
system. This is how you do it, now normalized in international trade
and financial dealings.

So, as posed at the beginning of this chapter, are international institutions coming to the rescue of democratic capitalism? Unfortunately,
the United States is enfeebling its leadership role in responsible free market ideology. The UN and the WCO are acquitting themselves well. For
the World Bank and the IMF, both heavily influenced by the decades-
long practice of the United States in welcoming dirty money from abroad,
not yet, with the World Bank in particular requiring some serious soul-
searching. Other institutions mentioned here likewise need to recognize
the stakes—quite literally, the survival of the democratic-capitalist
system—and widen and deepen their respective commitments.

11

Hiding in Silos

THIS IS THE SHORTEST CHAPTER in this book and contains the only sentence written in italics.

A most disturbing aspect of the problems surrounding the financial secrecy system and its impact on capitalism and democracy is how little attention foreign policy and national security communities devote to this reality.

Within the State Department in Washington and Whitehall in London and Quai d'Orsay in Paris and other Western seats of government, the role of capitalism, operating so determinedly through mechanisms of stealth and secrecy, compromising and undermining democracy, is given short shrift. Supposedly larger questions surrounding diplomacy, power relationships, military preparedness, and conflict are seen as far more important. The money moving through the shadow financial system, whether initiated or facilitated by citizens or foreigners though weakening scores of countries around the world, is hardly on the table. Many would like to believe that such matters are covered by other branches of their governments, but this very often is not the case. The foreign policy and national security communities, seeing disruptions around the world stemming in good part from economic deprivation, dislocation, and duplicity, should realize the point. Instead, the tolerance level for economic malpractices taking resources in and out of Russia, in and out of China, in and out of Nigeria, in and out of Mexico, in and out of the pockets of one's own American, European, and other citizens is to longtime observers absolutely extraordinary.

Diplomatic, military, and intelligence agencies in most Western nations believe that what they address is the "hard stuff" and what the economic and commercial people address is the "soft stuff." Money laundering, tax evasion, corruption, illicit financial flows—these are all presumably soft issues, all the concerns of other people, the economic and commercial types. Projecting power and undermining enemies is instead the real core of national concerns.

Furthermore, the diplomatic, military, and intelligence communities utilize the financial secrecy system for their own purposes. The US Central Intelligence Agency avails itself of the supposed advantages of corruption and money laundering on countless occasions. CIA operatives handed out cash bribes in Afghanistan and Iraq for almost two decades. Tens if not hundreds of millions of dollars obtained from US sources have been transported by corrupt foreign government officials for deposit into their private accounts, primarily in the UAE. The CIA and the State Department, initiating relationships and providing funds, argue that the information and support that such payments purchase saves American lives. The reality is the opposite—it costs American lives, as these conflicts and others drag on year after year. Those who receive bribes from the CIA in limitless stacks of $100 bills and then hide millions abroad have little incentive to pursue peace. Successfully combating the shadow financial system while using the shadow financial system is a nonstarter. Long years of bribery in these two countries and others are evidence of misguided foreign policy and national security efforts, not evidence of their success. Staggering poverty, rampant corruption, and incessant crime in scores of countries around the world, in good part facilitated by the global shadow financial system, used by the supposedly noble for thoroughly ignoble purposes, is a strategic failure.

To those in foreign policy and national security communities, with rare but occasionally notable exception, an utterly fundamental issue needs to be grasped. And I, speaking directly, am saying as straightforwardly as possible that you have missed it.

You have missed the degree to which the capitalist system operating increasingly beyond the rule of law undermines your own efforts to spread the rule of law.

Many experts in these fields, as I have heard repeatedly, fail to understand how gross illegalities in the economic arena, where we are participants and facilitators, cancel opportunities to secure peace and stability in the political arena. Hopefully, no one will rise in self-defense saying "Oh, we've understood this all along. It's just that we deal in the much more important realities of diplomacy and security. What you are talking about is merely the commercial side of international affairs." This is often the view, but it is certainly not correct. The fact is that what these communities consider the more important side of world affairs is severely weakened by what they dismiss as the less important side of world affairs. These two communities, to an overriding extent, have just plain missed it.

When you are in a silo, you cannot see ahead or behind or left or right. Foreign policy and national security communities are often in single-purpose silos that prevent them from assimilating the broader panorama of concerns that directly affect their ability to succeed at their chosen tasks. These disciplines must reach out and acquire a clearer understanding of how the capitalist system—for good and bad—is a determinative factor in their ability to accomplish their professional goals and advance their nations' interests.

Surely Ukraine, attacked by one of the darkest and most corrupted countries on Earth, provides a vivid yet tragic example of the linkage between global financial secrecy and the geopolitical calculus.

This book is in part a plea to foreign policy and national security communities to recognize that democratic capitalism can thrive and provide a positive example to the world only when both components comprising its structure are operating with transparency and accountability.

PART III

Renewing Democratic Capitalism

DEMOCRATIC CAPITALISM AS A TWO-PART POLITICAL and economic system is facing its most perilous doctrinal challenge since its creation more than 200 years ago. Previous pages have focused on the incentives and contrivances particularly within capitalism that are driving apart these two ideologies. In earlier years they worked rather well together. Can the sense of shared purpose be re-created?

Part III turns to what can be done to enhance the common good. Chapter 12 confirms just how fragile our situation has become. Chapter 13 asks whether change is now empowered or imperiled. Chapter 14 provides specific measures that can reform capitalism and return our economic system to maximizing its contributions to our political well-being. And we close with a summons to character and reason, which can be mustered anew given the popular and political will to do so.

12

The Precarious State
of Democratic Capitalism

H OW DO YOU SOLVE A PROBLEM that no one wants to solve? Or, to
put it more accurately, a problem that few want to solve? Or, to put it
more accurately still, a problem that few among the economic and
political elite want to solve? Capitalism has adopted motivations and
mechanisms that undermine democracy, concentrate wealth, drive inequality, and empower crime and corruption. Yet, grasp of these linkages
and their combined impacts is painfully narrow, subdued, and avoided.

Explanations, illustrations, and outcomes surrounding capitalism's financial secrecy system filled the preceding pages. Secrecy is treated not
as a matter of guarding binary snippets of data but more broadly as the
assembly and operation of a construct that organizes and propels an obscured motivation.

> Understood thus, secrecy is less about the pure withholding of informa-
> tion and more about the production of a social order. . . . [W]hat becomes
> important to understand about the secret is less its hiding per se, and more
> the way in which it structures social relations, regulates communication,
> and distributes political power.[1]

Secrecy contributes to separation, and separation contributes to social
disintegration. Capitalism's financial secrecy system has brought about
a fundamental change from the way the world was viewed in the mid-
twentieth century. Then, most saw the world as a north-south divide—
democratic northern countries versus unstable southern countries. But

the world is now more accurately viewed as a rich-poor divide, with economically privileged elites across the globe distancing from less fortunate masses of humanity. The ultimate product of a sense of economic segregation is a matching sense of social and political anomie, which characterizes the United States and many other countries today.

Within these pages I seek to frame issues affecting democratic capitalism with clarity. Modern-day motivations propelling capitalism inform the construction of this framework. Within this scaffolding, operative mechanisms are explained and outcomes elucidated. Understanding capitalism's motivations and mechanisms developed in recent decades is a necessary step toward understanding how to change the system.

This approach differs from commentary surrounding neoliberalism, often taken to mean laissez-faire economics or preferences for free markets over government controls. Nothing in the pages of this book should imply opposition to the profit motive or support for anticorporatist sentiment. What is criticized here is the way capitalism is operating today, wholly unanticipated and unintended by earlier designers of and practitioners in the capitalist system. Neoliberalism is sometimes mistakenly credited with economic growth and poverty alleviation recorded in recent decades. The fact is, every aspect of both accomplishments would have been realized, indeed exceeded, without neoliberalism in place. In the absence of financial secrecy there would have been considerably more economic expansion and social equity. The shadow financial system is less about growth for all and more about moving money in a hidden manner, serving the dishonest, the corrupt, and the criminal.

Democracy has largely maintained its essential motivations since first adopted, however imperfectly implemented. But capitalism has veered away from its original motivations, now fundamentally altered. Capitalism for the last half century has been building and perfecting secrecy structures that allow the commanding heights of the system to function well beyond effective oversight by representatives of democracy. These structures, cleverly and proudly erected to create, move, and shelter trillions of dollars in income and wealth, have concentrated power into capitalism's ranks, weakening democracy's standing. If this continues, the democratic-capitalist system will not survive the twenty-first century. Authoritarianism beckons as the logical amalgamation of economic and political systems seeking to operate with neither transparency nor accountability.

Consider what has happened over recent decades since secrecy became the shared goal along with profits in the capitalist system:

Tens of millions of disguised corporations without known owners are established worldwide.

Secrecy jurisdictions have grown from 3 or 4 handling minor transactions to now more than 100 facilitating perhaps half of international trade and capital movements.

Multinational corporations, led by those headquartered in the United States, conduct hundreds of millions of transactions for goods and services in violation of laws against schemes to defraud and offenses against property.

Enablers design and participate in financial arrangements comprising dozens of opaque steps specifically intended to disable comprehension and escape scrutiny.

Transnational organized crime groups, using the financial secrecy system provided by capitalism, grow exponentially, successfully defying global efforts to curtail drug trading, human trafficking, environmental crimes, arms flows, and more.

Western financial institutions encourage, organize, and welcome trillions of dollars gushing out of developing and authoritarian states even as Western governments then criticize and sanction poor and despotic regimes.

Banks create and participate in schemes intentionally cheating their own customers out of billions of dollars through false dealings.

Economic inequality, narrowing between countries, is widening within most countries as income and wealth flow to those at the top, those able to profit from opportunities offered by secrecy structures.

Tax burdens worldwide shift from capital to labor as corporations and the wealthy seek ever greater accumulations and continuously weakening oversight.

Tens of trillions of dollars sit in accounts earning little interest, no interest, or negative interest as most of the world's population yearns for greater productive investment and higher living standards.

When financial systems eventually collapse and when pandemics unexpectedly hit, a disproportionate burden falls immediately on the poor without savings.

Measures of freedom in the United States and scores of countries across the globe decline as faith in democracy decidedly wanes.

Capitalism buys the forbearance of democracy through legalized campaign contributions and sells the lure of democracy by exchanging citizenship for cash.

These are realities, not judgments, not speculations. None of this has arisen as the result of some giant conspiracy. It has arisen out of the motivation adopted within capitalism for secrecy, parallel in importance with profitability. Hiding money has become as material as making money.

The overarching purpose of secrecy mechanisms within capitalism is to drive money from the bottom to the top. Not a single element of the secrecy system is aimed at benefiting the poor. Extreme poverty viewed globally is already being reduced and could in fact be ended. But charity for the poorest is not the same thing as change for the whole. This book is about change.

Capitalism, taken as a current body of thought and practice, has no answer to widening inequality. Capitalism is making a mistake, offering something it cannot deliver, marketing shared prosperity but delivering inflated disparity. The truth is, we cannot reduce inequality via a system that is designed to produce inequality. Economic fairness does not exist within the machinations of the financial secrecy system, neither in fact nor in perception. A more equitable world cannot be realized while widespread secrecy pervades operations in one of the components of the democratic-capitalist equation, while the other component strives to operate with transparency. Secrecy and transparency are incompatible partners.

Capitalists themselves have not focused their attention on moderating the top of the economic scale, where money flowing through secrecy mechanisms comes to rest, giving the richest few more wealth than all the rest of humankind. Certainly some scholars and politicians seek means to lessen inequality, but this is pursued with scarce recognition among the wealthiest that lessening inequality is in fact necessary to preserving democracy. Are capitalists prepared to sacrifice any portion of wealth accumulation in order to enhance democracy? For some, the answer is no, readily accepting a diminution of democracy if needed to maximize and retain riches. Inequality undermines democracy, a price that a portion of the wealthiest are quite willing to pay.

Our chosen political system—democracy—will always need to hone its reach for justice, and shortcomings can be corrected within the democratic system's refreshing ideologies. Shortcomings evident in capitalism cannot be corrected within the frame of current capitalist thought and practice. Capitalism is not introspective, not self-correcting. Minor adjustments perhaps, but not the fundamental realignment with principles and goals compatible with democracy that is necessary. The democratic-capitalist system as a whole requires both parts to contribute to freedom and prosperity for all. This is not happening now.

Capitalism has become competitive with democracy, indeed suborning democracy, seeking to subordinate the influence of its counterpart. Instead of cooperative systems, mutually reinforcing, these have become confrontive systems, and democracy is losing. Capitalism has transformed from a force focusing primarily on economic progress to a force equally bent on political control. Capitalism has acquired enormous powers over democracy, and these powers are corrupting. Capitalism has bought democracy, paid for the concessions that give it dominion over democracy, making democracy a commodity that can literally be sold on the market. Capitalism, claiming that it is overregulated, is in fact running out of control. Nothing so clearly illustrates the triumph of capitalism over democracy as the massive structures that have enabled multinational corporations to operate for decades effectively beyond the rule of law. We are witnessing a separation between our two central ideologies, once linked but now engaged in conflict. Repeated blows could produce mutual destruction. Declining faith in democracy lies within the failings of capitalism. Steer capitalism toward equity or risk losing liberty. With declining democracy, nothing prevents capitalism's drift toward an alignment with authoritarianism.

Law enforcement has failed to curtail excesses of capitalism and explosions of crime powered by the financial secrecy system. The reason is fundamental: you cannot regulate a secret system. You cannot regulate what you cannot see. Attempts to do so belie logic. And attempts to do so are inevitably compromised by inadequate and porous legislation. In this arena, the vital role of law enforcement is playing whack-a-mole. You hit it in one place, and it pops up in several more places. For decades, law enforcement going one-on-one against selected miscreants has failed to curtail the magnitude of drug trading, human trafficking, resource theft, illegal logging, unregulated fishing, arms trafficking, counterfeiting, money laundering, tax evasion, and more, activities moving trillions upon trillions of dollars. There are not enough law enforcement agents to compete effectively with an entire system designed to function beyond the oversight of law enforcement. Instead, the secrecy structure must be eliminated before law enforcement and regulatory efforts have a real chance to succeed.

Can anything that is politically acceptable be done? Capitalists themselves will not dismantle the secrecy structures that make them wealthy. This has to be done by elected legislators, influenced by the votes and demands of citizens. There is an approach that, executed with purpose and courage, will work: transparency and accountability. Deconstruct secrecy. Require accountability. Enact systemic change around transparency and accountability. Instill into our shared world a capitalist system steeped in transparency and accountability, and we can look forward to the democratic-capitalist system building shared prosperity and freedom likely for ages to come.

Can the shattering crises occurring in this decade be marshaled in meaningful efforts to recast democratic capitalism for the twenty-first century? Let us hope, as chapter 13 addresses.

13

Change: Empowered or Imperiled?

ARE WE AT AN INFLECTION POINT IN HISTORY? Much depends on how we react to multiple challenges that have simultaneously struck America and the world. In this chapter, our focus will be on only two of these—the pandemic devastating the entire world and the putsch threatening American stability—because these two so clearly illustrate the fraying linkages between capitalism and democracy.

Consequential events do not necessarily produce historic change. Uprisings in Europe in 1848, sometimes called the Springtime of the Peoples, are often referred to as "the turning point at which modern history failed to turn." Beginning in France and spreading to 50 countries, urban workers rioted, monarchies were threatened, and Karl Marx published *The Communist Manifesto*. But lacking coordination among groups and across countries, reactionaries ultimately returned to power, essentially preserving much of the status quo ante. As Danish philosopher Søren Kierkegaard said, "So the king flees—and so there is a republic. Piffle."[1] What, therefore, might we expect from the global realities that are now shaking capitalism and democracy to their foundations?

Pandemics can alter the course of world history. COVID-19 has proven to be hugely confrontive to both democracy and capitalism. In the United States the pandemic became politicized, contributing to perhaps hundreds of thousands of people losing their lives, lives that could have been spared with simple preventive measures. The state of Florida, for example, with residents anxious to socialize outside, at one point had more cases than all the countries of the European Union combined. Other states closed public gatherings and reopened and then again closed and reopened, driving up infections and deaths. Republicans and Democrats waged bitter battles over simple precautionary procedures.

In an otherwise depressing picture, a bright image does arise. Doctors, nurses, and emergency medical teams showed incredible tenacity in fighting for patients' lives while often fighting back personal tears, tending to the mortally sick, isolated, suffering, and dying alone, removed from loved ones. Voluntary food banks sprung up, teachers gave online lessons, children made posters and wrote cards, sports and entertainment figures lifted the mood, the musically gifted sang from balconies and played in front of hospitals and nursing homes. Spontaneous decency and unselfishness stood in stark contrast to examples of poor leadership.

Journalist George Packer got it right:

> The fight to overcome the pandemic must also be a fight to recover the health of our country, and build it anew, or the hardship and grief we're now enduring will never be redeemed. . . . We can learn from these dreadful days that . . . in a democracy, being a citizen is essential work; that the alternative to solidarity is death.[2]

In addition to causing problems for democracy, the pandemic also illustrated stark weaknesses within capitalism. In the United States, Black Americans and Latinos died at rates far above their population percentages in most major cities, with income and wealth disparities cited overwhelmingly as the major reason. Unemployment rose to the highest percentage level of any other wealthy nation, with low-wage workers hit hardest.[3] State and local governments did a reasonably commendable job of providing some measure of support to workers out of jobs. Local communities stepped up with food assistance, reminiscent of bread lines in the Great Depression.

The financial and emotional distance between rich and poor was dramatically illustrated by what was going on in the life experiences of opposite sides of the economic spectrum during the early weeks of the crisis. *The Economist* called it "a dangerous gap; the markets v the real economy."[4] Bank of America called it "The Gaps of Wrath."[5] In 2020 conflicting realities accelerating Wall Street and decimating Main Street were simply stunning, as figure 13.1 depicts.

Frank Vogl, formerly with *The Times* in London and later the World Bank, put it clearly:

> The . . . U.S. stock market upsurge and the accompanying GDP nosedive show in what altered states the U.S. economy is currently operating. One

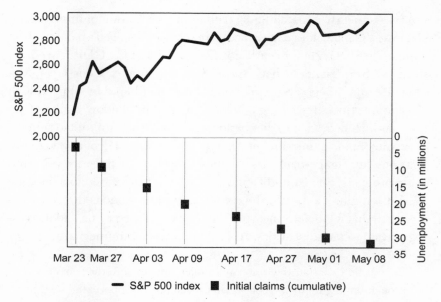

FIGURE 13.1 Rising stock market and unemployment
Source: Prepared by the author using data from the U.S. Employment and
Training Administration and the S&P Dow Jones Indices LLC, retrieved
from **FRED**. Used with permission.[6]

would usually expect that these two economic forces move in tandem, not
in opposite directions. The almost grotesque divergence between the U.S.
stock market and the country's real economy underscores dramatically
just how unequal the country has become.[7]

In the midst of the pandemic, the dominance of capitalism's influence in
the US Congress was dramatic. The $3 trillion Coronavirus Aid, Relief
and Economic Security (CARES) Act was anything but. Corporations
and banks receiving billions were essentially unconstrained in executive
salary increases, dividend payments, and share buybacks. The rich got
tax relief and even tax refunds, particularly benefiting hedge funds and
real estate developers. Representative Alexandria Ocasio-Cortez of New
York publicly decried the act as "crumbs for our families." And she was
right; the bill, ultimately passed into law, was a distressing demonstration of the degree to which wealth rules and the poor are treated unfairly.
Trickle down does not work in modern America; trickle up—or rocket-
ing up—prevails.

The Federal Reserve Board, expanding the role adopted in 2007–
2008, handed over some $3 trillion to banks, driving up excess banking

reserves to nearly a matching $3 trillion in anticipation of future financial losses. Capital adequacy ratios were relaxed. The Fed's balance sheet climbed to $8.8 trillion in early 2022, 42 percent of US GDP. Corporate securities from giants such as Apple, AT&T, Walmart, Coca-Cola, McDonald's and others, even junk bonds, were purchased by the Fed with abandon, artificially jacking up asset values. The shadow banking system was included, as in earlier bailouts, with virtually unlimited support of private financial instruments such as collateralized debt and loan obligations, mortgage-backed securities, commercial paper, repos, and other products. Some pundits said yes, this is a proper step to assure the market remains stable. On the contrary, by these actions the Fed demonstrated that it is determinedly in the business of preserving and increasing private wealth disparities. As critic Lawrence Summers argues,

> There is no case that the best way to inject money into the economy is through buying financial assets. That mechanism supports the wealthy who hold these assets, rather than the bulk of the population, at a moment of nearly unprecedented inequality.[8]

Out of the total of $6-plus trillion in economic support funds, barely 10 percent went to direct cash payments to citizens. Instead, the CARES Act vividly demonstrated how politically difficult it is to provide assistance to the poor and middle class unless disproportionate advantage is simultaneously given to the wealthy class. The Federal Reserve Board stepping in to support shadow banking, even derivatives, overwhelmingly protecting and benefiting the rich, is good policy only if one is determined to maintain and expand economic inequality in America. Distribution of wealth to the already wealthy seems to be politically advantageous even amid the most perilous economic straits affecting tens of millions of lower- and middle-class citizens. The pandemic was good for the 1 percent in America, who increased their collective net worth by more than $2 trillion.[9]

Even revisiting the issue of economic support for lower- and middle-class citizens in December 2020, Congress could not resist once again adding enormous benefits for the wealthiest. The $900 billion Coronavirus Response and Relief Act, part of the Consolidated Appropriations Act, included a provision to allow corporations that received funds for payroll support from the government in the March 2020 CARES Act to then deduct the amount of those distributions from profits. In other words, the money was free, and the corporations could expense the unearned money to reduce corporate taxes. The price tag on this wholesale giveaway is estimated at $200 billion.

Let it be clear: government borrowing to favor the rich ultimately comes out of the pockets of all the people, to be paid for by future generations through taxes or inflation. The federal debt burden in the United States reached 122.5 percent of GDP in 2021, the highest ever experienced, a massive encumbrance on future generations. Repayment of such debt will not materially affect Americans' share of the $120 trillion stashed away in broad money belonging mostly to the wealthiest.

Abroad, the pandemic, potentially breaking the European Union, was finally met with a nearly trillion-dollar recovery plan aimed at skirting crippling economic impacts on weaker, particularly southern, member states. Recalling that pandemics contributed to the fall of the Roman and Byzantine Empires, supporting the European Union, a hard-fought decision among member governments, was the correct decision. Many middle- and low-income countries faced severe and daunting sovereign debt crises as resource and commodity exports plunged, tourism dried up, and remittances from fellow countrymen abroad fell.

The pandemic hit developing countries especially hard. At a stroke an estimated 230 million were thrown into extreme poverty, perhaps even more, as economic prospects are set back by one or possibly two decades for billions of people. Ambitious UN Sustainable Development Goals adopted by 193 countries in 2015, promising progress for the world's majority, are threatened if not defeated. Of the world's two billion informal workers, many of whom spend 60–70 percent of their total income on food, the International Labor Organization estimates that half have lost opportunities for gainful work. Resource exports and their prices, the lifeblood of many developing countries, fell precipitously. Global trade in manufactured goods dived. Supply chains collapsed. Exchange rates for soft currencies plummeted. Sovereign debts went unpaid. Authoritarian regimes increased their powers. Remittances from family members living abroad to others at home, normally a half-trillion-dollar flow, declined.

While health and hunger are the immediate problems, inequality remains the continuing issue. In each of five major pandemics in this century—SARS (2003), H1N1 (2009), MERS (2012), Ebola (2014), and Zika (2016)—data indicates that Gini coefficients, which measure income disparity, worsened across each event's ensuing five years "despite the efforts of governments to redistribute incomes from the rich to the poor to mitigate the effects of pandemics."[10]

From Nigeria, I received the following emails in mid-2020:

Here, businesses and schools are closed. Many families have become beggars as people are dying of hunger every day. It is no longer coronavirus but hunger virus. People would walk along the road and suddenly fall down and die because of hunger. I lost two friends within a week. Our situation is suicidal.

I sent my wife and my daughter to market to buy some bags of rice and tin tomatoes. We all carried the food items joined by a few neighbors and distributed them to others. Emotions were so high; some were rolling on the floor with happiness while some were shedding tears of joy. This is so because in Nigeria now it's only the rich that can afford to eat rice. When we got back to our home my daughter who is in the university but presently at home because of this pandemic started to cry. When I asked her why she is crying she said two of the widows we just gave rice and tin tomatoes to told her that this is the first time in this year 2020 they will be eating rice.

In America, frustrations and emotions boiled over on January 6, 2021, in Washington, D.C., when thousands of rioters attacked the US Capitol. This day will be remembered alongside September 11, 2001, and December 7, 1941, as among the darkest moments in American history.

I have lived through five coup d'états, each conducted within less than a mile of where I was at the time. Whether we call the events of January 6 a coup or an insurrection or an uprising, an act of sedition or treason or revolt, it was an attempt to use violence to change the outcome of an election. Perpetrators in the thousands, spurred on by Donald J. Trump, voted out of office two months earlier, sought to prevent certification of the election of the new president, Joe Biden, and vice president, Kamala Harris, and in the process threatened to kill the outgoing vice president, Mike Pence, the Speaker of the House Nancy Pelosi, and others. They—the perpetrators—succeeded in breaching the Capitol, attacking protective officers, rampaging and ransacking, bringing about the deaths of 5 individuals and causing injuries to 140 more. Televised in real time, America and the world were absolutely traumatized. Democracy held on by its fingertips. With order restored hours later, legislators reassembled and at 4:00 a.m. the next morning confirmed the election of the country's new leadership. The national psyche remains deeply wounded and will likely continue to be so for years to come.

Who were the attackers, and why were they so angry? Answering these questions will be ongoing for decades. There is no indication that the rioters were drawn primarily from the ranks of the poor and home-less. On the contrary, initial impressions suggest this was rather more an expression of discontent within the middle class. I do ask the reader to look back at two points made earlier. Figure 4.9 depicts disturbingly the diminishing odds felt by those Americans in midlife, despairing of ever reaching the standards of living of their parents. Figures 5.7 and 5.8 illustrate that vast stretches of America are lagging in output and sug-gest that the people living in these areas sense they are falling behind other parts of the country. These economic anxieties undermine Amer-ican democracy.

Nor are economic anxieties limited only to the less affluent sectors of American society. The wealthy can also exhibit bitter determination to hold on to disproportionate gains achieved in recent decades. Indeed, some political alignment between favored elites and disadvantaged throngs is not hard to grasp.

Certainly, economic anxieties cannot be a complete explanation for prejudice, extremism, and violence. But central to the thrust of this book is that greater economic equality can ameliorate tendencies toward prej-udice, extremism, and violence. As said earlier, the individual who ex-periences and senses economic fairness will usually have little or no objection to fairness being experienced and sensed by others as well. A more equal America, a more balanced America, will be a more stable and productive America. Economic fairness is not a total solution, but it is, I believe, the most essential component of a solution.

Biden and Harris were sworn into office on January 20, 2021. Deliv-ering her poem "The Hill We Climb" at the inauguration, a young Black woman, Amanda Gorman, mesmerized the audience and the nation with her words, in part as follows:

We are striving to forge a union with purpose
To compose a country committed to all cultures, colors, characters and conditions of man.
We close the divide because we know, to put our future first,
we must first put differences aside
We lay down our arms
so we can reach out our arms
to one another
That even as we grieved, we grew
That even as we hurt, we hoped

With young people like Amanda Gorman, like Greta Thunberg, like millions of others, opportunities for a better world are indeed within reach.

The brief pages of this chapter relate just a small slice of the enormous challenges to the politics and economics—to democracy and capitalism—facing America and the world. Are conditions right for a renewal of the grand bargain between these two guiding tenets?

Susan Rice, former national security advisor in the Obama administration and now leading the Domestic Policy Council, expressed her uncertainties:

> This defining moment, unlike any since the 1960s, has the potential to transform the country into one that is far more just and equal for all its citizens. Yet this incipient movement also risks being reduced to a fleeting instant of heightened consciousness, one that dissipates in the fog of pandemic, economic recession and a bitter presidential campaign.[11]

Robert Samuelson, columnist for the *Washington Post*, put it clearly:

> What results—it has been building for years—is a crisis of democracy or, more precisely, a crisis of the liberal democratic states established since World War II. This democratic crisis subsumes all the crises I've mentioned—health care, economics and politics—and raises the profound question of whether we can govern in the common interest.[12]

Darren Walker at Ford Foundation, continuing his most articulate observations, said:

> Even before the coronavirus, before the lockdowns, and before the murder of George Floyd—during the longest sustained economic expansion in American history—income inequality in America had reached staggering levels. This contributes to a hopelessness and cynicism that undermines our shared ideals and institutions, pits us against one another, and drives communities further apart. That's why I am worried about our democracy, deeply and for the first time in my life.[13]

With extraordinary sensitivity to the moment, its place in history, and our shared future, UN secretary-general António Guterres delivered the 2020 Nelson Mandela lecture titled "Tackling the Inequality Pandemic: A New Social Contract for a New Era," from which the following excerpts are extensively quoted:

Dear friends.

Inequality defines our time. . . .

Multiple inequalities intersect and reinforce each other across the generations. The lives and expectations of millions of people are largely determined by their circumstances at birth. . . .

High levels of inequality are associated with economic instability, corruption, financial crises, increased crime and poor physical and mental
health. . . .

Enough of inequality and discrimination that treats people as criminals
on the basis of their skin colour[.]

Enough of the structural racism and systematic injustice that deny people
their fundamental human rights.

. . . Illicit financial flows, money-laundering and tax evasion must be prevented. A global consensus to end tax havens is essential.

Now is the time for global leaders to decide:

Will we succumb to chaos, division and inequality?

Or will we right the wrongs of the past and move forward together, for
the good of all?

We are at breaking point. But we know which side of history we are on.[14]

Breaking point? Rather than closing this chapter with a prediction, let
us instead recognize what a once-in-a-lifetime moment this is. It should
be unmistakably clear that the global political economy is not prepared
for the remainder of this century, with soaring populations and staggering disparities. Crises provide opportunities for political and economic
change but not necessarily the will to change. In the wake of this set of
crises, the democratic-capitalist system is literally at stake. It cannot survive massive and widening inequalities perpetually expanded by its capitalist component determinedly shifting money to the rich, even in the
midst of global threats to the lives of others. Democracy cannot survive

with an ideological partner committed to the opposite of democracy, that is, committed to an economic system pursuing a self-aggrandizing agenda for the wealthy despite raging harms caused to billions of people.

So, the question is this: Does the current confluence of events bode well or ill for change, change that is necessary if the democratic-capitalist system is to offer to the remainder of this century opportunities for prosperity and liberty for all? Social justice cannot be grafted onto economic injustice. Or, putting the point in the positive, economic justice is necessary to the achievement of all forms of social justice. Political tranquility cannot be achieved amid vast economic disparities. Set aside the idea that we can realize social justice and shared political ambitions while at the same time purposefully maintaining and increasing levels of economic injustice. We cannot. Economic justice—a much higher level of economic equality—is a precondition for achieving social justice and for ultimately preserving political democracy.

Yes, we are at an inflection point.

The message conveyed in this book is: Reform capitalism or forfeit democracy.

How do we reform the ill dealings that have settled into capitalism? Straightforward, uncomplicated measures undertaken with political will can accomplish the goal. To this we now turn.

14

Restoring Integrity

REESTABLISHING BALANCE BETWEEN CAPITALISM and democracy is necessary, such that each of these basic tenets serves to enhance prosperity and freedom for all. To accomplish this, primary focus is placed on the capitalist component, which has shifted far from its original intents.

Earlier pages have foreshadowed the instruments being advanced herein to renew capitalism: transparency and accountability. This is exactly what capitalism's operators within the financial secrecy system do not want. This is exactly what, if put firmly in place, they will find difficult to get around.

Instead, why not just leave secrecy mechanisms as they are and try to write more regulations to constrain them?

Two reasons. First, this has demonstrably failed across the last five or six decades. Well-meaning laws are riddled with loopholes or left unenforced, providing pathways for corporations and criminals alike. Second, even the best lawmakers and regulators are not nearly as agile, quick, or creative as the millions of operators in the secrecy system. These legions readily find ways around laws that leave the essentials of the secrecy system in place. Recall the examples in chapter 7 of multinational corporations for a quarter of a century using mechanisms established "nowhere," completely beyond the knowledge and understanding of the US Congress. Trying to regulate secrecy, repeating again, is simply unworkable.

Fundamental problems are not solved by tacking more directives and stiffer penalties onto defective laws and policies. A single norm requiring transparency or accountability in capitalist operations is worth far more than multiple statutes attempting to regulate ongoing secrecy structures entrenched in the system. The difference is between mechanisms and motivations. Focusing on the mechanisms by which dirty money moves has failed and will continue to fail. Constraining the new motivation for secrecy that has arisen with the capitalist system can succeed.

Deconstruct secrecy. Implement transparency and accountability. This is the repurposed structure necessary to achieve progress, a structure that can be built out of entirely logical component parts. This is how we renew capitalism's contributions to our shared world.

Examples of requirements for transparency and accountability already in place that work reasonably well include the following:

Sarbanes-Oxley, passed almost unanimously by the US Congress in 2002, requires CEOs and CFOs to sign and confirm the accuracy of their periodic financial reports. Marshaling the power of the signature, making executives accountable for their accounts, finally strengthened after capitalism had been in place for more than 200 years, was a step in the right direction.

The USA Patriot Act, passed in 2001, put almost all shell banks out of business. As explained in chapter 1, shell banks used to be central components of the financial secrecy system—banks operated by unknown owners yet given ready access to US and global financial institutions. The Patriot Act, while controversial in other aspects, took at least this portion of the financial secrecy system largely off the table. A "shell bank loophole" sometimes enables shell companies to operate as though they are financial entities, and this too needs to be eliminated.

FATCA, the Foreign Account Tax Compliance Act, operative since 2014, requires foreign financial institutions to submit to the Internal Revenue Service information on financial holdings of US taxpayers above designated threshold amounts. Bilateral agreements in five variations have been entered into with more than 100 foreign jurisdictions, and while imperfect, these agreements serve US interests.

Bank stress tests, since the financial crisis of 2007–2008, are now required annually by the Federal Reserve and must be made public. The viability of large US financial institutions is no longer clouded in secrecy. Investors and depositors alike can see if their money is safe.

Terrorist financing has been substantially pushed out of the legitimate financial system as the United States has forced banks and governments across the globe, even the Belgium-based financial messaging service SWIFT, to be cooperative and accountable in the fight against this threat.

On the following pages, transparency and accountability provisions are set forth that can very substantially improve the relationship of capitalism to democracy and therefore elevate prospects for democratic capitalism moving deeper into the twenty-first century. Several parameters guide the selections of and explanations surrounding each of these measures:

1. All recommended policies focus on capitalism or capitalism's direct relationship to democracy, without attempting to be fully comprehensive.
2. Primary though not exclusive emphasis is placed on what needs to be done by the United States.
3. Adoption of each step is a matter of political will; none are technically difficult to implement in practice.
4. Pending legislation addressing aspects of some of these proposals is not covered here simply because such details continue to evolve.
5. Emphasis is on the purposeful and the prompt rather than on the perfect.

With these parameters in mind, what specifically can be done to strengthen capitalism's contributions toward furthering the democratic-capitalist system? The following are addressed in order: corporations, financial institutions, enablers, tax matters, economic inequality, aspects of US democracy, and finally international institutions.

CORPORATIONS

Virtually every multinational corporation uses the financial secrecy system and other mechanisms for generating and moving money that cannot be seen, finally summarized into annual reports with scant details. Opacity has become the name of the game in much of capitalism's operations, unfortunately for some small and medium-sized businesses as well. Rising inequality and weakening democracy are the prices paid. These realities can be changed.

Disguised Corporations
Begin by eliminating disguised corporations no matter who owns them, citizens or foreigners. Whether structured as anonymous companies, shell companies, shelf companies, cell companies, portfolio companies, money-box companies, intermediary accounts, or any other iteration, end this

practice, a thoroughly destructive component of the current capitalist system.

The means for doing this has already been established and implemented and is close to wholly successful—the nearly complete elimination of shell banks. Accomplished via the Patriot Act, recalled above and elaborated upon in chapter 3, shell banks operated for decades throughout the financial system without their ownership being known. Most shell companies can be eliminated in the same way with legislation based on the Patriot Act as follows: no US financial institution can receive money from a shell company, and no financial institution in the world can send money to the United States that it has received from a shell company, defined as any company failing to identify natural persons in ownership and management in registries available publicly and digitally.

The question frequently arises, down to what percentage of ownership? Most logically, all owners with 5 percent or more of shares or ownership rights, which is consistent with requirements of the US Securities and Exchange Commission for identifying owners of listed companies.

Note also the requirement for registries available publicly and digitally. Public registries of shareholder information, accessible online, are already under way in many countries and should become the required global norm.

Note as well that no department of government need be tasked with massive regulatory oversight. US financial institutions simply cannot do business with shell companies. As with US banks, the onus is transferred to foreign banks to ensure that their transactions with the US financial system are in compliance, with severe penalties for noncompliance including loss of access to the US financial system. This worked to put shell banks out of business and can work to put millions of shell companies out of business. A period of months can be allowed to identify beneficial owners of shell companies if they wish to continue to do business. Predictably, the majority will identify their ownership and continue operations. Those that choose not to do so are just the ones the United States can do without.

Exceptions may occasionally be needed. Some foreigners of good repute have money deposited in foreign shell companies in order to escape economic, political, or personal harassment by dictators and despots. In such cases, upon petition by a bank and approval by the US Treasury Department, a longer period of perhaps three to five years could be permitted, leading to account closure or ownership disclosure, as preferred.

Another complication should be noted: the front company, often a company operated by a party acting on behalf of another party. Essentially, there is no way to prevent one individual from doing business on behalf of another individual, and little advantage in pursuing such a direction. For example, "landmen" frequently are used to purchase mineral rights on behalf of a major company wishing to keep its interest in a tract confidential. Or a family member may be the owner of record of a business actually belonging to another family member. Furthermore, intelligence agencies the world over currently use shell companies, which, if eliminated, would still leave the opportunity to use front companies. Perhaps in the future such front companies can also be eliminated, but at the moment the goal is the good, not the perfect.

Financial institutions have no grounds to complain of burdensome investigations or mounds of paperwork. Instead, simply provide a form to company account holders to be filled out with the names of natural persons who are beneficial owners and managers on the account. Highlighted in the form is a statement by the bank saying that should the information given subsequently be found to have significant errors or omissions, the account will be frozen until correct information is provided. The bank will almost certainly receive the correct information, or the account holders will seek a more accommodating institution elsewhere.

Fundamental to restoring integrity in capitalism is ending shell companies—whether in America or elsewhere—without delay.

Financial Reporting

Thousands of corporations operate tens of thousands of subsidiaries without reporting on the financial activities of these subsidiaries. Annual reports consolidate obscured results that financial regulators and tax collectors very often find impossible to decipher. This, another major component of secrecy mechanisms, must change. And the change is straightforward: report what you are doing and where you are doing it.

Agitation has arisen in recent years for country-by-country reporting, meaning that corporate results would be reported in each country where operations are conducted. This might require several subsidiaries within a country to consolidate statements for activities that are unrelated, producing an unhelpful picture. The preferable alternative is company-by-company reporting, which means that every entity operating in every country must file its annual financials with appropriate authorities in each country. Annual reports should include revenues, expenses, profits, and taxes payable on current results and paid on immediately preceding results.

Faced with such a possibility, multinational corporations have argued that filings for each entity in each country would be burdensome. This is nonsensical, since every MNC knows almost to the penny what every unit is doing in every country, and the burden would be little more than hitting "send" on the computer screen. MNCs also argue that such filings carry the risk of exposing trade secrets, whether to governments or competitors. Not correct. As the appropriately constituted authority, what you are doing financially in my country is not going to be a secret, and besides, your competitors have the same filing requirements placed on them.

In the United States, the US Securities and Exchange Commission allows corporations to avoid financial reporting on subsidiaries if their activities are not "material" to the overall business. This leaves MNCs themselves in a position to judge if tax avoidance and title passing operations are material, resulting in thousands of subsidiaries operating effectively beyond oversight. Incorporation or legal establishment itself—wherever—should be the definition of materiality and therefore require accountability.

Furthermore, corporations do not now have to publicly reconcile their financial and tax returns. Thus, there is advantage in maximizing income reported to shareholders and minimizing income reported to the Internal Revenue Service. The solution is straightforward: require public release of tax reconciliations along with annual reports.

The doctrine of economic substance is underutilized in US law. This is the notion that transactions should have substantial purposes beyond simply sheltering income or avoiding taxes. Logically, each reporting entity should make a statement affirming economic substance accompanying each annual filing. And economic substance has to be commensurate with assets invested, revenues generated, and staff employed: no more multibillion-dollar enterprises with no offices, no employees, and thus no substance.

Legitimate questions arise. Should all required annual reports by all entities be publicly accessible? Perhaps a workable answer is all reports for entities above certain threshold annual revenue levels. What about strictly representational offices and appointed agents? Reporting requirements can be left to the country or state.

Failures and laxities in financial reporting have harmed rich and poor countries alike. Enormous attention is given to tech and digital companies not paying proper taxes in scores of countries where they operate and sell their products. Developing countries often have little or no idea what resource exporters are doing as riches go out and little comes in. You cannot have accountability if you do not have the ability to count.

Together with eliminating shell companies, all companies must report what they are doing and where they are doing it.

For those who are particularly focused on ending tax havens, note that the combination of eliminating shell companies, requiring public owner-ship registries, company-by-company reporting, and declarations of economic substance accomplishes this. All of these are transparency and accountability measures, none requiring big government oversight struc-tures.

Trade Legitimacy

Chapter 1 carefully explained how falsified trade, sitting in the middle of the financial secrecy system, has become the most frequently used mechanism to shift corrupt, criminal, and commercial dirty money across borders. Having become so normalized in international business, how can this reality be changed? By clarifying that it is already illegal and applying principles of transparency and accountability to future cross-border trading activity.

Analysis presented in chapter 9 concerning the United States informs the following measure that can substantially curtail falsified trading. US multinational corporations should, with support from board and execu-tive levels, be required by law to adopt a policy and then give to employ-ees involved in any way in cross-border trade transactions the following statement:

> Taking into consideration laws in the United States against mail fraud, wire fraud, schemes to defraud, and offenses against property, and refer-encing court decisions reached in *Pasquantino, Georgiou,* and *Bengis,* this is to inform you that in performance of your duties required by the corpo-ration or expected by management the chance that you may be commit-ting or participating in a criminal offense is zero.

Today, this is exactly what US multinational corporations do not want to do. Without changing policies and practices, almost all would be ex-tremely hard-pressed to make such an assurance to executives and staff involved in many, many types and examples of international trade deci-sions. Think what this says: At the present time, we cannot assure you that you are not committing a crime. You may be committing a crime. Tens of thousands of our company's employees may be committing crimes. When we ask you to manipulate prices, volumes, weights, measures, or specifications in order to shift money across borders, we cannot guarantee that you are guiltless of any offense against US law.

Instead, adopting the above statement as a matter of clear corporate policy would eliminate by far the greater part of trade falsification, the centerpiece of the financial secrecy system. Let it be clear: There is no problem with trade priced and identified correctly conducted in order to make a profit without trying to evade any country's taxes or escape any country's exchange control laws or criminal prohibitions. No problem whatsoever. The problem arises when corporations and managers indulge in schemes to manipulate prices and specifications in order to manipulate taxes and circumvent financial regulations. So, the answer is simple: do not use trade manipulations in violation of US laws or the laws of other countries.

If a corporation does not want to give such assurances to management and staff, then employees involved in cross-border trade pricing and documentation should ask for such reassurance. A brief letter from an employee to top management or corporate counsel can include reference to US laws and court decisions as laid out above and then request as follows:

> Please give me a one-sentence letter confirming that in the performance of my duties required by the corporation, the chance that I may be committing or participating in a criminal offense is zero.

Is such transparency impractical, naive? No; Sarbanes-Oxley, requiring corporate CEOs and CFOs to sign their accounts confirming accuracy, was criticized and scorned, that is until it was passed and made into law and is now completely routine. In the same way, trade integrity can be made routine.

Corporations can be given a line of appeal. In situations where dividends or trade remittances are blocked by a recalcitrant foreign government, Treasury can be petitioned to permit manipulations necessary to recover payments or profits.

For countries other than the United States, developing countries, for example, adopting legislation such as the following would go far toward minimizing losses due to falsified trading:

> Whoever, in relation to the importation or exportation of goods or in relation to trade in services or intangible property, deliberately misstates, manipulates, falsifies, or omits a price, quantity, volume, grade or other material aspect of an invoice for the purpose of (1) evading or avoiding

value-added taxes, customs duties, income taxes, excise taxes, or any other form of tax or revenue collected by the government, (2) obtaining a tax benefit, export subsidy, or other benefit provided by the government, or (3) evading or avoiding capital or foreign exchange controls, shall be subject to civil or criminal fine or imprisonment.

Some developing countries have some fractions of such regulations in place, but imprecision and disorder prevent most developing countries from effectively addressing trade misinvoicing and manipulation. MNCs take advantage of this lack of clarity to pursue what they consider to be merely tax avoidance schemes, which cost developing countries hundreds of billions of dollars. In addition to governments adopting the kind of language above, developing country customs departments and central banks should avail themselves of global trade databases to check prices of imports and exports, ensuring that they are within global norms or enabling informed questions to traders.

Such laws should also require CEOs managing corporations, whether multinational or domestically owned, to confirm by signing annual reports or tax returns that the requirements of the above law have been fully adhered to in the preceding year. The power of the signature is more powerful than any law that governments can enact.

The same kind of requirement for signatures by CEOs on the annual reports or tax returns of US corporations would go far toward ensuring that trade is conducted honestly and legitimately for all, Americans and others alike. European and Asian countries would follow US leadership.

Trade agreements, bilateral and multilateral alike, should include prohibitions against falsified trading practices as well as requirements for the identities of natural persons owning all trading entities. Free trade makes a powerful contribution to global prosperity, and this contribution will be greatly heightened when trade is free of misappropriation and misidentification.

The importance of legitimizing trade, conducting trade with integrity, cannot be overemphasized. The importance of instilling responsible performance, high standards of ethics, into management ranks, cannot be overemphasized. The United States, most criticized of all countries for trade manipulations, should take the lead. As with the Foreign Corrupt Practices Act barring bribery of government officials, the United States was first and then other countries followed, and the prohibition has become global, imperfectly implemented but widely aspirational.

Free trade must become legitimate trade, and this can be significantly advanced with a one-sentence law backed up by the power of the signature.

Legal Entity Identifier, Plus
In promoting transparent and traceable trade, a number of additional systems need to be more widely utilized, enabled by growing digitalization of transaction documents and monitoring opportunities.

First, following the financial crisis of 2007–2008 and with subsequent decisions taken by the G20, financial institutions were urged to obtain Legal Entity Identifier numbers, to appear on transaction documents. LEIs, easily available from multiple providers, should now be required of all financial as well as commercial enterprises in cross-border trade and financial transactions utilizing mails or wires. This further curtails the use of disguised companies and unidentified owners.

Second, tracking data on ocean shipping needs to be more purposefully utilized. All oceangoing vessels are expected to operate with automatic identification systems, reporting where they are at all times. However, ship captains often turn off AIS transponders in order to enter waters or ports surreptitiously to take on or discharge suspect cargo. Furthermore, hundreds of ships entering US waters have disguised owners. The United States and other countries need to get tough and ban any ship from docking with unknown ownership or a broken or incomplete log covering some past number of months.

Third, special economic zones and free trade zones are abused all over the world, often providing smuggling routes and opportunities for illicit activity to thousands of businesses operating within. Originally conceived of as duty-free ports, these zones, whether in the United States, the United Kingdom, Israel, UAE, China, or anywhere else, have morphed into something much more problematic. They should be required to submit documentation to appropriate authorities in advance of import or export so that what comes in and what goes out can be reviewed and verified as complying to privileges accorded. Furthermore, these zones need to comply with best practices as overseen by a coordinating organization, with perhaps the Financial Action Task Force providing the model. As frequent contributors to illegal trafficking and counterfeiting, these appendages to the free market system need to be reined in.

A note of caution: Beware of cryptocurrencies in international trade. Specifically designed to delink buyers and sellers, nothing can so drive money laundering, illegitimacy, tax evasion, crime, and corruption as this. Widespread use of cryptocurrencies in international transactions can put democratic capitalism in serious jeopardy.

Trade, the bedrock of the capitalist system, has become deeply compromised, with a high percentage of global transactions intentionally priced, measured, or identified illegally or inaccurately. High returns of income and wealth accrue to perpetrators, but huge losses of income and wealth accrue to billions of other people. This has to change.

Board Reform

The intersection of capitalism and inequality is a defining issue of our times, with the impact of inequality on democracy its most troubling manifestation. Yet concerted efforts to interrelate these issues are sparse and inconclusive. Short of attempting to be all-embracing, several steps that focus specifically on governance in multinational corporations can accelerate the process of reconciling disparate outcomes.

Without question, put employees on corporate boards of directors. Senator Elizabeth Warren has introduced before the US Congress the Accountable Capitalism Act, which proposes that employees be empowered to elect 40 percent of the membership on their employers' boards. Whether this or some other level is finally agreed to, the time has come for corporations in America and elsewhere to hear clearly the voices of their workers, those whose take-home pay has stagnated in comparison to executive pay. Deny this, and the democratic-capitalist system itself is at rising risk.

In addition, corporations should be required to create stakeholder boards tasked with monitoring several aspects of corporate policy and performance, including environmental, social, and governance (ESG) issues, with periodic results publicly reported. This is essentially a successor to the corporate social responsibility movement, which had a limited voice and rather little influence on board decisions. These stakeholder boards should annually report on remuneration comparisons across corporate ranks, whether in quintile groupings or by employment grade levels. With executive compensation sometimes 300 to 400 times workers' pay or even more, this disparity needs to be a point of focus by workers and executives alike. Periodic meetings between stakeholder and fiduciary boards should be normalized.

Excessive, near-exclusive focus on share value needs to be addressed. With executive compensation so often tied to stock price, thousands of companies have held down wages, offshored production, and curtailed investment in order to drive up dividends and fund stock buybacks, disproportionally benefiting the already wealthy, sometimes even bordering on insider trading. A multiyear waiting period needs to be required before executives can cash in their stock awards, and limitations on stock buybacks should be considered.

In 2019 the Business Roundtable, with CEOs of major companies as its members, pledged to redefine "the purpose of a corporation" to include "customers, employees, suppliers, communities, and shareholders."[1] But another corporate group, the Conference Board, found in its 2019 survey that inequality was not even among the top 10 concerns of the polled senior executives. Board reform and wider corporate reform are mandatory if this gap in understanding, in reality, is to be narrowed.

FINANCIAL INSTITUTIONS

Recent revelations exposing how banks are actively transmitting and receiving ill-gotten gains in the hundreds of billions of dollars should dispel any notion that this major component of the capitalist system is operating responsibly. Even in the wake of the financial crisis of 2007–2008, many banks are back in the business of processing corrupt, criminal, and commercial dirty money with abandon.

In the United States, the first tool to be used in the bank repair kit has to be asking necessary questions before opening accounts and processing major transactions. Recall the explanation in chapter 6: following 9/11, the Treasury Department weakened US anti–money laundering oversight in order to allow suspect funds to come into the financial system, with banks then obligated to file Suspicious Activity Reports and Currency Transaction Reports, so that incoming terrorist funds could be traced back to their sources. The policy worked; virtually the whole world has cooperated in pushing terrorist money for the most part out of the legitimate financial system. The downside, however, is that these reports exploded to an average approaching 80,000 each business day, providing cover for billions of dollars in other forms of dirty money seeking to enter the US financial system. Since 9/11, the United States has become the preferred destination for illicitly generated funds smuggled out of authoritarian regimes and poor countries, an inexcusable reality.

And it is a reality that can be curtailed easily. Go back to the anti–money laundering policy in place before 9/11. Ask the right questions and require the right commitments before opening the account or handling the suspect money.

Bankers argue that they should not be overly burdened with owner-ship and transaction monitoring details. Agreed. Instead, provide to the account opener or customer the form referred to above that requires iden-tification of natural persons owning accounts and likewise contains a statement to be attested to by the opener or customer that funds have been legally earned and transferred and will be legally utilized. A dec-laration with a signature. Minimize the complicated, time-consuming investigative process. Transfer the burden to the customer, which in the great majority of cases eliminates the need to file reports on suspicious activities and gives the bank the right to halt transactions if information provided is found to be incorrect.

However—and this is a huge qualification—banks in fact do not want to stop receiving the dirty money. Most banks want to open the accounts and take in the funds, with plausible deniability provided by filing Suspi-cious Activity Reports. The United States has to move beyond this. Banks must be required to inform new and existing customers that dirty money passing through accounts, if suspected or confirmed, can be grounds for freezing accounts. For the good of capitalism and the democratic-capitalist system, again, put requirements for transparency and accountability in place, this time on the part of the banks and their customers alike.

Next, American banks have to return to being financial institutions and cease being corporations. Big banks today are in hundreds of nonfi-nancial ancillary activities, often competing directly with customers. The solution to this is straightforward: return to Glass-Steagall, which worked well for decades separating commercial and investment banking. This is a crucial component of measures necessary to clean up the financial sys-tem. Additionally, commercial banking should focus on business and con-sumer lending and abide by the Volcker Rule to avoid securities trading for their own profit. Investment banking should have a covenant requirement holding senior executives personally responsible in large part for fines and penalties assessed, reminiscent of partnerships in banking in years past.

Derivatives, many times larger than GDP, are a ticking bomb. At a minimum, banks guaranteed by the Federal Deposit Insurance Corpo-ration should be out of this business, leaving what is often pure gambling to other parts of the financial system.

Limitations on sharing information about suspicious transactions should be lifted, enabling banks and the Treasury Department's Finan-cial Crimes Enforcement Network to distribute data on suspect entities and transactions. Customers should be so advised; banking secrecy is not secrecy when data indicative of wrongdoing is evident.

Automatic exchange of tax information, the quite successful FATCA process mentioned at the beginning of this chapter, should be made fully reciprocal with foreign governments. If they are telling us of activity by US citizens, we should be telling them of activity by their citizens. Open doors to the money of their citizens flowing into US coffers should at least be matched with financial information flowing back to their governments. One-way agreements are insufficient in curtailing flows of dirty money.

Banks the world over, led and pushed by the United States, should get out of the business of opening accounts and handling significant funds of foreign government officials. Nothing would more effectively curtail grand corruption than this. Election to political office or employment by the government should mean giving up access to foreign financial dealings. Perhaps a moderate level of transfers executed with permission of heads of government or attorneys general for designated purposes such as children's education or medical treatment can be allowed. But the open door now existing for billions of dollars corruptly acquired and knowingly welcomed into foreign accounts simply has to end.

In recent years global banks have found themselves mired in misdeeds even more often than corporations. Mark Carney, when he was governor of the Bank of England, spoke of

a crisis of legitimacy. A series of scandals ranging from mis-selling to manipulation have undermined trust in banking, the financial system, and to some degree, markets themselves. Repeated episodes of misconduct have called the social license of finance into question.[2]

Pope Francis, continuing his remarkably insightful encyclicals, broadens the point:

The marketplace, by itself, cannot resolve every problem, however much we are asked to believe this dogma of neoliberal faith. Whatever the challenge, this impoverished and repetitive school of thought always offers the same recipes. Indeed, without internal forms of solidarity and mutual trust, the market cannot completely fulfil its proper economic function. And today this trust has ceased to exist.[3]

Future commentators are likely to look back on the decades since the fall of the Berlin Wall as the low point in the annals of financial integrity, the years when capitalism savored its ideological victory over competing economic systems with unprecedented shifts of wealth from poor to rich, with storied institutions serving as the vanguard.

Banks need to ask the right questions about their individual customers and also the right questions about their societal responsibilities. These would be epical changes from the way banking operates today. Necessary changes.

CORRALLING ENABLERS

American diplomats serving in foreign assignments are required to advise the State Department of information learned about bribes offered, anticipated, or paid by US citizens doing business abroad. Thus, diplomats avoid being party to corruption. Similar requirements need to be placed on enablers of corruption and money laundering in the private sector. Gatekeepers should be part of the solution, not proponents of the problem.

Lawyers
Early in this chapter, shell companies were singled out for elimination from the banking sector. Actually, the same must be true of every other sector of the economy. Doing business with shell companies has to be made illegal, incumbent upon lawyers and all others as well.

More broadly, lawyers have to be brought under anti–money laundering restrictions, required to file Suspicious Activity Reports and Currency Transaction Reports like other components of the capitalist system. The argument that attorney-client privilege precludes cooperation in anti–money laundering policies is frankly offensive and has contributed hugely to America becoming the preferred destination for dirty money in recent decades. The powerful American Bar Association offers all sorts of reasons why lawyers should not be obligated to report on laundering schemes planned or executed, basically asserting the right to earn legal fees despite illegalities. This has to change; the United States cannot continue permitting advocates of the law abetting or overlooking violations of the law.

Inclusion in AML requirements might be handled in such a way as to impact lawyers use or misuse of IOLA arrangements explained earlier: interest on lawyer accounts. Hundreds of millions of dollars of client money shielded from normal AML checks simply because it is in a lawyer's account is an intolerable breach of ethics and needs to be a breach of law.

Auditors

Chapter 8 identified the auditing profession as perhaps the single most compromised component of the capitalist system. The reason is obvious; most countries permit auditors to offer consulting services bordering on or overstepping into tax evasion and money laundering. Then, auditors review and approve accounts of clients so advised. There is no greater conflict of interest in all of free market economics.

Separate the two functions—totally—in all countries. Do not accept into consolidated corporate accounts audits performed by firms operating in countries allowing both advisory and audit functions to be performed by the same organization. The heavy hand of the United States or perhaps the G7 or the G20 needs to be brought to bear. Get out of the business of selling suspect services and simultaneously approving suspect accounts. Without delay.

Even after separation from consulting services, accounting firms would still be left with an inherent flaw: they can see illegal activities and not report them on audited statements. For example, auditors can observe falsified trades conducted on a regular basis, yet they are not obligated to note such activities on certified accounts. While auditors are not law enforcement agents, when illegal activity stares them in the face they should be obligated to footnote accordingly, calling attention to potential financial risks. Either through legislation or by revised codes of ethics, auditors should not continue to certify accounts without highlighting blatant legal problems that may compromise the accuracy of accounts or even threaten corporate viability.

Accounting firms have for decades sought to avoid accountability. This has to change.

Other Enablers

Real estate agents, appraisers, inspectors, title insurance companies, and others engaged in property transactions must be fully encompassed in anti–money laundering and disclosure requirements, now proposed by the US Treasury Department. Though focused primarily on fighting foreign corruption and eliminating criminals and kleptocrats from gaining access to US assets, the pending regulations do constitute an important step toward improving integrity in some aspects of US financial affairs.

Measures to achieve greatly enhanced transparency and accountability in operations of corporations, in financial institutions, and among enablers within economic systems are the key to rebuilding capitalism's contributions to equity and liberty. Transparency and accountability constrain opportunities for opacity and impunity. Each one of the steps laid out above is worth multiple attempts to regulate within the financial secrecy system. While secrecy structures remain utilized and continuously expanded, law enforcement efforts directed against perceived financial malfeasance will continue to fail. Instead, clear obligations requiring transparency and accountability are much more difficult to exploit and can change the way the world works.

Many of the above courses of action can be understood as forms of mandated disclosure. Require disclosure. Add a confirming signature. Transparency and accountability are greatly advanced in a split second.

TAX MATTERS

Each of the measures so far described are predistribution, that is, they function before taxes are assessed, rather than redistribution, functioning after taxes are assessed. Predistribution methods have one great advantage: they have no or minimal costs to government budgets. In fact, most contribute to enhancing government budgets. Alternatively, redistribution methods have to be paid for out of tax receipts.

Earlier pages explained the realities surrounding the generation, movement, and accumulation of criminal, corrupt, and commercial dirty money. Many people view the entirety of this issue as a tax question, that is, tax evasion hurting government revenues. While tax evasion and avoidance are critically important concerns, they are not the whole of the matter. Suppose $100 billion is taken illegally out of a country and kept abroad. What would happen if that $100 billion instead stayed in the country? Perhaps 20 or 30 percent or more of this money would eventually accrue as taxes to the country's government. But the other $70 billion or $80 billion that remains within the economy—having a multiplier effect through consumption, investment, and savings—is even more valuable. In other words, tax is fundamentally important, yes, but so is the rest of the money, even more so.

From this perspective and within the quite distinct agenda of helping capitalism contribute to curtailing inequality and promoting democracy, what sorts of tax measures make sense and are politically achievable? This section and the next on inequality address several useful steps, focusing primarily on the United States, not attempting to be all-inclusive.

Restore the Internal Revenue Service

Tax evasion and avoidance have risen in the United States in good part because the Internal Revenue Service has been defunded in successive administrations as capitalism exerting its power through the US Congress progressively subordinates democracy. Step one toward fiscal sanity is to increase the budget of the IRS, well above the modest levels approved in 2022. Tax evasion has become sport in America, driving wealth to the top and hurting middle- and lower-income groups. Changing this reality begins with curtailing tax evasion and collecting proper revenues.

Tax Cuts and Jobs Act

America's 2017 effort to change its corporate tax code needs to be changed again by reconsidering the 21 percent corporate tax rate. With budget deficits skyrocketing in the United States, a rate of 25 to 27.5 percent still leaves the United States competitive with other countries.

The notion that tax cuts pay for themselves through economic growth has been proven wrong time and again. As said previously, trickle-down economics does not work where trickle-out economics is the reality. Trickling out or, in fact, gushing out of sight is just what the financial secrecy system is designed to facilitate.

One approach that must never be seriously considered is elimination of corporate income tax altogether. No single step would so completely explode economic inequality as this one, multiplying income and wealth for the already rich and probably sounding the death knell for the democratic-capitalist system.

Financial Transaction Tax

For years, various governments have considered applying a minimal tax on financial transactions. This is an idea whose time has come. At 10 or 20 basis points, that is, 0.1 or 0.2 percent on each transaction, the burden is small and the benefits are considerable. In the United States, even the U.S. Securities and Exchange Commission is funded by a small tax on stock and futures trades. The United Kingdom has had a similar tax for centuries, and other countries have recently followed suit, while more are planning to do so.

Transactions in stocks, bonds, and derivatives are the logical targets. Imposed on stock trades, reductions in speculative activity and high-frequency trading should be realized. On bond trades, US government securities would probably be exempted. Derivatives should certainly be included in the tax, with some care in determining the base rate for futures, interest rate swaps, security-based swaps, currency derivatives, and options.

Estimates suggest that a financial transaction tax could raise perhaps $800 billion in US revenues over ten years.[4] By far the greater part of this tax falls on the wealthy, thus serving to address economic inequality. Whatever tax rate is agreed upon, it should be applied at the outset, not phased in over time, which might enable subsequent legislation to reduce the tax. Thought can be given to earmarking the proceeds of the tax directly to funding programs such as health care, child care, prekindergarten education, or other redistributive efforts, thus hopefully helping to retain support for the tax through political administrations.

Carried Interest

Hedge funds, private equity funds, and venture capital funds often distribute profits to their partners, who are then taxed at capital gains rates, which are lower than income tax rates. This is even the case when partners put no money into selected investments. Interests in such assets are carried and distributed sometimes annually or after investments are sold. Applying capital gains rates to such profits hugely benefits partners who argue that their sweat equity should be treated as capital input rather than compensation.

While this is a very brief explanation of a complex issue, the essential reality is that carried interest has been a major driver of income inequality, enabling thousands of immensely wealthy individuals to pay lower taxes on their labor than workers. Partners in such funds have been huge campaign contributors for years as they seek to preserve their preferential treatment, another example of capitalism buying democracy.

Changing carried interest to ordinary income might enable the fund industry to take defensive actions to preserve some of its advantages. Even with such actions, the Congressional Budget Office in the United States produced an estimate of revenue gains approaching $15 billion over 10 years.[5] While not a huge amount of money, making this change would be a hugely symbolic gesture.

Social Security

Some have suggested that the United States should increase Social Security taxes on high-income earners. One of the most popular programs in the country, Social Security and Disability Insurance offers what should be a politically acceptable means of increasing revenues without tackling other tax rates. From current levels of 6.2 percent, hiking to a higher percentage on higher incomes—incomes above $147,000, the current point at which further Social Security tax drops to zero—should not be too much to ask.

Estate Tax

Taxes on assets transferred to heirs at the time of passing have been in place in the United States for more than a century, but successive legislation has now upped the value at which the tax kicks in to $23.4 million per couple. This too serves to secure plutocratic outcomes. Already, some 40 percent of household wealth in the United States stems from inheritances. A handful of the richest Americans immediately grasp that this is unfair and limit what goes to their children to relatively modest levels, donating the rest to foundations and charitable efforts.

To put it simply, reinstate a proper estate tax, kicking in at a much lower figure.

Corporate Minimum Tax

The United States and other G7 countries have agreed on the need for a minimum tax on corporate profits, with 15 percent a likely goal. This is a long-brewing and laudable effort, and hopefully success can be achieved. There are, however, very serious issues that must be considered.

First, tax evasion and avoidance are symptoms of the problem in the corporate world, not the problem itself. The real problem is the financial secrecy system that enables, even encourages, evasion and avoidance. Trying to impose a minimum tax—in other words, treating the symptoms while leaving secrecy mechanisms in place, which are the causes—is unlikely to work. Instill transparency and accountability first, then a minimum tax regime can work.

Second, formulas for distributing corporate tax collections across multiple countries will be extremely difficult to structure and implement. If a minimum tax regime ends up collecting revenues mainly for countries where corporations have their headquarters, the program has the potential to hurt, not help, more people around the world.

Third, legislative commitments to minimum corporate taxes will be difficult if not impossible to maintain in the United States and other countries where corporate lobbyists operate with abandon. Clearly undesirable is a tax regime that, with changing legislative majorities, is voted in and out of existence.

Fourth, there is a great risk that establishing a minimum corporate tax at 15 percent could lead to permanently lowering the maximum rate to

15 percent. In fact, a maximum rate at 15 percent could then be just a vote away from eliminating corporate taxes altogether. No other step could so fully guarantee rising economic inequality as this. Executive pay would soar even beyond the stratospheric levels now prevailing, underlining the disparities and discontents currently characterizing political malaise.

Collecting proper corporate taxes is a mandatory component within democratic capitalism. Repeating the point above, transparency and accountability should come first, then corporate taxes will follow. On this issue of a minimum corporate tax, proceed with caution.

Wealth Tax?

In recent years scholars and politicians have lauded the benefits of a wealth tax perhaps coupled with global asset registries, which would be a straightforward assault on economic inequality in America and other countries. As attractive as this appears, there is something that has to be done first: dismantle the financial secrecy system; instill transparency and accountability.

Hastily imposing a wealth tax, no matter how modest, while secrecy jurisdictions, anonymous companies, fake foundations, money laundering techniques, purchased passports, and millions of legal and accounting enablers are still thriving is a formula for disaster. Doing so would undoubtedly strengthen and prolong the financial secrecy system. It will without question move more money out of America and indeed out of other countries into inaccessible caches than is collected in tax, leading to a loss rather than a gain for society. Several countries have tried and abandoned such efforts.

Matthew Collin at the Brookings Institution weighs in on the point:

> For those of us that worry about inequality, our ability to raise tax revenue on the richest in society is going to be affected by their ability to move that money offshore. . . . [W]e really have to figure out how to stop them from hiding money offshore before these policies are going to be effective.[6]

Do not, I repeat, do not impose a wealth tax until the major elements of the shadow financial system have been substantially removed.

Then, with transparency and accountability in place, a wealth tax makes eminent sense and should be enacted. Sequenced properly, this might be the single most important step toward curtailing the twenty-first century's greatest economic problem—raging inequality.

Pertaining to Resources

Linking capitalism quite directly to the twenty-first century's other greatest problem, a carbon tax is needed to fight climate change. Nothing else can so effectively push industry out of fossil fuel use as this. Of course, China, India, and other countries should be urged to curtail coal and oil consumption, but that is not a reason for delay, not an excuse for postponement of decisive actions by North America and Europe. Global warming will exacerbate global poverty and inequality, also threatening survival of the democratic-capitalist system.

Meanwhile, as resources continue to be exported from developing countries, the Extractive Industries Transparency Initiative and the Publish What You Pay movement need to be adhered to and strengthened. Both of these efforts seek to ensure that oil and mineral mining companies pay their proper taxes and royalties to exporting country governments. Recent efforts in the United States to weaken these obligations are disgraceful. Quite simply, extractive companies must account for their liftings and pay their bills, with full transparency.

FRONTAL ATTACK ON ECONOMIC INEQUALITY

A free market system operating transparently and accountably can make a decisive contribution toward curtailing economic inequality and thereby securing democracy. How might some of these advantages be directed toward reducing income disparities? For the United States, several steps are already politically achievable, and others could succeed with greater effort.

Minimum Wage

Pay workers $15 per hour, with increases from existing levels enacted over no more than two years. Just do it. Half of Americans in low-wage jobs are essential workers, more than demonstrating their value during the pandemic. Now, $15 per hour, on the way higher.

Universal Health Care

Inexcusably, the United States is the only wealthy country that has so far failed to care for the health requirements of all its citizens. Whether via an improved Affordable Care Act or Medicare for all or some other hybrid, this glaring gap in what it means to be an American has to change. COVID-19 took a disproportionate toll on the poor. Whatever the reasons for this reality, one of them cannot be disproportionate access to health care. As with increasing the minimum wage, get it done.

Student Debt

The 2007–2008 financial crisis resulted in bailing out financial institutions and leaving tens of millions of Americans with stagnating incomes for the next decade. Results better balanced for the majority need to emerge from the current crises. In addition to health care and the minimum wage, student debt has to be on the agenda.

Some 45 million Americans owe the U.S. government about $1.75 trillion in loans for higher education. Steps taken in 2022 cancel roughly $400 billion of this debt, resulting in full relief for about 20 million and partial relief for millions more. Though controversial, future cancellations focusing on lower-income brackets would be beneficial to the economy.

Racial Economic Gaps

The moment is right in the world's premier democracy and largest economy to undertake measures purposefully counteracting the history of slavery and addressing ongoing discrimination against Black Americans, thus making a fundamental contribution to reducing inequality and strengthening liberty. Establishing Juneteenth—June 19th—as a federal holiday marking the 1865 date when slaves in Texas were finally told they were free is certainly a step forward. Three basic components of a further plan would include the following.

First, acknowledge three centuries of slavery and its following century and a half of racial discrimination and render an official apology. This could come from the president or in the form of a congressional resolution. History is replete with similar actions. Surviving Japanese Americans interned during World War II received a formal apology signed by Ronald Reagan. Even as recently as 2020, Belgium's King Philippe apologized to the government and people of the Congo for the horrors of enslavement and exploitation carried out long ago by king and country. The United States will further heal its own domestic wounds and strengthen its global stature with a forthright acceptance of its economic and political wrongs and commitment to rights.

Second, allocate a portion of financial transaction tax collections to funding economic and educational development for Black Americans. Strengthening predominantly Black communities and universities can play a key role in securing prosperity and political participation for these persistently disadvantaged Americans for years to come.

Third, decisions on means and mechanisms of allocating funds should be determined by an ongoing commission of Black Americans drawn from politics, business, education, the arts, entertainment, and youths. A forward-looking focus contributing to progress should be politically viable.[7]

In the words of Martin Luther King Jr., "We are confronted with the fierce urgency of now."[8] This decade, the 2020s, with a strong Black Lives Matter movement, offers a chance to reduce economic disparities and strengthen political unions between races.

The Poorest of the World

For decades the governments of wealthy nations have loaned money to low-income countries, contributing to economic development. Paying interest and principal on such debts by these countries with per capita incomes of barely $1,000 a year will be impossible in the wake of the global pandemic. Already, many of these poor countries are seeing COVID-19 deaths in countless thousands. Holding on to such debts, anticipating rescheduling or repayment in future years, serves no purpose.

The US government may not have a clear accounting of such bilateral debts, probably on the order of $20–$30 billion or so. The United States should cancel bilateral debts owed by low-income countries and then encourage other wealthy bilateral lenders to do the same. The gesture and the reality, costing little, will be well received the world over.

DEMOCRACY NOT FOR SALE

This chapter has thus far addressed predistribution and redistribution measures that can collectively strengthen capitalism's relationship to democracy, helping to secure—even save—the democratic-capitalist system in this century. Each of the measures addressed has a direct financial component; that is, they will generate money or cost money. There are additional measures that need to be taken, less directly linked to fiscal concerns but nevertheless important in reframing the synthesis of capitalism and democracy. Focusing on the United States, if rebalancing capitalism and democracy is to be achieved, then capitalism has to relinquish some of the shackles it has, through years of effort, secured upon vital components of democratic processes.

Citizens United

Nothing so fully confirms capitalism's victory over democracy as *Citizens United*, the flawed 2010 US Supreme Court decision that essentially equates unlimited corporate political campaign spending with free speech. Not only did the ruling usher billions of dollars into electioneering, it also opened the door to dark money from disguised companies and secrecy jurisdictions abroad, contributing to foreign interference in US elections. American democracy has become to a significant extent a subsidiary of capitalism, with business interests working to sway elections to their advantage. This thwarts the fight against inequality, the greatest threat to democratic capitalism.

Amending the US Constitution to reverse *Citizens United* would require a two-thirds vote in the House and Senate and approval by three-fourths of the 50 states, a daunting prospect in the near term. While campaign finance reform efforts should continue, possibly including a new case reaching the Supreme Court, pursuing a proposed 28th amendment eliminating the notion that money is speech is essential.

Facilitate Federal Funding of Elections

One way to get around the billions of dollars raised by corporate interests and political action committees is to offer very substantial levels of federal funding for elections, with the proviso to candidates that they would wholly or partially forgo private money. Many states and cities have multiple variations of public financing programs for local elections, with some offering full funding and others shared funding.

In 1966 the United States established the Presidential Election Campaign Fund, which now enables taxpayers to check a box on tax forms to direct $3 to the Federal Election Commission for distribution to campaigns according to clear rules. Though neither a cost nor a refund, participation by taxpayers in this system has fallen to about 4 percent of filers, effectively a failed effort.

With this system still in place, however, the mechanism exists to facilitate full public funding of presidential elections. Increasing the amount and making it tax deductible would boost participation rates substantially. For example, a $25 deduction checked by half of filers would total around $2 billion annually, which should be adequately attractive to candidates and parties eschewing private donations. With good publicity, participation rates could be well above 50 percent. This money would then not be available for other federal programs, but this is a modest price to pay to escape much of the damage done to democracy by *Citizens*

United. In other words, while still working to pass a constitutional amendment, pull the rug out from under corporations and PACs with public funding of presidential elections. Cut back capitalism from the business of buying democracy.

Golden Visas Dropped

As said repeatedly, democracy should not be a commodity purchased and sold by capitalism. Nor are America's interests served by welcoming money so often stolen from other countries. Whether Russia, China, Nigeria, Brazil, Malaysia, or any other nation, their citizens are harmed by our passports for proceeds policy.

The EB-5 program is beyond repair. End it and do not replace it. The United States can welcome foreign investment without selling residence and citizenship in the process.

Consumer Protections Strengthened

The Consumer Financial Protection Bureau has been under assault by the financial industry ever since it was authorized in 2010 in the wake of the 2007–2008 economic disaster. But consumers still need protection, as the unbelievable Wells Fargo scandal hurting millions of Americans vividly illustrated for years during and following the crisis. So, instead of undercutting the CFPB, it should be self-funding in the same way as the Securities and Exchange Commission is self-funding. An annual assessment on U.S. banks and perhaps also other types of financial institutions will underline the fact that the industry should pay for a portion of its own oversight. What is good for the SEC is good for the CFPB.

Control Regulatory Capture

Industry will continuously strive to control regulatory mechanisms, a perpetual problem for every country operating under principles of democratic capitalism. In the United States the inspector general process, with IGs assigned to every department of government, usually works reasonably well. But subjecting IGs to departmental or executive control is fraught with risks—risks that cost people their lives, as earlier examples illustrated. How to protect against regulatory capture has been debated for years.

What is needed is an independent regulatory oversight board similar to the Federal Reserve Board. What ensures the Fed freedom of action is 14-year terms of service by its governors, meaning that each appointee crosses multiple election cycles and is therefore not subjected to undue political pressures.

A regulatory oversight board staffed with long-serving commission-ers would have several functions. First, it would be empowered to review the inspectors general and examine oversight processes in every depart-ment of government, ensuring effectiveness and rooting out industry in-fluence. Second, its annual and occasional reports should be public. And third, the board should be available to confidential whistleblowers, thus providing a safe and needed mechanism for receipt of insider infor-mation outside places of employment.

In countless ways, capitalism seeks opportunities to subordinate reg-ulation. Democracy is enhanced when such opportunities are limited. An independent oversight board can make a major contribution to this.

INTERNATIONAL ARENAS

All of this chapter thus far has focused on the United States as the world's primary proponent of democratic capitalism. This nation must take the lead in correcting the perilous clash between these two ideologies or risk losing its preferred system and giving way to authoritarianism, already rearing its ugly head in America and in countries around the world. In addition to US efforts, there are measures that need to be taken by in-ternational institutions influenced and pressured by the United States and by other democracies. A selection of such needed efforts, still focusing on making capitalism more responsive to democracy, follows.

World Bank
Release the US stranglehold on this underachieving institution. Rather than automatically naming an American as president of the bank, allow other candidates to vie for leadership as finally approved by the board of directors.

The US role in the World Bank has consistently served immediate US interests, meaning free flows of capital and protection of foreign invest-ments. This reality lies at the heart of the condition lamented in previous pages, noting that for half a century development economists focused on how much money they could direct into developing countries and com-pletely failed to note how much money comes out of developing countries. To stop this damaging myopia, require of the World Bank an annual analysis of illicit financial flows—their magnitudes and the means by which they flow—and relate this analysis directly to achieving sustainable development goals. Put the whole of the development equation on the table for the first time. The vast majority of the world's 8 billion people will be grateful, and capitalism and democracy will both be strengthened.

In order to ask the right questions and produce compelling metrics, the World Bank has to incorporate into its ranks a wider spectrum of talent, including sociologists, psychologists, political scientists, philosophers, and more, not just a few but in significant numbers. So frequently it is observed that the most forward-thinking individuals are those trained in and working in more than one discipline. The only way the World Bank can achieve its potential is to widen its intellectual pool, welcoming the tough questions asked by and answers offered by a broader array of talent encouraged to think creatively about the state of the world and its fullest potential. This does not describe the World Bank today. It needs to be the design of the bank tomorrow. Frankly, caution—and this is a very mild choice of words—needs to be replaced with courage.

United Nations

Building upon efforts already under way, a UN convention on transparency is achievable, provided it remains primarily focused on international economic relations and does not tread too heavily on sovereignty and fiscal concerns or attempt to become a global tax regime. Such a convention can contribute to dismantling the shadow financial system, the greatest brake on economic development for the majority of the world's people. Transparency can and must become a centerpiece within cross-border financial and commercial affairs in this century lest economic inequality defeat democratic capitalism and then authoritarianism, right on the threshold, becomes normalized. If this happens, humanity is set back for a long stretch into the future. The United Nations has a key role to play.

World Trade Organization

As explained in previous chapters, one of the greatest mistakes made within capitalism in recent decades is the separation of value and price in trade transactions. The arm's-length principle is supposed to be operative, meaning that the price of the traded goods should reflect what would be charged between unrelated buyers and sellers. No question, this is the most violated principle in global financial affairs. Trade pricing is unmoored from legitimate value. Trillions of dollars in goods and services move at prices that do not reflect real values, instead configured to shift revenues and profits across borders. Developing countries have lost trillions of dollars of foreign exchange, and richer countries have lost trillions of dollars in tax revenues.

The World Trade Organization should take the lead in correcting this basic flaw in the way the capitalist system functions. Policies should be adopted that 1) require customs duty documentation and payment documentation to be the same in identifying, measuring, and pricing goods and services and 2) require buyer and seller signatures on documentation confirming that prices conform to legitimate values. These measures will go far toward curtailing widespread trade misinvoicing. Multinational and even many smaller corporations will fight against this, preferring to stick to the practice of manipulating trade for the purpose of shifting money.

Within the WTO, a drive for change would have to be led by a consortium of nations. Leadership by the United States, already the world's richest economy, would make all the difference. Americans can prosper without cheating others and, in the process, can sustain democratic capitalism for future generations.

World Customs Organization

The WCO already has some momentum in analyzing and addressing trade pricing manipulations. It should join the WTO in driving for regularization of trade valuations.

In addition, the WCO is the right organization to take up another matter—the misuse of free trade zones and special economic zones all over the world, violating customs regimes, contributing to smuggling, and facilitating trafficking. There is currently no effective regulatory effort directed toward these zones, and therefore rampant illegalities surround what goes in and out of thousands of small geographic enclaves, making it impossible to control much of transnational criminal activity. What is needed is a regimen of statistics, inspections, and sanctions, with the Financial Action Task Force, global anti–money laundering body, serving as a model.

The WCO and the WTO have crucial roles to play if trade, the very essence of capitalism, is to maximize its contributions to prosperity and liberty going forward.

Organisation of Economic Co-operation and Development

As said earlier, the OECD is maligned by some as a rich man's club. At least the OECD is in the arena seeking to move its rich club members toward a more responsible world. Progress is slow, incomplete, and fraught with diplomatic difficulties.

The OECD needs to insert basic requirements for transparency and accountability in trade transactions into its proposals to reduce profit shifting by multinational corporations, as laid out at the beginning of this chapter. Trade integrity, accomplished with commitments and confirmed with signatures, can go far in maximizing capitalism's contributions toward a free world.

Similarly, the OECD needs to push transparency and accountability measures in financial transactions. Eliminate banking for disguised entities and transactions for unknown customers, with the OECD taking a leading role in pushing for fast adoption of ironclad commitments and sanctions. The Common Reporting Standard identifying assets held across borders needs to be universalized, with the OECD continuing a leading role.

The OECD's headquarters in Paris and quality of staff give it a unique opportunity to be of maximum influence, particularly on richer countries and increasingly on developing countries. Combining economic prowess with a measure of independence from diplomatic pressures, the OECD can be a leader in rebuilding capitalism and thereby strengthening democracy. After all, it is the richer countries that most need to change.

Financial Action Task Force

Established to encourage global anti–money laundering efforts, the FATF needs to move from its alliance status into a treaty organization of member nations, fully empowered to require and oversee adherence to higher AML standards. Such a move requires leadership by the US Treasury Department, which should at the same time elevate the US financial intelligence unit, FinCEN, to a seat on the National Security Council.

Revisit and Revise Bretton Woods

Guiding economic principles adopted during and immediately after World War II have given way under pressures exerted by floating exchange rates, the rise of multinational corporations, global supply chains, instant transfers of information and money, trillions upon trillions of dollars hidden from proper records, and secrecy structures and mechanisms now embedded within the heartbeat of capitalism. A new Bretton Woods agreement is called for, a new gathering of global economic and political leaders addressing the very different world of the twenty-first century.

Such a move would require adequate preparation at the UN, G7, and G20. As currently operating, the World Bank and the International Monetary Fund are incapable of dealing with the reality of financial secrecy, the deep involvement of the West in creating and advancing the secrecy system, and the damage done to geoeconomic and geopolitical affairs by ill dealings within this system.

As the whole of humanity shares in recovering from its current crises, the time is right to begin rebuilding economic systems and their relationships to political affairs for a better future for all.

REALIZING INTEGRITY

Transparency and accountability must be central components within the ideologies and operations of thriving capitalism. This goal is the opposite of the financial secrecy system now so deeply imbedded in trade and financial affairs. If this secrecy system prevails, then capitalism will continue to undermine democracy, and the democratic-capitalist system as a whole risks failure.

Transparency and accountability do not threaten initiative and competition in free market affairs, and no argument supporting these flawed notions has credence. Privacy and confidentiality as part of business dealings are one thing; asking employees, financiers, lawyers, accountants, and customers to cooperate in illicit transactions is quite another. In the early paragraphs of this chapter, multinational, multibillion-dollar, multiproduct corporations are called on to tell their employees involved in trade and finance that the chance they may be committing any criminal offense is zero. Millions of smaller companies can already do so. The first multinational to respond is awaited. Reality is that crossing into already illegal and illicit dealings has become normalized.

Maintaining the financial secrecy system within capitalism has the effect of widening economic inequality, which is the greatest threat to democratic capitalism going forward. Narrowing inequality cannot be achieved within a system that is specifically designed and operated to move money from the bottom to the top. Change the system, and then the world has a chance to offer economic justice to its growing billions.

Who should lead? Without question, the United States. The opening years of this decade highlight the experiences, insights, and reflections needed to drive economic and political renewal.

A few hundred words establishing transparency and accountability in each of perhaps a dozen pieces of legislation in US law can change the way American capitalism works and secure the democratic-capitalist system for the rest of the century. Preservation of democracy is at stake.

Equally confronting the twenty-first century is the issue of climate change, threatening the well-being of billions. As temperatures likely continue rising for decades, there is at least the possibility of technical innovation eventually halting the rise, particularly with solar power holding out prospects for efficiency levels perhaps even reaching 50 percent, converting half of incoming energy to outgoing energy. In other words, technology, coupled with political will, may play a role in finally alleviating the climate problem. No such technical fix exists to help solve deep-seated problems within democratic capitalism. This is entirely a matter of political will and demands the same or even greater degree of reckoning. The existential threat of climate change is matched by the existential threat of losing democratic capitalism and collapsing into a world of authoritarianism.

A very purposeful round of national and global leadership is now needed. Embedding transparency and accountability into trade and financial operations can be easily accomplished with requisite purpose and courage, enhancing equality and freedom.

All of the measures put forward in this chapter center on capitalism and its relationship with democracy. This is not to suggest that democracy itself has little need of improvement. On the contrary, democracy is always an evolving concept. Major issues surround concerns for racial justice, gender rights, voter protections, even free speech in its modern manifestations, and more. These are issues for a different book. This book is about capitalism's obligations and opportunities to strengthen democracy and to share good fortune.

A core assertion within these pages is that we cannot have rising economic inequality in perception and in fact and at the same time have a strengthening democracy. Or, to put the point in positive terms, improving economic equality and fairness in perception and in fact is a necessary—mandatory—component of strengthening democracy.

I believe that the most critical problems we face must be solved essentially from the bottom up. Or, again, to put it another way, from the perspective of average citizens rather than from the perspective of the most elite. With a greater sense of equality both in voice and in well-being, we can sustain the better angels of the century we now inhabit. Shared advantages for coming generations can achieve and maintain prosperity and peace.

From where will the motivation for change, for integrity and character, arise, within our heads or our hearts? We conclude with the urgency of this question.

Conclusion:
Character Is Destiny

ERACLITUS, SOMETIMES CONSIDERED the first genuine philosopher, lived in the community of Ephesus, now in modern-day Turkey, passing away around 475 BCE. Fragments of his only known work, *On Nature*, have survived, as well as commentaries on his thought by Plato, Aristotle, and others. Heraclitus explored the space between sense perceptions and thought:

> Learning many things does not teach understanding.

> Sound thinking is the greatest virtue and wisdom: To speak the truth and to act on the basis of an understanding of the nature of things.[1]

Perhaps most often quoted from Heraclitus's writings is the phrase *Ethos anthropoi daimon*, usually translated as "character is destiny." John McCain and Mark Salter chose this familiar phrase as the title of their book telling stories of courageous personages of recent centuries. I choose it as the title of this concluding chapter. Preceding pages have explored critically the construct of the capitalist system as it has become perverted in recent decades. I have asserted as strongly as possible that such character flaws within capitalism must be substantially altered or the destiny of capitalism and with it the destiny of the democratic-capitalist system is at risk. If character is indeed destiny, then we, in this decade and this century, have much work to do.

Should the current quest for change, the thrust for new order in the democratic-capitalist system, be pursued primarily through the application of morality or reason? Merely asking the question opens the door to thousands of years of philosophical debate, far beyond the intent of this book. So, here we limit the notion of morality to conceptions of right and wrong and the notion of reason to pursuits of logical and rational thought.

In the earliest paragraphs of this book, I said that the writings offered here strive to be both analytical and evocative, because both our intellects and our passions are required to solve our shared problems. Let us now explore this question further. Upon what traits of character—morality or reason—do we draw in order to bring about a renewal of democratic capitalism, able to meet the enormous challenges of this century?

Fundamental advance arising from the awakening of morality is a long, long process. The slavery issue is cautionary. Timelines for slavery run from the beginning of recorded history to the present day, as the reality of enslaved conditions has never been fully expunged. Abolition movements began in earnest in the early 1800s in England, France, the Scandinavian countries, and America. Defenders of slavery offered as many logical reasons for its continuance, drawing upon biblical, economic, and social arguments, as opponents put forward for ending slavery. Ultimately the abolitionists won with moral appeals centering on the rights of man, but that process consumed nearly the entire nineteenth century and did not result in a complete revision of social norms even up to the present day.

The point is, trying to utilize moral arousals to alter the acceptance of and practice of illicit dealings now firmly established within capitalism will have a difficult time producing change in the near term. Resolving this issue is not about what we "ought" to do, disparaged as "impotence of the ought" by nineteenth-century German philosopher G.W.F. Hegel. What we ought to do stemming from moral convictions conveys less urgency that what we can and must do for practical reasons.

Defenders of the status quo, such as Michael Novak, a distinguished scholar who made the case for moral capitalism, are often unaware of what prevails in the real world:

> Capitalism teaches people to show initiative and imagination, to work cooperatively in teams, to love and to cherish the law; what is more, it forces persons not only to rely on themselves and their own moral qualities, but also to recognize those moral qualities in others and to cooperate with others freely.[2]

This does not describe or even recognize the domineering presence and use of anonymous companies, tax havens, secrecy jurisdictions, money laundering techniques, ubiquitous trade manipulations, and more that today are widely utilized by corporations and handle perhaps half of global free market affairs. Moral argument couched in these terms will not move fast enough to get us where we need to go.

Many of the preceding pages describe examples of moral failings within capitalism. So, drawing on these stories, if the moral case for re-modeling capitalism is to be summoned, I would put it in much more present-day and concrete terms. The following kinds of questions bear careful thought.

> What part, what percent, of your standard of living, my standard of
> living, is worth someone else's liberty, someone else's life? Whether
> that someone is a serving American military officer improperly
> forced from her home by a corrupted bank, or an unemployed
> opioid addict in Appalachia unable to care for his family, or a
> drowned Guatemalan child and her father washed up on the north
> banks of the Rio Grande, or a homeless Venezuelan girl fleeing her
> country to an uncertain life, or an ambitious young engineer in
> Brazil seeing his career prospects disappear, or a grandmother in
> the Niger Delta watching the land of her birth destroyed, or an
> elderly man in a captured South Africa losing hope for his children
> and grandchildren, or a Mozambique laborer reading of massive
> theft and unable to find even casual work, or an imam in Iran
> seeing his fellow citizens involved in drugs and crime, or a confused
> little Rohingya boy wondering where or if he belongs in this world,
> or a Malaysian civil servant watching massive wealth stolen by
> politicians from his country's coffers, or a young educated Chinese
> democracy advocate whose voice is silenced, or even a proud
> Russian woman emigrating from her country in utter despair over
> its turn to violence and conquest?

> What of their reality is worth our reality? What of their loss is worth
> our gain?

In order for the moral case to be compelling, it needs to be drawn in this manner from today's world, a world of rising economic inequality and declining political liberty.

But the drive for change presented in terms of morality, even in terms of urgent and unconscionable realities, will be slow in effecting meaningful progress. Instead, in this instance, on these issues surrounding capitalism, the moral case for transformation should be secondary to reason, because with its underperforming capitalist component as currently functioning, democratic capitalism simply cannot get us through the remaining years of the twenty-first century intact. We have many opportunities to alter our behaviors based on logic and rational thought, and these approaches can be marshaled much more quickly in pursuit of meaningful reform.

In my judgment, the democratic-capitalist system is the best invention within political economy yet devised. But it is being damaged, terribly damaged if not destroyed, by ill motivations and dealings within one of its components, capitalism, far more so than within its other component, democracy. Rather than dwelling on what we ought to do in a moral sense, these pages are about what we are compelled to do in a practical sense if we are to secure economic well-being and personal freedom for all.

Edmund Husserl, German philosopher born in 1859, watched the politics of his country come apart in the 1920s and 1930s. In 1935 at a perilous moment foreshadowing World War II and the Holocaust, he delivered what came to be known as "The Vienna Lecture," saying

> it is important . . . to show how . . . the 'modern age,' . . . so proud of its successes in theory and practice, has itself finally fallen into a growing dissatisfaction and must even look upon its own situation as distressful.[3]

He then in his final sentences calls for the "heroism of reason." Confronting the issues of his time, Husserl stood, not on distant moral ground, but on the immediacy of reason as the path forward.

Pause for a moment to absorb Husserl's words—"modern age," "proud of its successes," "finally fallen," "growing dissatisfaction," "distressful." These words describe our time in this century as well. And our time calls for a similar grounding, a similar "heroism of reason," lest we lose democratic capitalism and decline increasingly into the arms of authoritarianism, the most unreasonable of ideas for peace and prosperity.

A renewal of high character within capitalism can bring about the strengthening of democracy. This is the fulcrum, the determinant of destiny, around which a major part of economic and political affairs in the twenty-first century will pivot, a hinge in human affairs.

Invisible Trillions Discussion Guide

PART I

1. Shouldn't capitalists have the right to conduct their affairs in secret?
2. Why is it important to care about income inequality in addition to poverty? Why is a focus on only poverty, while neglecting inequality, inadequate?
3. Is democracy in the United States diminishing? What evidence supports this view?
4. What danger does the financial secrecy system pose to capitalism? To democracy?
5. Why is it important/necessary for capitalism to benefit the widest range of people? What are the risks to a stable society if capitalism does not fairly benefit the majority?

PART II

1. What business practices enable the financial secrecy system? What business-as-usual practices need to change to rein in the financial secrecy system?
2. Certain business practices, such as falsified trading, are entrenched as acceptable. What would it take to make such practices unacceptable?
3. Are multinational corporations asking/requiring their staffs to break the law?
4. Is there a disconnect between national security and corrupt capitalist practices? If so, how should this disconnect be remedied?
5. What gaps do you see between ideal capitalism, as taught in business schools, and the corrupted capitalism as practiced in the real world?

PART III

1. Western countries take for granted that capitalism and democracy work in tandem. What is the danger in splitting the two-part system? Do other

systems, such as China's, present a viable option? What would the world look like if illiberal capitalism was the dominant force?

2. What do you think are the most realistic solutions to subdue the financial secrecy system? What solutions/actions would you add?

3. What would create more political will?

4. What, if anything, does capitalism owe to the stability of the societies in which it operates?

5. Is real change possible in America or elsewhere?

List of Abbreviations

1MDB	1 Malaysia Development Berhad
AIG	American International Group
AML	anti–money laundering
AOI	Apple Operations International
CARES	Coronavirus Aid, Relief and Economic Security
CCP	Chinese Communist Party
CICIG	Comisión Internacional contra la Impunidad en Guatemala (International Commission against Impunity in Guatemala)
CTR	Currency Transaction Report
DEA	Drug Enforcement Administration
DOJ	Department of Justice
DRC	Democratic Republic of the Congo
EY	Ernst & Young
FAA	Federal Aviation Administration
FATF	Financial Action Task Force
FBI	Federal Bureau of Investigation
FCPA	Foreign Corrupt Practices Act
FIFA	Fédération Internationale de Football Association
FinCEN	Financial Crimes Enforcement Network
GDP	gross domestic product
ICIJ	International Consortium of Investigative Journalists
IMF	International Monetary Fund
IOLA	Interest on Lawyer Account
IRGC	Islamic Revolutionary Guards Corps
IRS	Internal Revenue Service
MCAS	Maneuvering Characteristics Augmentation System
OECD	Organisation of Economic Co-operation and Development
OML	Oil Mining Lease
OPL	Oil Prospecting License
PDVSA	Petroleos de Venezuela, S.A.

PwC	PricewaterhouseCoopers
RBS	Royal Bank of Scotland
RICO	Racketeer Influenced and Corrupt Organizations Act
SAR	Suspicious Activity Report
SEC	Securities and Exchange Commission
SWIFT	Society for Worldwide Interbank Financial Telecommunication
UAE	United Arab Emirates
UN	United Nations
WCO	World Customs Organization
WTO	World Trade Organization

Notes

FOREWORD

1. Larry Diamond, *Ill Winds: Saving Democracy from Russian Rage, Chinese Ambition, and American Complacency* (New York: Penguin, 2019).

2. Larry Diamond, "Democratic Regression in Comparative Perspective: Scope, Methods, and Causes," *Democratization* 28, no. 1 (September 2020): 22–42.

3. R. S. Foa, A. Klassen, M. Slade, A. Rand, and R. Collins, "The Global Satisfaction with Democracy Report 2020," Centre for the Future of Democracy, 2020, https://www.cam.ac.uk/system/files/report2020_003.pdf.

4. Richard Wike, Laura Silver, and Alexandra Castilo, "Many across the Globe Are Dissatisfied with How Democracy Is Working," Pew Research Center, April 29, 2019, https://www.pewresearch.org/global/2019/04/29/many-across-the-globe-are-dissatisfied -with-how-democracy-is-working/.

CHAPTER 1

1. Javier Garcia-Bernardo, Jan Fichtner, Frank W. Takes, and Eelke M. Heernskerk, "Uncovering Offshore Financial Centers: Conduits and Sinks in the Global Corporate Ownership Network," *Scientific Reports* 7 (2017), doi:10.1038/s41598-017-06322-9.

2. "Financial Secrecy Index—2020 Results," Tax Justice Network, n.d., https://fsi .taxjustice.net/en/introduction/fsi-results.

3. Emile van der Does de Willebois, J. C. Sharma, Robert Harrison, Ji Won Park, and Emily Halter, *The Puppet Masters: How the Corrupt Use Legal Structures to Hide Stolen Assets and What to Do about It* (Washington, DC: World Bank, 2011).

4. Rachel Louise Ensign and Serena Ng; "Law Firms' Accounts Pose Money-Laundering Risk," *Wall Street Journal*, December 26, 2016.

5. "Not So Special," *The Economist*, April 4, 2015.

6. National Association of Foreign-Trade Zones, "U.S. Foreign-Trade Zones: Expanding U.S. Exports, Jobs, & Economic Development," https://www.naftz.org/wp-content /uploads/2021/01/FTZ-Facts-2021-final.pdf.

7. Paul Krugman, *Arguing with Zombies: Economics, Politics, and the Fight for a Better Future* (New York: Norton, 2020), 6, 8–9.

CHAPTER 2

1. World Bank, GDP (current US$): World Bank national accounts data, and OECD National Accounts data files; calculations made from broad money (% of GDP): International Monetary Fund, International Financial Statistics and data files, and World Bank and OECD GDP estimates.

2. Gabriel Zucman, "Taxing Multinational Corporations in the 21st Century," Economics for Inclusive Prosperity, Policy brief no. 10, February 2019.

3. Economic Policy Institute, "Corporate Tax Chartbook: How Corporations Rig the Rules to Dodge the Taxes They Owe," June 1, 2017, epi.org/107544.

4. Valeria Pellegrini, Alessandra Sanelli, and Enrico Tosti, "Unreported Assets Held Abroad and Tax Evasion: Hints from External Statistics," VoxEU, March 14, 2016, https://voxeu.org/article/balance-payments-statistics-and-hidden-assets.

5. James S. Henry, "Let's Tax Anonymous Wealth! A Modest Proposal to Reduce Inequality, Attack Organized Crime, Aid Developing Countries, and Raise Badly Needed Revenue from the World's Wealthiest Tax Dodgers, Kleptocrats, and Felons," in *Global Tax Fairness*, ed. Thomas Pogge and Krishen Mehta (Oxford, UK: Oxford University Press, 2016), 79.

6. Board of Governors of the Federal Reserve System (US), Market Yield on U.S. Treasury Securities at 1-Year, 5-Year, and 10-Year Constant Maturity [GS1], [GS5], and [GS10], Organization for Economic Co-operation and Development, Consumer Price Index: Total All Items for the United States [CPALTT01USM657N], retrieved from FRED, Federal Reserve Bank of St. Louis, January 26, 2022.

7. Cormac Mullen, "World's Negative-Yielding Debt Pile Hits $18 Trillion," Bloomberg, December 10, 2020.

8. Lawrence Summers, "The Global Economy Has Entered Unexplored, Dangerous Territory," *Washington Post*, October 9, 2016.

9. Daniel Gross, "What Happens When Money Breaks the Rules?," Slate, September 28, 2016.

10. "Youth Not in Employment, Education or Training (NEET) by Sex—ILO Modelled Estimates," International Labour Organization, https://ilostat.ilo.org/data; the World Bank, "Broad Money (% of GDP): International Monetary Fund, International Financial Statistics and Data Files," https://data.worldbank.org/indicator/FM.LBL.BMNY.GD.ZS; and World Bank and OECD GDP estimates.

11. J. B. Maverick, "How Big Is the Derivatives Market?," Investopedia, November 23, 2021.

12. "Derivatives for Leading Domestic Financial/Bank Holding Companies," ibanknet.com, as of January 15, 2021, https://www.ibanknet.com/scripts/callreports/filist.aspx?type=derivatives.

13. J. B. Maverick, "How Big Is the Derivatives Market?," Investopedia, November 23, 2021.

14. Warren Buffett, "2002 Chairman's Letter," Berkshire Hathaway website, 15.

15. Caux Round Table, "2016: An Inflection Point in History?," Fondazione Centesimus Annus–Pro Pontifice, https://www.centesimusannus.org/media/2eupn1472643121.pdf.

16. "The Anti-Fiat Punto," *The Economist*, May 29, 2021, 66.

17. "The 2022 Crypto Crime Report," Chainalysis, February 2022, 3.

18. "The 2022 Crypto Crime Report," 3.

19. Sean Foley, Jonathan R. Karlsen, and Talis J. Putnins, "Sex, Drugs, and Bitcoin: How Much Illegal Activity Is Financed through Cryptocurrencies?," *Review of Financial Studies* 32, no. 5 (May 2019): 1847.

20. Eric Lipton and Ephrat Livni, "Crypto Nomads: Surfing the World for Risk and Profit," *New York Times*, July 25, 2021, 3.

21. J. Christopher Giancarlo and Daniel Gorfine, "Why a Digital Dollar Could Be Just What the Economy Needs," CNBC, June 9, 2021.

22. "The RIC Report: Rise of the Unknowns," BofA Global Research, February 9, 2021, 8.

CHAPTER 3

1. Rick Rowden and Jingran Wang, "The Global Crisis of Corruption," Global Financial Integrity, July 13, 2020.

2. Transparency International, "Corruption Perception Index," https://www.transparency.org/en/cpi/2020/index/nzl.

3. Foreign Corrupt Practices Act Clearinghouse, "Enforcement Actions," Stanford Law School.

4. "Selling England (and Wales) by the Pound," Private Eye, https://www.private-eye.co.uk/registry.

5. "Faulty Towers: Understanding the Impact of Overseas Corruption of the London Property Market," Transparency International UK, March 2017, 11.

6. "Impact of Tax Evasion and Money Laundering on Local Real Estate Markets, in Particular in European Cities," Special Committee on Financial Crimes, Tax Evasion and Tax Avoidance, European Parliament, public hearing, February 5, 2019, 5.

7. "Impact of Tax Evasion and Money Laundering," 6. See also "German Real Estate Market a Hotbed of Money Laundering, Transparency Reports," Deutsche Welle, December 7, 2018.

8. "Impact of Tax Evasion and Money Laundering," European Parliament, 6–8.

9. Tyler Stiem, "Race and Real Estate: How Hot Chinese Money Is Making Vancouver Unlivable," The Guardian, July 7, 2016.

10. Expert Panel on Money Laundering in BC Real Estate, "Combatting Money Laundering in BC Real Estate," final report to the Minister of Finance, May 2019, 1.

11. "Opacity: Why Criminals Love Canadian Real Estate (and How to Fix It)," Transparency International Canada, March 2019, 12.

12. Sean McCaughan, "The Big Problem of Dirty Money in Miami Real Estate," The Big Bubble Miami, October 14, 2018.

13. Patrick Farrell, Marta Oliver Craviotto, and Nicolas Nehamas, "Russian Allegedly Involved in Major Tax Fraud Bought South Florida Real Estate," Miami Herald, March 11, 2019.

14. Katherine Kallergis, "US Government Sells Palm Beach Home of Convicted Venezuelan Money Launderer," The Real Deal, June 14, 2019.

15. TRD Staff, "Former Ecuadorian Official Accused in Bribery Scandal Has Ties to SoFla Properties," The Real Deal, March 28, 2019.

16. "FBI Establishes Permanent Task Force to Investigate Corruption and Money Laundering in Miami's Real Estate Market," Barbosa Legal, April 1, 2019.

17. Louise Story and Stephanie Saul, "Stream of Foreign Wealth Flows to Elite New York Real Estate," New York Times, February 7, 2015.

18. Story and Saul, "Stream of Foreign Wealth."

19. Financial Crimes Enforcement Network, "FinCEN Targets Shell Companies Purchasing Luxury Properties in Seven Major Metropolitan Areas," press release, August 22, 2017.

20. Sean McGoey, "'A Kleptocrat's Dream': US Real Estate a Safe Haven for Billions in Dirty Money, Report Says," International Consortium of Investigative Journalists, August 10, 2021.

21. Ryan Cooper, "How Foreign Investors Launder Their Money in New York Real Estate," The Week, November 13, 2017.

22. Alison Fitzgerald, Marina Walker Guevara, Simon Bowers, et al., "New Leak Reveals Luxembourg Tax Deals for Disney, Koch Brothers Empire," International Consortium of Investigative Journalists, December 9, 2014.

23. Jérémie Barch, Maxime Ferrer, Maxime Vaudano, and Anne Michel, "OpenLux: The Secrets of Luxembourg, A Tax Haven at the Heart of Europe," Le Monde, February 8, 2021.

24. Jeremy Singer-Vine, John Templon, Scott Pham, et al., "We Got Our Hands on Thousands of Secret Documents. Let's Break Them Down," BuzzFeed News, September 20, 2020.

25. "Offshore Havens and Hidden Riches of World Leaders and Billionaires Exposed in Unprecedented Leak," International Consortium of Investigative Journalists, October 3, 2021.

26. Disclaimer for "Offshore Leaks Database," International Consortium of Investigative Journalists.

27. Doug Henwood, "How the Rich Stay Rich: An Interview with Brooke Harrington," *Jacobin*, November 20, 2017.

28. "Offshore Trove Exposes Trump-Russia Links and Piggy Banks of the Wealthiest 1 Percent," International Consortium of Investigative Journalists, November 5, 2017.

29. Channing May, "Transnational Crime and the Developing World," Global Financial Integrity, March 2017, xi.

30. Steve Morgan, "Cybercrime to Cost the World $10.5 Trillion Annually by 2025," Cybersecurity Ventures, November 13, 2020.

31. "Deforestation and Forest Degradation," World Wildlife Fund.

32. Matt Sandy, "The Amazon Rain Forest Is Nearly Gone," *Time*, September 23, 2019, 76–77.

33. "Money to Burn," Global Witness, September 23, 2019.

34. Sandy, "Amazon Rain Forest," 75.

35. Channing May, "Transnational Crime and the Developing World," Global Financial Integrity, March 2017, 62, 64.

36. "IUU Fishing Index," Global Initiative against Transnational Organized Crime.

37. May, "Transnational Crime," 33.

38. George Wittemyer et al., "Illegal Killing for Ivory Drives Global Decline in African Elephants," *Proceedings of the National Academy of Sciences* 111, no. 36 (2014): 13119. See also "End Wildlife Trafficking: Recommendations for an EU Action Plan on Illegal Wildlife Trade," Born Free Foundation, April 2015, 3.

39. Global Financial Integrity, confidential report submitted to the Central Bank of Nigeria, December 2015.

40. Dana Priest and William M. Arkin, "Top Secret America Part 1: A Hidden World, Growing Beyond Control," *Washington Post*, July 19, 2010.

41. Opening statement of Senator Chuck Grassley, *Anti-Terrorism Financing: Progress Made and Challenges Ahead; Hearing Before the U.S. Senate Committee on Finance*, 110th Cong. 4 (2008).

42. Hardin Lang, Peter Juul, and Trevor Sutton, "Confronting the Terror Finance Challenge in Today's Middle East," Center for American Progress, November 2015, 6–7.

CHAPTER 4

1. Alice M. Rivlin, Allan Rivlin, and Sheri Rivlin, "To Unite a Divided Nation, We Must Tackle Both Vertical and Horizontal Inequality," Brookings Institution, November 5, 2019.

2. Francois Bourguignon, *The Globalization of Inequality*, trans. Thomas Scott-Railton (Princeton, NJ: Princeton University Press, 2015), 29.

3. Max Roser, Hannah Ritchie, and Esteban Ortiz-Ospina, "World Population Growth," OurWorldInData.org, 2020, https://ourworldindata.org/world-population-growth. Based on estimates by the History Database of the Global Environment and the United Nations.

4. Branko Milanovic, "True World Income Distribution, 1988 and 1993: First Calculation Based on Household Surveys Alone," World Bank Development Research Group, 1999; The World Bank Gini index (World Bank estimate); the University of Texas Inequality Project Estimated Household Income Inequality Data Set; and the United Nations University World Institute for Development Economics Research World Income Inequality Database.

5. World Inequality Database, "Top 10% Share," https://wid.world/.

6. World Inequality Database, "Top 1% Share," https://wid.world/.

7. Angus Deaton, "The Threat of Inequality," *Scientific American*, September 2016, 48.

8. Jean-Paul Sartre, *War Diaries: Notebooks from a Phoney War 1939–40* (New York: Verso: 2000), 85.

9. Thomas Piketty, *Capital in the Twenty-First Century* (Cambridge, MA: Harvard University Press, 2014), 32.

10. Piketty, 294, 264.

11. Lawrence Mishel and Jori Kandra, "CEO Pay Has Skyrocketed 1,322% Since 1965," Economic Policy Institute, August 10, 2021.

12. Lawrence Mishel and Jori Kandra, "CEO Compensation Surged 14% in 2019 to $21.3 Million," Economic Policy Institute, August 18, 2020.

13. International Labour Organization, "SDG Indicator 10.4.1—Labour Income Share as a Percent of GDP (%)," accessed February 3, 2022, https://ilostat.ilo.org/data.

14. Deborah Hargreaves, *Are Chief Executives Overpaid?* (Cambridge, UK: Polity, 2018), 127.

15. Raj Chetty, David Grusky, Maximilian Hell, Nathaniel Hendren, Robert Manduca, and Jimmy Narang, "The Fading American Dream: Trends in Absolute Income Mobility since 1940," *Science* 356, no. 6336 (April 2017): 400.

16. Chetty et al., "The Fading American Dream," 406.

17. Chetty et al., "The Fading American Dream," 404.

18. David Leonhardt, "The American Dream, Quantified at Last," *New York Times*, December 8, 2016.

19. *Global Wage Report 2018/19: What Lies behind Gender Pay Gaps?* (Geneva: International Labour Organization, 2018), xiv.

20. *Global Wage Report 2020–21: Wages and Minimum Wages in the Time of COVID-19* (Geneva: International Labour Organization, 2020), 34.

21. Lawrence Mishel, "Growing Inequalities, Reflecting Growing Employer Power, Have Generated a Productivity-Pay Gap Since 1979," Economic Policy Institute, September 2, 2021.

22. Carter C. Price and Kathryn Edwards, "Trends in Income from 1975 to 2018," Rand, working paper WR-A516-1, November 20, 2020, 1, 10, 11.

23. Nick Hanauer and David M. Rolf, "The Top 1% of Americans Have Taken $50 Trillion from the Bottom 90%—And That's Made the U.S. Less Secure," *Time*, September 14, 2020.

24. Emmanuel Saez and Gabriel Zucman, "The Rise of Income and Wealth Inequality in America: Evidence from Distributional Macroeconomic Accounts," *Journal of Economic Perspectives* 34, no. 4 (2020): 15.

25. Andrew Van Dam, "The Unluckiest Generation in U.S. History," *Washington Post*, June 7, 2020.

26. William G. Gale, Hilary Gelfond, Jason Fichtner, and Benjamin H. Harris, "The Wealth of Generations, with Special Attention to the Millennials," Brookings Economics Studies, working paper, May 2020, 10.

27. Stephanie Clegg, "The Nation's Income Inequality Challenge Explained in Charts," Just Taxes (blog), Institute on Taxation and Economic Policy, September 27, 2019.

28. Piketty, *Capital*, 244.

29. John Cassidy, "Piketty's Inequality Story in Six Charts," *New Yorker*, March 26, 2014.

30. Credit Suisse, Global Wealth Databook 2021.

31. Credit Suisse, Global Wealth Databooks 2019 and 2021.

32. Annette Alstadsæter, Niels Johannesen, and Gabriel Zucman, "Tax Evasion and Inequality," NBER working paper no. 23772, September 2017, https://www.nber.org/system/files/working_papers/w23772/w23772.pdf.

33. Alstadsæter, Johannesen, and Zucman, "Tax Evasion and Inequality."

34. "International Community Continues Making Progress against Offshore Tax Evasion," OECD, June 30, 2020.

35. Tax Justice Network, "Revealed: Global Super-Rich Has at Least $21 Trillion Hidden in Secret Tax Havens," press release, July 22, 2012.

36. Credit Suisse, Global Wealth Databook 2021.

37. Fight Inequality, "Open Letter: World Leaders Must Stop Fuelling Inequality," July 2019, https://www.fightinequality.org/world-leaders-must-stop-fuelling-inequality.

38. Gregory Clark, "The Surest Cure for Inequality," *Wall Street Journal*, January 20, 2017.

39. Peter S. Goodman, "Davos Elite Fret about Inequality over Vintage Wine and Canapés," *New York Times*, January 18, 2017.

40. Darren Walker, "The Coming of Hope: A Vision for Philanthropy in the New Year," Ford Foundation, January 9, 2019.

41. Paul Krugman, "What's the Matter with Trumpland?," *New York Times*, April 2, 2018.

42. Joseph E. Stiglitz, "A Rigged Economy," *Scientific American* 319, no. 5 (November 2018).

CHAPTER 5

1. Freedom House, "Freedom in the World Scores 2019," https://freedomhouse.org /report/freedom-world/2019/scores; and United Nations Development Programme, "Income Inequality, Gini Coefficient," https://hdr.undp.org/en/indicators/67106.

2. Freedom House, "Freedom in the World Scores 2019."

3. Sarah Repucci and Amy Slipowitz, "Freedom in the World Report 2021: Democracy under Siege," Freedom House, 2.

4. Repucci and Slipowitz, "Freedom in the World Report 2021," 6.

5. "Global Trends in Democracy: Background, U.S Policy, and Issues for Congress," Congressional Research Service, report R45344, October 17, 2018, 13.

6. Freedom House, "Freedom in the World Report 2019: Democracy in Retreat," 19, https://freedomhouse.org/sites/default/files/Feb2019_FH_FITW_2019_Report_ForWeb -compressed.pdf.

7. "Democracy Index 2020: In Sickness and in Health?," Economist Intelligence Unit, 2020, 9.

8. "Fragile States Index 2020," Fund for Peace, https://fragilestatesindex.org/country -data/.

9. Freedom House, https://freedomhouse.org/report/freedom-world; and the US Census Bureau, "Current Population Survey, 1968 to 2021 Annual Social and Economic Supplements (CPS ASEC)," table A-5. The year (x-axis) refers to the year for which data are collected, not when the reports were published.

10. Mark Muro and Sifan Liu, "Another Clinton-Trump Divide: High-Output America vs Low-Output America," Brookings Institution, November 29, 2016.

11. Mark Muro, Eli Byerly Duke, Yang You, and Robert Maxim, "Biden-Voting Counties Equal 70% of America's Economy. What Does This Mean for the Nation's Political-Economic Divide?," Brookings Institution, December 8, 2020.

12. "Public Trust in Government: 1958–2021," Pew Research Center, May 17, 2021, https:// www.pewresearch.org/politics/2021/05/17/public-trust-in-government-1958-2021/.

13. John Sides, Michael Tesler, and Lynn Vavreck, *Identity Crisis: The 2016 Presidential Campaign and the Battle for the Meaning of America* (Princeton, NJ: Princeton University Press, 2018), 7.

14. Ryan Cooper, "Why Did You Vote?," *The Nation*, August 26, 2019.

15. Lawrence H. Summers, "We No Longer Share a Common Lived Experience," *Washington Post*, October 9, 2019.

16. Karl Vick, "8 Questions," *Time*, June 14, 2019, 56.

17. Ronald W. Dworkin, "Driven to the Edge," *American Interest*, December 4, 2019.

18. Benjamin I. Page, Larry M. Bartels, and Jason Seawright, "Democracy and the Policy Preferences of Wealthy Americans," *Perspectives on Politics* 11, no. 1 (2013): 68.

19. Pope Francis, "Encyclical Letter Laudato Si' of the Holy Father Francis on Care for Our Common Home," The Vatican, May 24, 2015.

20. Attila Ágh, "The Long Road from Neoliberalism to Neopopulism in ECE: The Social Paradox of Neopopulism and Decline of the Left," *Baltic Journal of Political Science* 7–8, no. 1 (2018): 7.

21. Alf Gunvald Nilsen, "Social Movements and Global Capitalism: Popular Struggles North and South," discussion, Department of Law, University of Jaffna, Sri Lanka, January 23, 2017.

22. "Populism: The Phenomenon," Bridgewater Associates, March 22, 2017, 2.

23. Emilio Ocampo, "The Economic Analysis of Populism: A Selective Review of the Literature," Unversidad del CEMA, working paper, 2019.

24. Jeffrey Gedmin and Sean Keeley, "Arch Puddington: 'There's No Such Thing as Illiberal Democracy,'" American Interest, February 4, 2020.

25. Arch Puddington, "Surging Autocrats, Wavering Democrats," Atlantic Council, June 13, 2017.

26. Puddington, "Surging Autocrats, Wavering Democrats."

27. *Combating Kleptocracy with Incorporation Transparency: Hearing before the Commission on Security and Cooperation in Europe*, 115th Cong. (2017), statement by Charles Davidson, executive director, Kleptocracy Initiative, Hudson Institute.

28. Marc F. Plattner, "Illiberal Democracy and the Struggle on the Right," *Journal of Democracy* 30, no. 1 (January 2019): 10.

29. Richard Wike and Janell Fetterolf, "Global Public Opinion in an Era of Democratic Anxiety," Pew Research Center, December 7, 2021.

30. "The Global State of Democracy 2021: Building Resilience in a Pandemic Era," International Institute for Democracy and Electoral Assistance, iv, 3.

31. The desire to hide wealth without financial transparency or accountability produced the financial secrecy system. In other words, the motivation for secrecy produced the mechanisms to achieve it. Today, however, the mechanisms of secrecy can indeed propel the motivation for secrecy.

CHAPTER 6

1. Ross Delston quoted in Peter Stone, "How America Became the Money Laundering Capital of the World," *New Republic*, May 7, 2021.

2. "Don't Look, Won't Find: Weaknesses in the Supervision of the UK's Anti–Money Laundering Rules," Transparency International, 2015, 5.

3. "Basel AML Index 2021: 10th Public Edition; Ranking Money Laundering and Terrorist Financing Risks around the World," Basel Institute of Governance, 11.

4. "The Politics of AML—Socio-Political Considerations for Money Laundering Regulation," Trulioo, March 13, 2018.

5. *U.S. v. HSBC Private Bank (Suisse) SA*, no. 0:19-cr-60359-RKA, U.S. District Court, Southern District of Florida, deferred prosecution agreement filed December 10, 2019.

6. Gerold Grasshoff, Zubin Mogul, Thomas Pfuhler, Norbert Gittfried, Carsten Wiegand, Andreas Bohn, and Volker Vonhoff, "Global Risk 2017: Staying the Course in Banking," Boston Consulting Group, March 2, 2017.

7. Kirstin Ridley, "In FX Rigging—'If You Ain't Cheating, You Ain't Trying,'" Reuters, May 20, 2015.

8. "JPMorgan Pays $100M, Admits Fault in 'London Whale' Trades," CBS News, October 16, 2013.

9. U.S. Department of Justice, "JPMorgan Chase & Co. Agrees to Pay $920 Million in Connection with Schemes to Defraud Precious Metals and U.S. Treasuries Markets," press release no. 20-1018, September 29, 2020.

10. *U.S. District Court, District of Connecticut, U.S. v JPMorgan Chase & Co.* deferred prosecution agreement, September 29, 2020. See also Rob Lenihan, "JPMorgan to Pay $920 Million in Spoofing Case," Thestreet.com, September 29, 2020.

11. Katie Benner, "3 From JPMorgan Accused in Scheme to Game Precious Metals Market," *New York Times*, September 16, 2019.

12. European Securities and Markets Authority, "Final Report: On Cum/Ex, Cum/Cum and Withholding Tax Reclaim Schemes," report ESMA 70-155-10272, September 23, 2020, 21.

13. Alex Simpson, "The Robbery of the Century: The Cum-Ex Trading Scandal and Why It Matters," The Conversation, November 12, 2019.

14. U.S. House Committee on Financial Services, "The Case for Holding Megabanks Accountable: An Examination of Wells Fargo's Egregious Consumer Abuses," report prepared by the Democratic staff, 115th Congress, September 29, 2017, 5.

15. Bethany McLean, "How Wells Fargo's Cutthroat Corporate Culture Allegedly Drove Bankers to Fraud," *Vanity Fair*, Summer 2017.

16. Editorial, "The Wells Fargo Spillover Effect," *New York Times*, September 22, 2016.

17. Stacy Cowley, "At Wells Fargo, Complaints about Fraudulent Accounts since 2005," *New York Times*, October 11, 2016.

18. "Violation Tracker Parent Company Summary," Good Jobs First, n.d., accessed November 17, 2020, https://violationtracker.goodjobsfirst.org/parent/wells-fargo.

19. Wells Fargo Multistate Settle Agreement with Attorneys General, December 28, 2018.

20. Michael S. Gibson to John Stumpf, February 2, 2018.

21. McLean, "Wells Fargo's Cutthroat Corporate Culture."

22. Emily Flitter, Stacy Cowley, and David Enrich, "Wells Fargo C.E.O. Timothy Sloan Abruptly Steps Down," *New York Times*, March 28, 2019.

23. In the Matter of John Stumpf, former chairman and chief executive officer, Wells Fargo Bank N.S., no. 2020-004, U.S. Department of the Treasury, Office of the Comptroller of the Currency, consent order, January 22, 2020, 5, 6.

24. U.S. Department of Justice, U.S. Attorneys' Offices, Central District of California and Western District of North Carolina, deferred prosecution agreement with Wells Fargo, A-6, February 20, 2020.

25. U.S. House Committee on Financial Services, "The Real Wells Fargo: Board and Management Failures, Consumer Abuses, and Ineffective Regulatory Oversight," report prepared by the Majority Staff, 116th Congress, March 2020.

26. "Wells Fargo—A Timeline of Recent Consumer Protection and Corporate Governance Scandals," Congressional Research Service, report IF11129, February 27, 2020.

27. Frederic Spohr and Mathias Peer, "Deutsche Bank Exec Linked to Malaysia Fund Scandal," *Handelsblatt Today*, September 19, 2018.

28. Spohr and Peer, "Deutsche Bank Exec."

29. Ahmad Naqib Idris, "Special Report: Names Could Be Deceiving," The Edge Markets, August 23, 2018.

30. Roomy Khan, "Goldman Sachs an Unwitting Villain? 1MDB and Rogues: It Takes More Than One to Tango," *Forbes*, January 23, 2018.

31. David Crow, "Goldman Sachs's Lloyd Blankfein Met 1MDB's Jho Low in 2012," *Financial Times*, November 22, 2018.

32. "Malaysia Probing Audit Firms' Conduct in 1MDB Scandal," Reuters, January 27, 2019.

33. U.S. Department of Justice, "Former Justice Department Employee Pleads Guilty to Conspiracy to Deceive U.S. Banks about Millions of Dollars in Foreign Lobbying Funds," press release no. 18-1586, November 30, 2018.

34. Shamim Adam, Yudith Ho, and Cedric Sam, "How the 1MDB Scandal Led to Goldman's First Criminal Charges," Bloomberg, December 21, 2018.

35. Ben Chu, "Goldman Sachs Is Implicated in History's Largest Financial Con—But Will It Be Held Accountable?," *The Independent*, November 13, 2018.

36. *U.S. v. The Goldman Sachs Group, Inc.*, no. 20-437 (MKB), U.S. District Court, Eastern District of New York, deferred prosecution agreement filed on October 22, 2020.

37. Goldman Sachs, "Goldman Sachs' Statements Relating to 1MDB Government and Regulatory Settlements," press release, October 22, 2020.

38. Yantoultra Ngui, "JPMorgan, Deutsche Bank among Firms Sued by 1MDB over $23-bn Loss," Bloomberg, May 11, 2021.

39. "Malaysia's 1MDB, Former Unit File Suits to Recover $23 Bln," Associated Press, May 10, 2021.

40. "KPMG Denies Alleged Breaches, Negligence after Reported 1MDB Lawsuit," Reuters, July 9, 2021.

41. Privinvest.com.

42. *U.S. v. Jean Boustani, et al.*, no. 18-cr-00681-WFK, U.S. District Court, Eastern District of New York, indictment filed December 19, 2018, 12, 19, 20, 29.

43. "Independent Audit Related to Loans Contracted by ProIndicus S.A., EMATUM S.A. and Mozambique Asset Management S.A.," Kroll, report prepared for the Office of the Public Prosecutor of the Republic of Mozambique, June 23, 2017, 50.

44. "Independent Audit," Kroll, 47.

45. Harry Holmes, "Mozambique Charges 18 in 'Tuna Bonds' Scandal," Organized Crime and Corruption Reporting Project, January 9, 2019.

46. Joseph Cotterill, Laura Noonan, and Kadhim Shubber, "Ex-Credit Suisse Bankers Charged over $2bn Mozambique 'Tuna Bond' Scandal," *Financial Times*, January 3, 2019.

47. *U.S. v. Credit Suisse Group AG*, U.S. District Court, Eastern District of New York, deferred prosecution agreement filed October 19, 2021, 5–6.

48. Cate Reid, "Mozambique: The Anatomy of Corruption," Africa Report, June 26, 2018.

49. "Costs and Consequences of the Hidden Debt Scandal of Mozambique," Centro de Integridade Pública, May 2021, 6–7.

50. U.S. Department of Justice, "Israel's Largest Bank, Bank Hapoalim, Admits to Conspiring with U.S. Taxpayers to Hide Assets and Income in Offshore Accounts," press release no. 20-412, April 30, 2020. See also U.S. Department of Justice, Southern District of New York, deferred prosecution agreement for Bank Hapoalim, April 22, 2020.

CHAPTER 7

1. "Former Shell VP Indicted in Nigeria's OML 42 Scandal," Sweet Crude Reports, March 28, 2018.

2. Kelly Gilblom, "Shell Suspects Former Executive Committed Crime in Nigeria Deal," Bloomberg, March 28, 2018.

3. "Former Shell VP Indicted," Sweet Crude Reports.

4. "Shell Knew: Emails Show Senior Executives at UK's Biggest Company Knew It Was Party to a Vast Bribery Scheme," Global Witness, April 2017, 2.

5. "Shell Knew," Global Witness, 12.

6. "Shell Knew," Global Witness, 6–8, 11, 12, 14.

7. "Education," UNICEF, https://www.unicef.org/nigeria/education.

8. Will Fitzgibbon, "Paradise Papers Research Raises Questions over Glencore's $440m Congo Discount," International Consortium of Investigative Journalists, December 14, 2017.

9. Sherri Lee, "Case Study: Och-Ziff's African Bribery," Seven Pillars Institute, March 3, 2018.

10. Franz Wild, Vernon Silver, and William Clowes, "Trouble in the Congo: The Misadventures of Glencore," Bloomberg, November 16, 2018.

11. Uri Blau and Daniel Dolev, "Israeli Diamond Tycoons Mentioned in Leaked Panama Papers," *Haaretz* [Israel], April 6, 2016. See also "Dan Gertler," Wikipedia, https://en.wikipedia.org/wiki/Dan_Gertler.

12. Will Fitzgibbon, Oliver Zihlmann, Petra Blum, Edouard Perrin, Frederik Obermaier, and Bastian Obermayer, "Room of Secrets Reveals Mysteries of Global Commodity Giant," Organized Crime and Corruption Reporting Project, November 5, 2017.

13. *Jane Doe 1 et al v. Apple Inc. et al.*, no. 1:19-cv-03737, U.S. District Court for the District of Columbia, class complaint filed for injunctive relief and damages filed on December 16, 2019, 2, 60.

14. "Swiss Prosecutor Finds 300 Bank Accounts Linked to Petrobras Scandal," Reuters, March 18, 2015.

15. David Segal, "Petrobras Oil Scandal Leaves Brazilians Lamenting a Lost Dream," *New York Times*, August 7, 2015.

16. David Barstow, "Wal-Mart Hushed Up a Vast Mexican Bribery Case," *New York Times*, April 21, 2012.

17. Barstow, "Wal-Mart Hushed Up."

18. David Barstow and Alejandra Xanic von Bertrab, "How Wal-Mart Used Payoffs to Get Its Way in Mexico," *New York Times*, December 17, 2012.

19. Barstow, "Wal-Mart Hushed Up."

20. Barstow, "Wal-Mart Hushed Up."

21. Ben W. Heineman Jr., "Walmart's Massive Bribery Scandal: What Happens Now?" *Atlantic*, April 22, 2012.

22. Walmart, "Walmart Global Responsibility Report," 2011, 1, https://corporate .walmart.com/global-responsibility/global-responsibility-report-archive.

23. U.S. Department of Justice, "Walmart Inc. and Brazil-Based Subsidiary Agree to Pay $137 Million to Resolve Foreign Corrupt Practices Act Case," press release no. 19-691, June 20, 2019.

24. Securities and Exchange Commission, "Walmart Charted with FCPA Violations," press release 2019-102, June 20, 2019. See also U.S. District Court, Western District of Arkansas, Fayetteville Division, order and final judgment in re: *City of Pontiac General Employees' Retirement System v. Wal-Mart Stores, Inc. and Michael T. Duke*, case no. 5:12-cv-5162, filed April 8, 2019, 7.

25. U.S. District Court, Southern District of New York, decision on appeal in re: Purdue Pharma, L.P., filed December 16, 2021, 4.

26. U.S. District Court, Northern District of Ohio, Eastern Division, abatement order in re: National Prescription Opiate Litigation, case no. 1:17-md-2804, filed August 17, 2022, 6.

27. U.S. District Court, Northern District of Ohio, Eastern Division, abatement order in re: National Prescription Opiate Litigation, case no. 1:17-md-2804, filed August 17, 2022, 8.

28. Associated Press, "Judge Rules CVS, Walgreens, and Walmart Owe $650M in Opioids Suit," Statnews.com, August 17, 2022.

29. Jesse Eisinger and James Bandler, "Walmart Was Almost Charged Criminally over Opioids. Trump Appointees Killed the Indictment," ProPublica, March 25, 2020.

30. Eisinger and Bandler, "Walmart Was Almost Charged Criminally."

31. U.S. District Court for the Northern District of Illinois, Eastern Division, compliant for permanent injunction, monetary relief, civil penalties, and other relief in re: *Federal Trade Commission v. Walmart Inc.*, case no: 1:22-cv-3372, filed June 28, 2022, 26.

32. U.S. District Court for the Northern District of Illinois, Eastern Division, compliant for permanent injunction, monetary relief, civil penalties, and other relief in re: *Federal Trade Commission v. Walmart Inc.*, case no: 1:22-cv-3372, filed June 28, 2022, 5, 7.

33. Federal Trade Commission, "FTC Sues Walmart for Facilitating Money Transfer Fraud That Fleeced Customers Out of Hundreds of Millions," press release, June 28, 2022.

34. "Violation Tracker Current Parent Company Summary," Walmart statistics, Good Jobs First, n.d., accessed September 6, 2022, https://violationtracker.goodjobsfirst.org /?parent=walmart&order=pen_year&sort=.

35. Elise J. Bean, *Financial Exposure: Carl Levin's Senate Investigations into Finance and Tax Abuse* (New York: Palgrave Macmillan, 2018), 348.

36. Permanent Subcommittee on Investigations, "Offshore Profit Shifting and U.S. Tax Code—Part 2 (Apple Inc.)," memorandum, 113th Congress, May 21, 2013, 23.

37. *Offshore Profit Shifting and the U.S. Tax Code—Part 2 (Apple Inc.): Hearings before the Permanent Subcommittee on Investigations of the Committee on Homeland Security and Governmental Affairs*, 113th Congress 2 (2013) (opening statement of Senator Carl Levin).

38. European Commission, "State Aid: Ireland Gave Illegal Tax Benefits to Apple Worth up to €13 Billion," press release, August 30, 2016.

39. European Commission, "State Aid."

40. "Fact Sheet: Apple and Tax Avoidance," Institute on Taxation and Economic Policy, November 2017.

41. Theodore F. DiSalvo, "The Apple-Ireland Tax Case: Three Stories on Sovereign Power," *Duke Journal of Comparative & International Law* 28 (2018): 371–72.

42. Michael E. Miller, "How a Curmudgeonly Old Reporter Exposed the FIFA Scandal That Toppled Sepp Blatter," *Washington Post*, June 3, 2015.

43. U.S. Attorney's Office, Eastern District of New York, "Former Managing Director at Swiss Bank Pleads Guilty to Money Laundering Charge in Connection with Soccer Bribery Scheme," press release, June 15, 2017.

44. U.S. Attorney's Office, Eastern District of New York, "Former Managing Director at Swiss Bank Pleads Guilty."

45. John Miller, "Swiss Watchdog Raps Credit Suisse for Anti-Corruption Failings," Reuters, September 17, 2018.

46. Miller, "How a Curmudgeonly Old Reporter Exposed the FIFA Scandal."

CHAPTER 8

1. "Lowering the Bar: How American Lawyers Told Us How to Funnel Suspect Funds into the United States," Global Witness, January 2016, 1.

2. "Lowering the Bar," Global Witness, 6–10.

3. Neil Gluckman, "The US Lawyer Who Said, 'This Ain't for Me,'" iNews (Cayman), February 3, 2016.

4. *U.S. v. "The Wolf of Wall Street" Motion Picture*, no. 2:16-cv-05362, United States District Court for the Central District of California, verified complaint forfeiture filed July 20, 2016, 35–37, 90, 113, 116, 126–127.

5. Ben Seal, Brenda Sapino Jeffreys, Scott Flaherty, and Miriam Rozen, "The 2018 Dealmakers of the Year," *American Lawyer*, April 2018, 36.

6. Laura Smith, FBI Special Agent, affidavit in support of criminal complaint sworn before US magistrate judge M. Page Kelley, March 11, 2019, 22.

7. Smith, affidavit, 24.

8. Smith, affidavit, 28.

9. Kathryn Rubino, "Co-Chair of Biglaw Firm Charged in College Admissions Scandal," Above the Law, March 12, 2019, https://abovethelaw.com/2019/03/willkie-farr-chair-caught-in-college-admissions-scandal/.

10. Adam Leaver, Leonard Seabrooke, Saila Stausholm, and Duncan Wigan, "Auditing with Accountability: Shrinking the Spaces for Audit Failure," https://www.sheffield.ac.uk/polopoly_fs/1.884025!/file/Auditing-with-Accountability.pdf.

11. In re the Bear Stearns Companies, Inc. Securities, Derivative, and ERISA Litigation, document relates to Securities Action 08-Civ-2793 (RWS), master file no. 08 M.D.L. No. 1963 (RWS), United States District Court, Southern District of New York, consolidated class action complaint for violation of the federal securities laws filed February 27, 2009, 4.

12. *New York v. Ernst & Young LLP*, no. 451586/2010, New York Supreme Court, complaint filed December 21, 2010, 23.

13. In re Washington Mutual, Inc. Securities Litigation, no. 2:08-md-1919 MJP, United States District Court, Western District of Washington at Seattle, consolidated class action complaint filed August 5, 2008, 30.

14. Edvard Pettersson, "Washington Mutual Reaches $208.5 Million Class-Action Accord," Bloomberg, July 1, 2011.

15. Francine McKenna, "PwC Cashes in on AIG; Taxpayers Lose, Again," Medium, November 29, 2014.

16. David McAfee, "PwC to Pay $10.5M as Part of AIG Class Action Deal," Law360, September 12, 2014.

17. *MF Global Holdings LTD, as Plan Administrator v. PriceWaterhouseCoopers LLP*, no. 1:14-cv-02197-VM, United States District Court, Southern District of New York, complaint filed March 28, 2014, 1–2.

18. Michael Cohn, "PwC Settles MF Global Lawsuit for $65 Million," *Accounting Today*, April 20, 2015. See also Jonathan Stempel, "Corzine, Others Settle MF Global Lawsuit for $64.5 Million," Reuters, July 7, 2015.

19. Tammy Whitehouse, "PwC Reduces Damages in Colonial Bank Failure," *Compliance Week*, March 21, 2019.

20. Nate Raymond, "PwC Reaches Mid-Trial Deal in Lawsuit by Taylor Bean Trustee," Reuters, August 26, 2016.

21. Jonathan Stempel, "Deloitte to Pay $149.5 Million to U.S. over Failed Mortgage Lender," Reuters, February 28, 2018.

22. Austin Mitchell and Prem Sikka, *The Pin-Stripe Mafia: How Accountancy Firms Destroy Societies* (Essex, UK: Association for Accountancy and Business Affairs, 2011), 3, 9.

23. Economic Affairs Committee, "Bank Audits and the Financial Crisis," in *Auditors: Market Concentration and Their Role*, chap. 6 (London: The Stationery Office Limited, 2011).

24. U.S. Department of Justice, "Rolls-Royce Plc Agrees to Pay $170 Million Criminal Penalty to Resolve Foreign Corrupt Practices Act Case," press release no. 17-074, January 17, 2017. See also Kirstin Ridley, "British Accounting Watchdog Investigates KPMG over Rolls-Royce Audits," Reuters, May 4, 2017.

25. "Carillion: Second Joint Report from the Business, Energy and Industrial Strategy and Work and Pensions Committees of Session 2017–19," UK House of Commons, May 16, 2018, 5, 51, 53, 56, 68.

26. Emma Smith, "Auditors 'In the Dock' over Carillion as Report Calls for Big Four Break-up," *Accountancy Age*, May 16, 2018.

27. Madison Marriage, "MPs Turn Fire on KPMG and Deloitte Partners over Carillion," *Financial Times*, February 22, 2018.

28. Tabby Kinder, "PwC and EY Accused of Complicity in Thomas Cook Collapse," *Financial Times*, October 22, 2019.

29. Mark Taylor, "'Nothing Has Changed': Two Years on from Carillion Collapse," AccountingWEB, January 15, 2020.

CHAPTER 9

1. Richard Nixon, "How to Lose the Cold War," Richard Nixon Foundation, 1992, https://www.nixonfoundation.org/artifact/how-to-lose-the-cold-war/.

2. "The Reform of the Administration of the President of the Russian Federation," trans. Petr Podkopaev, Karen Dawisha and James Nealy, *Kommersant*, May 5, 2000, 3–4.

3. "The Structure of the Administration of the President of the Russian Federation," 3, 4, 5.

4. "Trade-Related Illicit Financial Flows 2009–2018," Global Financial Integrity, 2021, Table E.

5. Scott Johnson, "Capital Flight from Russia Carries $750 Billion Price Tag," Bloomberg, March 12, 2019.

6. Oliver Bullough, interview by Terry Gross, *Fresh Air*, NPR, May 1, 2019.

7. Filip Novokmet, Thomas Piketty, and Gabriel Zucman, "From Soviets to Oligarchs: Inequality and Property in Russia, 1905–2016," NBER, working paper no. 23712, August 2017, 22.

8. Anders Åslund, "Vladimir Putin Is Russia's Biggest Oligarch," *Washington Post*, June 5, 2019.

9. UK House of Commons Foreign Affairs Committee, "Moscow's Gold: Russian Corruption in the UK," 8th report of session 2017–2019, May 21, 2018, 7.

10. "Median Income by Country 2020," World Population Review.

11. John Herbst and Sergei Erofeev, "The Putin Exodus: The New Russian Brain Drain," Atlantic Council, February 2019, 41.

12. Anders Åslund, "The Illusions of Putin's Russia," Atlantic Council, May 6, 2019.

13. Marius Laurinavičius, "Weaponizing Kleptocracy: Putin's Hybrid Warfare," Hudson Institute, June 14, 2017, 27, 34.

14. Catherine Belton, *Putin's People: How the KGB Took Back Russia and Then Took On the West* (New York: Farrar, Straus and Giroux, 2020), 285.

15. Fatima Hussein, "U.S. Works to 'Seize and Freeze' Wealth of Russian Oligarchs," *Associated Press*, March 16, 2022.

16. Gordon Brown, "An International Anti-Corruption Court Would Bring Putin to Justice, *The Times* (UK), March 25, 2022.

17. "Trade-Related Illicit Financial Flows 2009–2018," Global Financial Integrity, Table E, 56.

18. Karl Russell and Keith Bradsher, "China's Exodus of Capital," *New York Times*, April 7, 2016.

19. Livia Yap and Ran Li, "China Quietly Revamps Tools for Controlling Capital Outflows," Bloomberg, May 31, 2019.

20. "Shadow Banker Exclusive: Leaked DEA, HSI, and FBI Report Exposes 'New Fusion' of Mexican Cartels Contracting Chinese Money Laundering Organizations in Chicago," Shadow Banker, August 2020.

21. Edward Wong, "New Communist Party Chief in China Denounces Corruption in Speech," *New York Times*, November 19, 2012.

22. "Charting China's 'Great Purge' under Xi," BBC, October 23, 2017.

23. Marina Walker Guevara, Gerard Ryle, Alexa Olesen, Mar Cabra, Michael Hudson, Christoph Giesen, Margot Williams, and David Donald, "Leaked Records Reveal Offshore Holdings of China's Elite," International Consortium of Investigative Journalists, January 21, 2014.

24. Peter Lorentzen and Xi Lu, "Personal Ties, Meritocracy, and China's Anti-Corruption Campaign," *SSRN*, November 21, 2018, 25, https://ssrn.com/abstract=2835841.

25. Cheng Li, "China's New Politburo and Politburo Standing Committee," Brookings Institution, October 26, 2017.

26. Charlie Campbell, "Why the Ex-Husband of a Missing Chinese Billionaire Is Risking All to Tell Their Story," *Time*, October 13, 2021, commenting on Desmond Shum's book *Red Roulette: An Insider's Story of Wealth Power, Corruption, and Vengeance in Today's China* (New York: Scribner, 2021).

27. Xiao Qiang, "The Road to Digital Unfreedom: President Xi's Surveillance State," *Journal of Democracy* 30, no. 1 (January 2019): 57.

28. Michael Pillsbury, *The Hundred-Year Marathon: China's Secret Strategy to Replace America as the Global Superpower* (New York: Henry Holt, 2015), 12.

29. "'Like We Were Enemies in a War': China's Mass Internment, Torture and Persecution of Muslims in Xinjiang," Amnesty International, ASA 17/4137/2021, 2021, 7. See also "The Uyghur Genocide: An Examination of China's Breaches of the 1948 Genocide Convention," Newlines Institute for Strategy and Policy, March 2021, 3.

30. Vicky Xiuzhong Xu, "Uyghurs for Sale," ASPI International Cyber Policy Centre, policy brief report no. 26/2020, 2020, 5.

31. "Full Text of Xi Jinping's Speech on the CCP's 100th Anniversary," Nikkei Asia, July 1, 2021.

32. Claudia Rosett, "China's Takedown of Hong Kong Is Part of a Strategy of World Domination," *Dallas Morning News*, December 27, 2020.

33. "New Report Exposes China's Malign Influence and Corrosion of Democracy Worldwide," International Republican Institute, June 27, 2019.

34. *Chinese Malign Influence and the Corrosion of Democracy: An Assessment of Chinese Interference in Thirteen Key Countries*, ed. David Shullman, International Republican Institute, 2019, 3.

35. U.S. Attorney's Office, Southern District of New York, "Manhattan U.S. Attorney Announces Extradition of Former President of Guatemala, Alfonso Portillo, on Money Laundering Charge," press release no. 13-190, May 28, 2013.

36. Steven Dudley, "The Zetas, Drug Money and the Colom Campaign in Guatemala," InSight Crime, August 9, 2018.

37. Arron Daugherty, "Guatemala's Big Corruption Scandal, Explained," InSight Crime, July 20, 2015.

38. Michael Lohmuller, "Guatemala's Government Corruption Scandals Explained," InSight Crime, June 21, 2016.

39. "An Attack on Corruption Sleuths in Guatemala Is Also Aimed at Judges," *The Economist*, January 10, 2019.

40. "Jimmy Morales's War on Guatemala's Graft Busters," *The Economist*, August 31, 2017.

41. "11ᵗʰ Annual Work Report of CICIG," International Commission against Impunity in Guatemala (CICIG), November 12, 2018.

42. "Hunger Hotspots: FAO-WFO Early Warnings on Acute Food Insecurity, March to July 2021 Outlook," World Food Programme and Food and Agriculture Organization, 2021, 16.

43. "Kingpins and Corruption: Targeting Transnational Organized Crime in the Americas," American Enterprise Institute, June 2017, 20.

44. Holly Yan, "$270 Million Worth of Cocaine Found on Air France Flight," CNN, September 24, 2013.

45. U.S. Attorney's Office, Eastern District of New York, "Former Top Leaders of Venezuela's Anti-Narcotics Agency Indicted for Trafficking Drugs to the United States," press release, August 1, 2016.

46. "Kingpins and Corruption," 21.

47. "Miami Media Says $800 Million in Assets of Diosdado Cabello Frozen in the US, but He Flatly Denies the Version," MercoPress, June 14, 2018. See also "Kingpins and Corruption," 22.

48. "Venezuelan President's Nephews Sentenced in New York to 18 Years in Jail for Drug Trafficking," Univision, December 14, 2017.

49. *U.S. v. Francisco Convit Guruceaga, et al.,* no. 18-cr-20685-KMW, U.S. District Court, Southern District of Florida, criminal complaint filed July 24, 2018, 15, 18.

50. Bram Ebus, "Militarization and Mining a Dangerous Mix in Venezuelan Amazon," Mongabay, December 7, 2017.

51. Cali Haan, "Bank of England Refusing to Hand Over Venezuela's Gold; Protestors in Toronto Denounce 'Interference' in Venezuela," Crowdfund Insider, January 27, 2019.

52. Associated Press, "US Sanctions Maduro's Stepsons for Alleged Food Corruption," Courthouse News Service, July 25, 2019.

53. Joshua Goodman, "As Venezuelans Go Hungry, Trump Targets Food Corruption," Associated Press, September 24, 2018. See also U.S. Department of the Treasury, "Treasury Disrupts Corruption Network Stealing from Venezuela's Food Distribution Program, CLAP," press release, July 25, 2019.

54. U.S. Department of Justice, "Former Swiss Bank Executive Pleads Guilty to Role in Billion-Dollar International Money Laundering Scheme Involving Funds Embezzled from Venezuelan State-Owned Oil Company," press release no. 18-1089, August 22, 2018.

55. *U.S. v. Francisco Convit Guruceaga, et al.,* 2–3.

56. Brianna Lee, "HSBC Leaks: Venezuela Had Third-Largest Amount of Money Stored in Swiss Banks, Report Says," International Business Times, February 10, 2015.

57. U.S. Department of Justice, "Venezuelan Billionaire News Network Owner, Former Venezuelan National Treasurer and Former Owner of Dominican Republic Bank Charged in Money Laundering Conspiracy Involving over $1 Billion in Bribes," press release no. 18-1527, November 20, 2018. See also Douglas Farah and Caitlyn Yates, "Maduro's Last Stand: Venezuela's Survival through the Bolivarian Joint Criminal Enterprise," IBI Consultants and the National Defense University, May 2019, 9.

58. François Pilet, "Venezuelan Ex-Minister Hoarded Money in Switzerland," SWI, December 12, 2018.

59. Jay Weaver, "Alejandro Andrade, Venezuela's Ex-National Treasurer, Likely to Be Released from U.S. Prison in Spring," *Miami Herald*, October 20, 2021.

60. "Condiciones de vida de los venezolanos: Entre emergencia humanitarian y pandemia," Universidad Católica Andrés Bello, September 2021.

61. Maurice O. Dassah, "Theoretical Analysis of State Capture and Its Manifestation as a Governance Problem in South Africa," *Journal for Transdisciplinary Research in Southern Africa* 14, no. 1 (2018): 2.

62. Anonymous interview by the author, 2017.

63. Open Secrets, *The Enablers: The Bankers, Accountants and Lawyers That Cashed In on State Capture*, February 2020, 65, https://www.opensecrets.org.za/wp-content/uploads /TheEnablers_web.pdf.

64. Zondo Commission, *Report of the Judicial Commission of Inquiry into State Capture: Part IV*, April 2022.

65. Rene Vollgraaff and Loni Prinsloo, "Eskom Calls for More Arrests After Ex-ABB Employees Apprehended," Bloomberg, July 13, 2022.

66. Reuters, "KPMG International Chairman Apologizes for South Africa Failings," September 19, 2017.

67. Leela Jacinto, "From India to 'Buying' South Africa: The Rise and Fall of the Guptas," France 24, February 15, 2018.

68. Lameez Omarjee, "State Capture: 4 Companies That Owe SA Millions," News24, September 10, 2018.

69. Associated Press, "Global Companies Snared in South Africa's Corruption Scandal," Mint, December 13, 2017.

70. "Bank of Baroda Played Key Role in SA's Gupta Scandal," Corruption Watch, March 1, 2018.

71. "State of Capture," Public Protector South Africa, report no. 6 of 2016/17, 89.

72. Jacinto, "From India to 'Buying' South Africa."

73. Karyn Maughan, "'We Are in Control of Everything,' Guptas Told Jonas," Sowetan Live, August 24, 2018.

74. Zondo Commission, *Report of the Judicial Commission of Inquiry into State Capture: Part 1; Vol. 1*," January 2022, 809.

75. Andrew Buncombe, "Burmese Generals Pocket $5bn from Total Oil Deal," *The Independent*, September 10, 2009. See also Saw Yan Naing, "Burma Govt Denies Reports That It Holds $11B in Singaporean Banks," Irrawaddy, September 13, 2013.

76. "Myanmar-China Pipelines," Hydrocarbons Technology.

77. "Jade: Myanmar's 'Big State Secret,'" Global Witness, October 23, 2015, 33.

78. "Methamphetamines from Myanmar Are Causing Problems across Asia," *The Economist*, December 15.

79. Vanda Felbab-Brown, "Myanmar Maneuvers: How to Break Political-Criminal Alliance in Contexts of Transition," United Nations University, Crime-Conflict Nexus Series no. 9, April 2017.

80. Marie Chêne, "Overview of Corruption in Burma (Myanmar)," Transparency International, updated October 1, 2012.

81. "Myanmar Opium Survey 2018: Cultivation, Production and Implications," United Nations Office on Drugs and Crime, 2018, 3–4.

82. Greg Constantine, "Between Burma and Bangladesh: Rohingya, a Stateless People," Pulitzer Center, April 18, 2012.

83. "Report of the Independent International Fact-Finding Mission on Myanmar," United Nations Human Rights Council, report A/HRC/39/64, September 12, 2018, 8. See also "Myanmar's Civilian, Military Leaders Meet, Vow to 'Crush' Rakhine Rebels," Reuters, January 7, 2019.

84. Hannah Ellis-Petersen, "Myanmar's Military Accused of Genocide in Damning UN Report," *The Guardian*, August 27, 2018.

85. "Report of the Independent International Fact-Finding Mission on Myanmar," United Nations Human Rights Council, report A/HRC/39/64, September 12, 2018, 1, 17.

86. Agence France Presse, "Canada, Netherlands to Formally Join Gambia ICJ Case Against Myanmar," *Barron's*, September 2, 2020.

87. Emanuele Ottolenghi, Saeed Ghasseminejad, Annie Fixler, and Amir Toumaj, "How the Nuclear Deal Enriches Iran's Revolutionary Guard Corps," Foundation for Defense of Democracies, October 2016, 7.

88. Adam Klasfeld, "In the Age of Trump, Judge Reflects on D'Souza and the 'New Rudy,'" Courthouse News Service, June 22, 2018.

89. Kenneth Katzman, "Iran Sanctions," Congressional Research Service, report RS 20871, updated April 22, 2019, 31, https://crsreports.congress.gov/product/pdf/RS/RS208 71/290.

90. Sirvan Ahmadi and Masoud Zahed, "Part I—Rostam Ghasemi: The Brigadier General of Sanctions Evasion," *Al Arabiya*, April 15, 2019.

91. United Nations Office on Drugs and Crime, *World Drug Report 2015* (New York: United Nations, 2015), 159.

92. US Attorney's Office, Southern District of California, "Wells Fargo Banker Pleads Guilty to Money Laundering Charges," press release no. CAS19-0516-Figueroa, May 16, 2019.

93. "Money-Laundering Methods of Drug Cartels and the Capture of El Chapo," Thomson Reuters, n.d., https://legal.thomsonreuters.com/en/insights/white-papers /money-laundering-methods-of-drug-cartels-and-the-capture-of-el-chapo.

94. Luis Gómez Romero, "The U.S.-Mexico Drug Trade Is Booming. Here Is Why," *National Interest,* July 21, 2019.

95. Eli Moskowitz, "Long Sought US Anti-Money Laundering Bill to Ban Anonymous Companies," Organized Crime and Corruption Reporting Project, January 5, 2021.

96. Oliver Bullough, *Moneyland: Why Thieves and Crooks Now Rule the World and How to Take It Back* (London: Profile Books, 2018), 245.

97. 18 U.S.C. § 1343 (2012).

98. *United States v. Pasquantino*, 336 F.3d 321 (4th Cir. 2003).

99. *United States v. Georgiou*, 777 F.3d 125 (3d Cir. 2015).

100. *United States v. Bengis*, 631 F.3d 33 (2d Cir. 2011).

101. Opinion of Justice Stevens, *Citizens United v. Federal Election Comm'n*, 558 U.S. 310 (2010).

102. Kent Greenfield, *Corporations Are People Too (And They Should Act Like It)* (New Haven, CT: Yale University Press, 2018), 23.

103. Lincoln Caplan, "A Workable Democracy," *Harvard Magazine*, March–April 2017.

104. Ellen L. Weintraub, "Taking On Citizens United," *New York Times*, March 30, 2016.

105. Steven Pearlstein, *Can American Capitalism Survive? Why Greed Is Not Good, Opportunity Is Not Equal, and Fairness Won't Make Us Poor* (New York: St. Martin's, 2018), 174–75.

106. Joseph Falcone, letter to the editor, *New York Times*, December 27, 2018.

107. *Hearings on the Disappearing Corporate Income Tax before the House Committee on Ways and Means*, 116th Cong. 1 (2020) (testimony of Chye-Ching Huang, Senior Director of Economic Policy, Center on Budget and Policy Priorities), February 11, 2020, 2, 4.

108. Calculations of IRS data, Center on Budget and Policy Priorities, https://www .cbpp.org/irs-enforcement-severely-depleted.

109. Natasha Sarin and Lawrence H. Summers, "Shrinking the Tax Gap: Approaches and Revenue Potential," NBER, working paper no. 26475, November 2019.

110. *The Financial Crisis Inquiry Report: Final Report of the National Commission on the Causes of the Financial and Economic Crisis in the United States* (Washington, DC: Financial Crisis Inquiry Commission, 2011), xix.

111. *Financial Crisis Inquiry Report*, xx.

112. *Financial Crisis Inquiry Report*, xx.

113. *The Financial Crisis Inquiry Report*, 32.

114. *Financial Crisis Inquiry Report*, xxii.

115. Gillian B. White and Bourree Lam, "Could Reviving a Defunct Banking Rule Prevent a Future Crisis?," *The Atlantic*, August 23, 2016.

116. White and Lam, "Could Reviving a Defunct Banking Rule."

117. Regis Barnichon, Christian Matthes, and Alexander Ziegenbein, "The Financial Crisis at 10: Will We Ever Recover?," Federal Reserve Bank of San Francisco, economic letter, August 13, 2018.

118. Jonathan Hopkin, *Anti-System Politics: The Crisis of Market Liberalism in Rich Democracies* (New York: Oxford University Press, 2020), 99.

119. Satish Thosar and Bradley Schwandt, "Has 'Too Big to Fail' Been Solved? A Longitudinal Analysis of Major U.S. Banks," *Journal of Risk and Financial Management* 12, no. 1 (February 2019): 3.

120. Noelle Straub, "Interior Probe Finds Fraternizing, Porn and Drugs at MMS Office in La.," *New York Times*, May 25, 2010.

121. Sheldon Whitehouse, "Sheldon Discusses Regulatory Capture in Response to the Gulf Oil Spill and the Financial Meltdown," press release, July 13, 2010.

122. Aircraft Certification Process Review and Reform Aviation Rulemaking Committee, "Recommendations on the Assessment of the Certification and Approval Process," report to the Federal Aviation Administration, May 22, 2012, xv, 12.

123. Natalie Kitroeff and David Gelles, "Before Deadly Crashes, Boeing Pushed for Law That Undercut Oversight," *New York Times*, January 6, 2020.

124. FAA Reauthorization Act 2018, Pub. L. 115-254 Sec. 202(c)(11) (2018).

125. U.S. House Committee on Transportation & Infrastructure, "The Design, Development & Certification of the Boeing 737 Max," final committee report prepared by the majority staff, September 2020, 19, 20, 25.

126. U.S. Department of Transportation Office of the Inspector General, "Timeline of Activities Leading to the Certification of the Boeing 737 MAX 8 Aircraft and Actions Taken after the October 2018 Lion Air Accident," report no. AV2020037, June 29, 2020, 15.

127. U.S. House Committee on Transportation & Infrastructure, "The Design, Development & Certification of the Boeing 737 Max," 11.

128. U.S. Department of Justice, "Boeing Charged with 737 Max Fraud Conspiracy and Agrees to Pay over $2.5 Billion," press release no. 21-17, January 7, 2021.

129. David Gelles, "Boeing's Saga of Capitalism Gone Awry," *New York Times*, November 29, 2020, 2.

130. Max de Haldevang, "Two Years into Trump's Tax Cut, the Results Are Not Promising," Quartz, December 22, 2019.

131. *Hearings on the Disappearing Corporate Income Tax Before the House Committee on Ways and Means*, 116th Cong. 2 (2020) (testimony of Rebecca M. Kysar, professor at Fordham University School of Law).

132. Peter Cary, "Republicans Passed Tax Cuts—Then Profited," Center of Public Integrity, January 24, 2020.

133. Rosa DeLauro, "We Must Repeal Trump's $135 Billion Hidden Tax Giveaway for Wealthy Real Estate Investors," *Fortune*, May 3, 2020.

134. Jessica Goodheart, "Two Years Later: What Has Trump's Tax Law Delivered?," Capital and Main, January 6, 2020.

135. Dylan Scott, "The GOP Tax Law's Lopsided Giveaway to Corporations, Explained in One Sentence," Vox, May 29, 2019.

136. Aimee Pichi, "The U.S. Tax System Is 'a New Engine of Inequality,'" CBS News, October 16, 2019.

137. Max de Haldevang, "Two Years into Trump's Tax Cut, the Results Are Not Promising," Quartz, December 22, 2019.

138. William R. Cline, "The New Tax Law's Impact on Inequality: Minor but Worse if Accompanied by Regressive Spending Cuts," Peterson Institute for International Economics, policy brief 18-3, February 2018, 2.

CHAPTER 10

1. Jason Mack, "U.S. National Statement at the High-Level Panel on International Financial Accountability, Transparency and Integrity for Achieving the 2030 Agenda," United States Mission to the United Nations, March 2, 2020.

2. Steven Friedman, "What the World Bank's Shift from Public to Private Funding Means for Development," The Conversation, July 9, 2017.

3. "About WTO," World Trade Organization, https://www.wto.org/english/thewto_e /thewto_e.htm.

4. "Technical Information on Customs Valuation," World Trade Organization, https:// www.wto.org/english/tratop_e/cusval_e/cusval_info_e.htm.

5. "G20 Leaders' Communique Hangzhou Summit," European Commission, September 6, 2016, https://ec.europa.eu/commission/presscorner/api/files/document/print/en/state ment_16_2967/STATEMENT_16_2967_EN.pdf.

6. World Customs Organization, *Illicit Financial Flows via Trade Mis-invoicing: Study Report 2018*, http://www.wcoomd.org/-/media/wco/public/global/pdf/media/newsroom/reports /2018/wco-study-report-on-iffs_tm.pdf?la=fr.

CHAPTER 12

1. Marieke de Goede and Mara Wesseling, "Secrecy and Security in Transatlantic Terrorism Finance Tracking," *Journal of European Integration* 39, no. 3 (2017): 257.

CHAPTER 13

1. Søren Kierkegaard, *Papers and Journals: A Selection,* tr. Alastair Hannay (New York: Penguin, 1996), 293.

2. George Packer, "We Are Living in a Failed State," *The Atlantic,* June 2020.

3. Jonathan Rothwell and Hannah Van Drie, "The Effect of COVID-19 and Disease Suppression Policies on Labor Markets: A Preliminary Analysis of the Data," Brookings Institution, April 27, 2020.

4. "The Market v the Real Economy," *The Economist,* May 9, 2020, https://www .economist.com/leaders/2020/05/07/the-market-v-the-real-economy.

5. "The RIC Report: The Gaps of Wrath," BofA Global Research, May 12, 2020, 1.

6. US Employment and Training Administration, Initial Claims, retrieved from FRED, Federal Reserve Bank of St. Louis, April 7, 2022, https://fred.stlouisfed.org/series /ICSA, and S&P Dow Jones Indices LLC, S&P 500, retrieved from FRED, Federal Reserve Bank of St. Louis, April 6, 2022, https://fred.stlouisfed.org/series/SP500. BofA Research, "The RIC Report: The Gaps of Wrath," May 12, 2020.

7. Frank Vogl, "March 23, 2020: The Day the US Economy Did Not Crash," The Globalist, May 14, 2020.

8. Lawrence H. Summers, "It's Time for the Fed to Rethink Quantitative Easing," *Washington Post*, August 26, 2021.

9. Chuck Collins, "Updates: Billionaire Wealth, U.S. Job Losses and Pandemic Profiteers," Inequallity.org, October 18, 2021.

10. Davide Furceri, Prakash Loungani, and Jonathan D. Ostry, "How Pandemics Leave the Poor Even Farther Behind," IMF Blog, May 11, 2020.

11. Susan E. Rice, "Take the Next Step toward Racial Justice," *New York Times,* July 21, 2020.

12. Robert J. Samuelson, "This Crisis Is about Democracy Itself," *Washington Post*, March 22, 2020.

13. Darren Walker, "Are You Willing to Give Up Your Privilege?," *New York Times,* June 25, 2020.

14. "Secretary-General's Nelson Mandela Lecture: 'Tackling the Inequality Pandemic: A New Social Contract for a New Era,'" United Nations, July 18, 2020, https://www.un.org/sg /en/content/sg/statement/2020-07-18/secretary-generals-nelson-mandela-lecture-%E2%

80%9Ctackling-the-inequality-pandemic-new-social-contract-for-new-era%E2%80%9D
-delivered.

CHAPTER 14

1. Business Roundtable, "Business Roundtable Redefines the Purpose of a Corporation to Promote 'An Economy That Serves All Americans,'" press release, August 19, 2019.
2. Mark Carney, "Remarks at the Banking Standards Board Panel 'Worthy of Trust?
Law, Ethics and Culture in Banking,'" speech, Bank of England, London, March 21, 2017.
See also Mark Carney, "Turning Back the Tide," speech, FICC Market Standard Board,
London, November 29, 2017.
3. Pope Francis, "Encyclical Letter Fratelli Tutti: On Fraternity and Social Friendship,"
October 3, 2020.
4. "Impose a Tax on Financial Transactions," Congressional Budget Office, December 9, 2020, https://www.cbo.gov/budget-options/56876.
5. "Tax Carried Interest as Ordinary Income," Congressional Budget Office, December 13, 2018, https://www.cbo.gov/budget-options/2018/54795.
6. Matthew Collin, "Dirty Money in Offshore Banks," Brookings Institution, Brookings
Cafeteria podcast transcript, July 2, 2021, 14–15.
7. I recommend an influential thinker to serve on such a commission, Dr. Rashawn Ray,
professor of sociology at the University of Maryland and a David M. Rubenstein Fellow at
the Brookings Institution.
8. Martin Luther King, Jr., "Beyond Vietnam: A Time to Break Silence," speech, Clergy
and Laity Concerned, Riverside Church, New York, April 4, 1967.

CONCLUSION

1. Stanford Encyclopedia of Philosophy, "Heraclitus," https://plato.stanford.edu
/entries/heraclitus/#Kno.
2. Michael Novak, "Who Are the Neoconservatives? A Conversation with Michael Novak," *Crisis Magazine*, March 1, 2007.
3. Edmund Husserl, "Philosophy and the Crisis of European Man," lecture, Vienna,
May 10, 1935.

Acknowledgments

I am obligated to many people who have influenced me over the years since my first book was published in 2005, and I will thank each of them personally. Here, I offer my appreciation to those who worked with me specifically on this book.

Jennifer Nordin has again contributed her extraordinary language skills, mathematical aptitude, and attention to detail, making this a far better work. I simply could not have executed this effort without her.

A team of interns worked with us: Chris Raslavich, Eric Ward, Nicole Calvario, Takhmina Nasimova, John Fuller, Shreya Walia, Jiaqi Feng, R. Daniel Jones, and Hanchen Zheng, and to each I express my great appreciation.

Within the Global Financial Integrity team, Tom Cardamone offered outstanding advice and comment. Also helpful have been Dev Kar, Rick Rowden, Joe Spanjers, and two previous GFI colleagues, Heather Lowe and Clark Gascoigne.

Others who read the manuscript and offered broad commentary and detailed suggestions are Huguette Labelle, William Gale, Arvinn Gadgil, Françoise Valérian, John Cassara, Harald Tolan, Olav Lundstøl, John Stremlau, and Steve Young.

Considerable thanks go to Larry Diamond for his generous foreword and indeed for his decades of contributions toward making the world a better place.

T. M. Hawley provided absolutely superb editorial advice.

At Berrett-Koehler, Steve Piersanti immediately grasped what I was saying and added his considerable experience guiding publication of this book. Jeevan Sivasubramaniam ably made it all come together.

My wife Pauline has shaped my thinking more than anyone. My greatest thanks are owed to her.

Index

Note: Page numbers followed by *f* indicate a figure on the designated page.

ABN AMRO, 97, 107
abolition movements, 254
American dream, fading of, 63–66
American International Group (AIG), misstating of accounts, 135
Apple Inc., tax-avoidance strategy, 123–125
arms/weapons trade, Islamic Revolutionary Guards Corps (IRGC), 167–168
auditors, 133–139
Austria, 73, 76, 97
authoritarianism, 83–86, 152, 206, 209, 248, 252

Bair, Sheila, 183
Bank Hapoalim, 107–108
Bank of America, 35, 92, 93, 94, 212
banks/banking sector, 20–21, 35, 44–45, 79, 89–109, 181–182, 214, 222
Banks Secrecy Act (1970) (U.S.), 90
Bartels, Larry, 81
Belton, Catherine, 145
"Bermuda black hole" scheme, 16
Biden, Joe, 22, 216, 217
Blatter, Joseph "Sepp," 126
Bloomberg Economics, 31, 143–144
BNP Paribas scandal, 97
Borisovich, Roman, 144
Bourguignon, François, 53
Brazil, 126, 138–139
Bretton Woods agreement, 250–251
bribery, participating countries, 100, 104, 112, 153–154, 200
British Virgin Islands, 11–13
broad money, 27–34
Brookings Institution (Washington, D.C.), 52, 66, 77, 78f, 100, 190, 241
Brown, Gordon, 146
Buffet, Warren, 33
Bullough, Oliver, 143, 175

Canada, 39, 76f, 165, 176
"Capital Allowances for Intangible Assets" (CAIA) scheme, 17–18
capitalism: contributions to economic divisions, 52; fundamental forces of, 25; growing conflict with/undermining of democracy, 3–7, 72, 82, 84, 140, 152, 208; growth of secrecy motivation, 5; impact on income inequality, 55; law enforcement's failure to curtail, 209; modern-day motivations for, 206; need for repurposing of, 73; rogue capitalism, 7, 26; role in invisibly sheltering wealth, 1, 2. *See also* democratic-capitalist system; financial secrecy system
Capitalism's Achilles Heel (Baker), 2–3
Capital without Borders: Wealth Management and the One Percent (Harrington), 43
Caplan, Gordon, 131–133
Carney, Mark, 234
Cayman Islands, 11–13, 157
"cell" companies, 13, 223–224
Central Intelligence Agency (U.S.), 45, 200
Chang, Manuel, 104–105
Chavez, Hugo, 156–158
Chetty, Raj, 63
China, 11, 20, 24, 39, 44, 47, 53, 57–58, 57f, 147–152, 197
Chinese Communist Judicial Prosecution Committee, 174
CICIG. *See* United Nations (UN) Comission Internacional contra la Impunidad en Guatemala (CICIG), anti-impunity body
Citibank, 49, 91, 180, 184
Citigroup, 93–94
Citizens United v. Federal Election Commission (2010) (U.S.), 177–179, 245
Ciudad del Este, free trade zones/special economic zones, 20

civil liberties, 6, 75

climate change, 1, 3, 7, 192, 242, 251–252

Cline, William, 190–191

Collin, Matthew, 241

Commodity Futures Modernization Act (2000), 180

Commodity Futures Trading Commission (CFTC) (U.S.), 95, 184

Commonwealth Bank of Australia, 107

Communications Act (1934) (U.S.), 176

Congressional Budget Office (U.S.), 52, 239

Congressional Research Service, 76, 100

Consumer Protection Act (2010) (U.S.), 93, 184

Control of Corruption Index (World Bank), 37

Cooper, Ryan, 79

Coronavirus Aid, Relief and Economic Security (CARES) Act, 211–212, 214

corporations, 12–13, 109–127. *See also* multinational corporations

corruption, 1, 37–43, 68, 72, 110–113, 163–164

Corruption Perception Index (Transparency International), 37

Corzine, John, 135–136

counterfeiting, 44, 167, 209, 230

COVID-19 (Coronavirus) pandemic, 28, 117–118, 151, 211–212, 214–216, 242–244

Credit Suisse, 92, 93, 97; Mozambique, financial corruption, 103–106, 126, 127, 158

Credit Suisse/Mozambique, financial corruption, 103–106

crime, 43–49; counterfeiting, 44, 167, 209, 230; human trafficking, 1, 21, 28–29, 44, 45, 207, 209; illegal logging, 44, 46, 164–165, 209; organ trade, 47; plundering of resources, 48–49; promotion of by financial secrecy, 6; unregulated fishing, 46–47; wildlife poaching/trafficking, 1, 44, 47, 164–165

cryptocurrencies, 34–36, 230–231

Cum-Ex scam, 96–97

Currency Transaction Reports (CTR), 90, 170

Danske Bank, 106

dark money, 178, 245

Deaton, Angus, 56

Deloitte, 41, 102–103, 133f, 134–138

Delta Land and Investment Co., Ltd. v. Todd, 10–11

democracy: conflict with capitalism, 3–7, 4, 5–7, 72, 82, 84, 140, 152, 205–206; Freedom House measures of, 73, 74f, 75f; global decline of, 7, 73–78; strategies for survival of, 219–220

democratic-capitalist system, 1–7, 81–86, 205–210, 206, 252; role of corporations in restoring integrity, 223–232; role of economic equality in restoring integrity, 242–244; role of financial institutions in restoring integrity, 232–234, 232–235; role of international institutions in restoring integrity, 247–251; role of taxes in restoring integrity, 237–242; role of the U.S. in restoring integrity, 244–247; traits of character required for renewal of, 254–256

democratic socialism, 83–85, 152

Denmark, 73, 76, 97

derivatives, 21, 33–36, 102, 180–181, 182, 214, 233

Deutsche Bank, 42, 46, 92–96, 101, 103, 106

Diamond, Larry ("Mr. Democracy"), 81

dirty money, 2, 39, 48–51, 89, 90, 108, 170, 221–222, 227, 233, 234

disguised corporations, 12–13, 58, 169, 223–224

Disney, 41

DLA Piper, 131

Dodd-Frank Wall Street Reform, 93, 95, 184

Drug Enforcement Administration (DEA) (U.S.), 45, 121, 170–172

drugs/drug trafficking: in Guatemala, 153–155; in Iran, 167; in Myanmar, 164–165; in the United States, 50, 171; in Venezuela, 156

Dworkin, Ronald, 81

East Asia, declining poverty levels, 53

EB-5 employment creation visa program, 173–174, 246

Economic Policy Institute (EPI) (Washington, D.C.), 61, 65

Economist Intelligence Unit, 76

employment: abuses related to, 14; impact of COVID-19 pandemic, 28; issuance of employment visas to foreigners, 173–174; post–World War II data, 5; unemployment and underemployment, 32–33, 212, 213f

England, 38, 136, 157, 254

Enron, bankruptcy, 134

Eskon, 161
EY, 41, 102, 133f, 134, 136–138

Falcone, Joseph, 179
False Claims Act (U.S.), 176
FBI (Federal Bureau of Investigation), 39–40, 126, 131–132
Federal Reserve Board, 30f, 52, 67f, 239; impact of repeal of Glass-Steagall Act, 180–181; protection of derivatives, 214; requirement of bank stress tests, 222; response to COVID-19 pandemic, 213–214
Federal Trade Commission, 122
FIFA (Fédération Internationale de Football Association), money laundering, 126–127
Fight Inequality, 71
Financial Action Task Force (FATF), anti-money laundering watchdogs, 20, 90, 196, 250
Financial Crimes Enforcement Network (FinCEN), 40, 42, 90, 172, 233
Financial Crisis Inquiry Commission (U.S.), 181–182, 182f
Financial Secrecy Index, 12
financial secrecy system, 9–27; anonymous trust accounts, 13; black holes, sandwiches, malts, 16–18; China, hawala system/flying money (fei chien), 24; development/ components of, 21–26, 23f; disguised corporations, 12–13; enablers of, 128–139; fake foundations, falsified trades, 14; goal of, 9–10; government complicity, 140–191; impact on income inequality, 6, 58–66, 72; strategies and methods, 19–20, 209–210, 221–252; tax havens/ secrecy jurisdictions, 10–12; trade misinvoicing, 18–19, 58
Financial Services Modernization Act (1999) (U.S.), 180
Financial Stability Oversight Council (U.S.), 185
First Indochina War, 11
Florida, servicing of corrupt, criminal money, 39–40
food banks, 28, 212
Foreign Account Tax Compliance Act (FATCA) (U.S.), 222, 234
Foreign Corrupt Practices Act (FCPA) (U.S.), 38, 117
forex, manipulation of foreign currency rates, 94–95
Fragile States Index (Fund for Peace), 77

France, 73, 76, 91, 97, 254
Freedom House, measures of global democracy, 73, 74f, 75f, 76f
"Freedom in the World" measures (Freedom House), 73

Gale, William, 66, 189–190, 190
Gelles, David, 189
gender discrimination, 1
Germany, 38–39, 57f, 73, 76, 91, 97, 126
Giuliani, Rudy, 112, 168
Glass-Steagall Act (U.S.), repeal of, 180–183
Glencore, illicit business dealings, 112–114
Global Financial Integrity, 40
global pandemic. See COVID-19 (Coronavirus) pandemic
Global Wage Report 2018/19, 64
Global Wealth Report 2021 (Credit Suisse), 68
Global Witness (NGO), 128
gold, 31, 34
golden visas, 148, 170, 173–175, 246
Goldman Sachs, 92; 1MDB scandal, 94–95, 100–103
Gorbachev, Mikhail, 142
Gorman, Amanda, 217–218
Grassley, Senator Charles (Chuck), 49, 51
Great Recession (2007–2008), 213–214, 230, 232, 246; description, 79, 92–93, 183–185; impact of Glass-Steagall repeal, 180; impact on incomes, 243; impact on regulatory oversight, 183; impact on student debt, 243; impact on wages, 66; shadow banking system and, 181–182; subprime mortgage crisis and, 92
Green, Pincus, 112–114
Greenberg Traurig, 131
Guatemala, 116, 153–158
Gurria, José Ángel, 196
Guterres, António, 218–219
Guzmán, Joaquín Archivaldo ("El Chapo"), 172

Hargreaves, Deborah, 62
Harrington, Brook, 43
Harris, Kamala, 22, 216, 217
Henry, James, 68–69, 196
Heraclitus, 253
Hong Kong, tax haven services, 11
Hudson Institute, 145, 152
Human Development Index (UNDP), 73

human trafficking, 1, 21, 28–29, 44, 45, 164, 207, 209
Husserl, Edmund, 256

IDEA's Global State of Democracy report, 85–86
Identity Crisis: The 2016 Presidential Campaign and the Battle for the Meaning of America (Sides, Tesler, Vavreck), 78–79
identity politics, 78–80
illegal logging, 44, 46, 164–165, 209
illiberalism, 81–83, 85, 152
illicit financial flows (IFFs): countries committed to dealing with, 2, 192–193; global conference on, 197; global estimates of, 28–29; role of the IMF in dealing with, 195–196, 198; role of the WCO in dealing with, 197–198; role of the World Bank in dealing with, 193–195, 198; role of the WTO in dealing with, 197; UN's embrace of dealing with, 192
Illicit Financial Flows via Trade Misinvoicing (IFFs/TM), 197–198
Immigration Act (1990) (U.S.), 173
income inequality, 7, 52–58, 56f, 63–66, 73–75; impact of COVID-19 pandemic, 211–212; impact of financial deregulation on, 55; impact of population growth, capitalism on, 55, 55f; impact of technology on, 55; impact of wealthy countries, 60–62; impact on democracy, 1; impact on financial secrecy, 6; Krugman's comment on, 71; trade misinvoicing and, 18–19, 58, 59f; World Inequality Index data, 56, 57f. *See also* wealth inequality
India, 31, 44, 57–58, 57f
ING, 97, 107
Internal Revenue Service (IRS), 175, 179–180
International Consortium of Investigative Journalists, 41
International Monetary Fund (IMF): estimates on global corruption, 37–38; estimates on money laundering, 90; role in dealing with illicit financial flows, 195–196, 198
International Republican Institute, 152
Iran/Islamic Revolutionary Guards Corps (IRGC), 166–169
Ireland, 12, 13, 123
Italy, increasing inequalities, falling freedoms in, 73, 76

January 6, 2021, attempted coup, U.S., 3, 216–217
Japan, 57f, 76f, 93, 184
Jennings, Andrew, 126, 127
Joint Comprehensive Plan of Action (JCPOA) (U.S.-Iran), 169
JPMorgan Chase, 42, 49, 92, 93, 94, 95, 96, 103, 111

Keynes, John Maynard, 34
Kierkegaard, Søren, 211
King, Martin Luther, Jr., 244
KPMG, 41, 103, 133f, 136–138, 161
Krugman, Paul, 22, 71
Kumar, Lakshmi, 40

lawyers: leaking of documents, 41; Malaysia, Goldman Sachs, 1MDB scandal, 100–103, 130–131; money laundering and, 40; opacity of pooled accounts of, 20; questioning of Apple's lawyers, 123; role in enabling financial secrecy, 4, 10, 22, 128–133; role in manipulation of tax laws, 12, 19, 96; "Varsity Blues" college admission scam, 131–132
Lazarus, Emma, 174
Lehman Brothers, 92, 134, 136, 183
Leissner, Timothy, 100–102. *See also* Goldman Sachs, 1MDB scandal
Le Monde, 41
LIBOR, London interbank offered rate, 93
Liechtenstein, fake foundation in, 14
liquid assets, 27–28
"London Whale" scandal, 95
Low, Jho, 101–102. *See also* Goldman Sachs, 1MDB scandal
Luxembourg, tax haven services, 11

Maduro, Nicholas, 156–159
Malaysia, 100–103, 130–131, 138–139
Malta, tax haven services, 11
Mandela, Nelson, 48, 159–160, 218
Marx, Karl, 211
Mauritius, tax haven services, 11
McCutcheon v. Federal Election Commission (2014) (U.S.), 178
Mexico, cigarette counterfeiting, 44
MF Global, 135
Mikuriya, Kunio, 197
Minerals Management Service (MMS), 185–186
Moneyland (Bullough), 175

money laundering, 20–21; anti-money
laundering (AML) laws, efforts, 18, 20, 49,
89–90; by banks, 89; by bearer share
companies, 13; in Canada, 39; in China,
148; by Citibank and Riggs National
Bank, 91; of cryptocurrencies, 34; drugs/
drug trafficking and, 171; failures at
halting, 25; fights against, 1; in Germany,
38–39; global anti-laundering efforts, 91;
in Guatemala, 153–155, 158; by halawa
dealers, 24; by HSBC, 91–92; illicit drug
trade and, 20–21; IMF global data, 90; by
the IRGC of Iraq, 168; by multinational
corporations, 87; by Odebrecht/Operação
Lava Jato, 114–118; in real estate, 38–40;
terrorism and, 49–50; in Turkey, 85; in the
U.S., 39–40, 85
multinational corporations: booking of profits
through tax havens, 29–30; impact of
financial secrecy on, 2; manipulations of
taxes by, 18–19; post–World War II growth
of, 9; trade misinvoicing by, 14–15; use of
falsified trades, 15
Myanmar, 162–166; amassing of wealth
for military personnel, 163, 164; drug
trafficking in, 164–165; The Gambia's
complaint against, 165; gem trade/jade
exports-related corruption, tax evasion,
money laundering, 163–164; genocide
against the Muslim Rohingyas, 165;
human/wildlife trafficking, 164; illegal
logging in, 164; military/Tatmadaw
"leadership of the state," 162–163, 165–166;
Yadana Gas Project, 163

narrow money: defined/types of, 27; global
savings glut and, 32; inclusion as broad
money, 28
National Bureau of Economic Research, 143,
180
NatWest, 106
Ndikumana, Léonce, 60
neoliberalism, 82–83, 206
Netherlands, 12, 38, 91
New Jersey, fake mutual funds scheme, 157
New York, real estate-related corruption, 40
New York Times, 71
Nigeria/Shell Oil, bribery and corruption,
110–112
Nixon, Richard, 141
nonfungible tokens (NFTs), 35

Norway, global share of income, 57f
Novak, Michael, 254

Obama, Barack, 169, 218
Ocasio-Cortez, Alexandria, 213
Odebrecht/Operação Lava Jato (Operation
Car Wash), 116–117
OECD. See Organisation of Economic
Co-operation and Development
Office of Foreign Assets Control (U.S.
Treasury Department), 97
Offshore Leaks Database (ICIJ), 43
1Malaysia Development Berhad (1IMDB),
100–1003, 130–131. See also Goldman
Sachs, 1MDB scandal
On Nature (Heraclitus), 253
Orbán, Viktor, 85
Organisation of Economic Co-operation
and Development (OECD), 68–69, 90,
195, 249

Packer, George, 212
Page, Benjamin, 81
Panama, 11, 12, 14, 20
Panama Papers (ICIJ), 42, 68
Panel on International Financial
Accountability, Transparency, and
Integrity, 193
Paradise Papers (ICIJ), 42
Pearlstein, Steven, 178
Pearse, Andrew, 104–105
Pelosi, Nancy, 216
Pence, Mike, 216
Pew Research Center, 77, 85
Philippines, cigarette counterfeiting, 44
Piketty, Thomas, 60–61, 67
Pogge, Thomas, 54
Pope Francis, 81, 234
populism/populists, 81–83, 156
poverty, 52–54; in Brazil, 117; deaths due to,
54, 54f; global decline of, 52–53; impact
of COVID-19 pandemic, 215; impact
of financial secrecy on, 58, 200; in
Mozambique, 106; multidimensional
definitions of, 53; in Nigeria, 112, 197;
organizational fights against, 1; in
Venezuela, 59, 159; World Bank report
(2018) findings, 53
PriceWaterhouseCoopers (PwC), 41, 102, 133f,
135–138
Privinvest Group, 103–105

Puddington, Arch, 83–84
Puerto Rico, fake mutual funds scheme, 157
Putin, Vladimir: accusation of kleptocracy
  against, 145; Belton's comment on, 145;
  Hudson Institute's accusation of kleptocracy
  against, 145; launch of attack on Ukraine,
  141, 145–147, 159, 201; rise to power/robbery
  of Russian assets, 141–147; robbery of assets
  within Russia, 141
Putin's People (Belton), 145

Qualified Intermediary (QI) Program, 175

Rabobank, 93, 107
Racketeer Influenced and Corrupt Organ-
  izations Act, 96
Rand Corporation, 65
ransomware attacks, 34, 48
real estate corruption, 38–41
Reeves, Rachel, 137–138
Reich, Robert, 182–183
Rice, Susan, 218
Rich, Marc, 112–114
Rivlin, Alice, 52
Rosenstein, Rod, 121–122
Rossett, Claudia, 152
Rubin, Robert, 175, 180
Russia, 141–147; abdication of wealthy
  oligarchs from, 142–143; authoritarianism
  in, 144; Borisovich's comment on
  plundering, 144; description of methods
  of robbery, 143; fictitious trade pricing
  practices, 143; illegal logging in, 46; illicit
  banking practices, 106–107; impact of war
  with Ukraine, 145; income comparison
  with ex-communist neighbors, 144;
  plundering of resources, 48; Putin's
  rise to power/robbery of assets, 141–145;
  U.S. launch of REPO Task Force/
  KleptoCapture, 146. *See also* Putin,
  Vladimir
Russian Elites, Proxies and Oligarchs
  (REPO) Task Force (U.S. Treasury
  Department), 146

Saez, Emmanuel, 66
Samuelson, Robert, 218
Sarbanes-Oxley legislation (2002), 133–134,
  222
Sartre, Jean-Paul, 60

Saul, Stephanie, 40
Scandinavian countries, 68, 83, 254
Seawright, Jason, 81
Securities and Exchange Commission (SEC):
  claims against Glencore, 113; claims
  against Odebrecht, 117; self-funding by,
  246; warnings to Bear Stearns, 134
"segregated portfolio" companies, 13
September 11, 2001 attack, 49, 77, 90
shadow banking/financial system, 181–182,
  182f, 199, 214
Shearman & Sterling, 130–131
"shelf" companies, 13, 223–224
Shell Oil/Nigeria, bribery and corruption,
  110–112
Sikka, Prem, 136, 138
Sinaloa (drug) Cartel, 148, 171–172
Singapore, tax haven services, 11
"Single Malt" scheme, 17
slavery, 26, 45, 243, 254
Sloan, Timothy, 99
Smith, Adam, 23
Social Security, 239–240
South Africa: audit failings in, 138; bribery
  and corruption in, 113; failure of auditors
  in, 138–139; global share of income, 57f;
  government-imposed sanctions against,
  159; Gupta brothers' companies illicit
  dealings, 160–162; Mandela's positive
  guidance of, 159–160; state capture
  of, 159–162; Zuma's state capture of,
  160–162
Spain, 39, 73, 76, 97
S&P Global Ratings, 104
spoofing/misleading about price movements,
  95–96
St. Kitts, West Indies, anonymous trust
  businesses, 13
Statue of Liberty, 174
Stiglitz, Joseph, 71
stock market: unemployment and, 213f; U.S.
  "flash crash," 33–34; wage growth *vs.*
  stock growth, 67f
Story, Louise, 40
Stumpf, John, 98–99
Sub-Saharan Africa: increasing poverty
  levels, 53; trade misinvoicing in, 59f
Sullenberger, Chesley, 188
Sullivan & Cromwell, 131
Summers, Larry, 31, 80–81, 180, 214

Supreme Court (U.S.) decisions: *Citizens United v. Federal Election Commission,* 177–179; *McCutcheon v. Federal Election Commission,* 178; *United States v. Pasquantino,* 176
Suspicious Activity Reports (SARs), 42, 90, 170, 215
Suu Kyi, Daw Aung San, 165–166
Swedbank, 106
Switzerland: bank investigations in, 102; bank secrecy laws in, 12; as a conduit country, 12; freezing of depositors' accounts, 117; Glencore scandal and, 112; Odebrecht scandal and, 116; settlement for tax fraud conspiracy, 92; U.S. investigations of corruption in, 127

"Tackling the Inequality Pandemic: A New Social Contract for a New Era" lecture (Mandela), 218–219
Tax Cuts and Jobs Act (2017) (U.S.), 189–191, 238
taxes and tax avoidance: by Apple Inc., 122–125; avoidance schemes, 15–16, 18–19; corporate inversion strategy, 20; creation of hybrids strategy, 19; "deduction/deduction mismatch," 19; "deduction/noninclusion mismatch," 19; of double taxation, 19; evasion of, 1; free trade zones/special economic zones, 20; money laundering, 20; strategy for avoiding double taxation, 11
tax havens, 10–12, 15–16, 29–30, 38, 41–43, 58, 68–69
terrorism, 1, 49–51, 72, 222. *See also* September 11, 2001 attack
Terrorist Finance Tracking Program (U.S.), 50
Thomson Reuters, real estate corruption report, 38
Thunberg, Greta, 3, 218
trade (trades): construction of trade manipulation, 16–18, 22–23; falsification of, 14–16; motivations for manipulations of, 18; post–World War II growth of, 9; trade misinvoicing, 18–19, 58, 59f
Transparency International, Corruption Perception Index, 37
trickle-down economics, 60, 213, 238
Troubled Assets Relief Program (TARP), 92
Trump, Donald J., 168–169, 216

UBS, 93, 94, 96, 106–107, 108
underemployment, 6, 32–33
United Arab Emirates (UAE), 20, 76f, 174–175
United Kingdom (UK): anti-money laundering efforts, 91; Cum-Ex scam, London, 96–97; failure of auditors in, 138–139; global share of income, 57f; increasing inequalities, falling freedoms in, 73, 75; real estate-related corruption, 38; sales of permanent residence, 174; tax haven phenomenon, 10–11; U.S. investigations of corruption in, 127
United Nations (UN), 153–154, 159
United States (U.S.), 28, 34, 48, 78–80, 170–191, 254; attempted coup (1/6/21), 3, 216–217; Banks Secrecy Act, 90; *Citizens United v. Federal Election Commission,* 177–179; Commodity Futures Modernization Act, 180; Communications Act, 176; decline of democracy in, 76–78; democracy comparison, 76f; False Claims Act, 176; "flawed democracy" ranking, 75; flawed Golden Visa Program, 173–175, 246; Foreign Corrupt Practices Act, 38, 117; Immigration Act (1990), 173; Minerals Management Service, 185–186; real estate-related corruption, 39–40; regulatory capture, 183–188, 246–247; repeal of the Glass-Steagall Act, 180–183; Sarbanes-Oxley legislation, 133–134; Tax Cuts and Jobs Act, 189–191; Walmart stores, 122; Wire Fraud Statute, 176
USA Patriot Act, 49, 222, 224
US Bancorp, 108

"Varsity Blues" college admission scam, 131–132
Venezuela, 45, 48, 76f, 116, 155–159
Vietnam War, 11
Vogl, Frank, 212–213

Walker, Darren, 71, 218
Wall Street Journal, 71
Walmart, 118–123
Warren, Senator Elizabeth, 99
Washington Mutual, 134–135
WCO. *See* World Customs Organization
wealth inequality, 67–70
Weintraub, Ellen, 178
Wells Fargo, illegal practices, 98–100

Westpac Bank, 107
whistleblowers, 41, 98, 247
Whitehead, John, 100, 103
wildlife poaching/trafficking, 1, 44, 47,
    164–165
Wire Fraud Statute (1952) (U.S.), 176
World Bank: average Gini data, 59f; Control
    of Corruption Index, 37; growth of global
    GDP, broad money, 29f; income inequality
    data, 56f; report (2018) on global poverty,
    53; role in dealing with illicit financial
    flows, 193–195, 198; role in restoring
    integrity to to democratic-capitalist
system, 247–248; suspension of support for
    Mozambique, 104; U.S. influence on, 193;
    youth not in education, employment,
    training *vs.* broad money, 32f
WorldCom, bankruptcy, 134
World Trade Organization (WTO), 197,
    248–249

Xi Jinping, 148–152. *See also* China

Yakuza crime syndicate, Japan, 184

Zucman, Gabriel, 40–41, 66, 68, 190, 196

About the Author

Raymond W. Baker, founding president of Global Financial Integrity, is a businessman, author, and internationally respected authority on corruption, money laundering, and foreign policy issues.

Baker's international business career began in 1961 in Nigeria, where he owned an investment company that bought and built manufacturing and financing ventures, two of which became Harvard Business School case studies. In 1976, Baker returned to the United States and founded a trading company doing business in dozens of countries in Africa, Latin America, and Asia. For more than a decade, he advised on confidential economic matters at the presidential level for developing country governments. His consulting work focused principally on anticorruption strategies, international terms of trade, and developing country debt.

These business and consulting experiences revealed practices, both legal and illegal, that funnel money out of poorer countries into richer countries. In 1990 Baker undertook an in-depth survey of this issue, interviewing 550 business-people in 11 countries on import and export mispricing, tax-evading capital flows, and money laundering. He received a grant from the John D. and Catherine T. MacArthur Foundation in 1996 to continue his research and associated as a guest scholar in economic studies at the Brookings Institution. Baker traveled to 23 countries to interview 335 central bankers, commercial bankers, government officials, economists, lawyers, tax collectors, security officers, and sociologists on the relationships between bribery, commercial tax evasion, money laundering, and economic growth. This project culminated in his first book, *Capitalism's Achilles Heel: Dirty Money and How to Renew the Free-Market System*, cited by the *Financial Times* as one of the "best business books of 2005."

Together with Tom Cardamone, Baker founded Global Financial Integrity (GFI) in 2006 to broaden international understanding of issues surrounding harmful economic practices. GFI coined the term "illicit financial flows," now used by virtually all countries and international institutions and embedded into the UN's Sustainable Development Goals. The GFI team has produced dozens of economic analyses of how resource transfers affect countries around the world. A 2009 analysis focusing on Africa led to formation of the High Level Panel on Illicit Financial Flows from Africa, on which Baker has served since its inception, under the able leadership of Thabo Mbeki and Abdalla Hamdok.

Across long years of writing and speaking, Baker has testified often before legislative committees in the United States, Canada, the United Kingdom, and the European Union. He has commented frequently on global news outlets, including ABC's *Nightline*, Bloomberg TV, the CBS *Evening News*, CNN, NPR, PBS, BBC, and Al Jazeera.

Baker is a graduate of Harvard Business School and Georgia Institute of Technology. He earlier served on the Policy Advisory Board of Transparency International–USA and on the Advisory Board of the Ethical Research Institute. His wife, Pauline, a political scientist, is the creator of the Fragile States Index and president emeritus of the Fund for Peace. They live in Bethesda, Maryland. Their daughter Gayle lives with her family in Washington, D.C., and their son Deren and his family are in San Francisco. This book is dedicated to Pauline and Raymond's grandchildren, as said in the book's dedication, "their friends, and their generation, again the best reason for optimism."

Berrett–Koehler
Publishers

Berrett-Koehler is an independent publisher dedicated to an ambitious mission: *Connecting people and ideas to create a world that works for all.*

Our publications span many formats, including print, digital, audio, and video. We also offer online resources, training, and gatherings. And we will continue expanding our products and services to advance our mission.

We believe that the solutions to the world's problems will come from all of us, working at all levels: in our society, in our organizations, and in our own lives. Our publications and resources offer pathways to creating a more just, equitable, and sustainable society. They help people make their organizations more humane, democratic, diverse, and effective (and we don't think there's any contradiction there). And they guide people in creating positive change in their own lives and aligning their personal practices with their aspirations for a better world.

And we strive to practice what we preach through what we call "The BK Way." At the core of this approach is *stewardship,* a deep sense of responsibility to administer the company for the benefit of all of our stakeholder groups, including authors, customers, employees, investors, service providers, sales partners, and the communities and environment around us. Everything we do is built around stewardship and our other core values of *quality, partnership, inclusion,* and *sustainability.*

This is why Berrett-Koehler is the first book publishing company to be both a B Corporation (a rigorous certification) and a benefit corporation (a for-profit legal status), which together require us to adhere to the highest standards for corporate, social, and environmental performance. And it is why we have instituted many pioneering practices (which you can learn about at www.bkconnection.com), including the Berrett-Koehler Constitution, the Bill of Rights and Responsibilities for BK Authors, and our unique Author Days.

We are grateful to our readers, authors, and other friends who are supporting our mission. We ask you to share with us examples of how BK publications and resources are making a difference in your lives, organizations, and communities at www.bkconnection.com/impact.

Dear reader,

Thank you for picking up this book and welcome to the worldwide BK community! You're joining a special group of people who have come together to create positive change in their lives, organizations, and communities.

What's BK all about?

Our mission is to connect people and ideas to create a world that works for all.

Why? Our communities, organizations, and lives get bogged down by old paradigms of self-interest, exclusion, hierarchy, and privilege. But we believe that can change. That's why we seek the leading experts on these challenges—and share their actionable ideas with you.

A welcome gift

To help you get started, we'd like to offer you a **free copy** of one of our bestselling ebooks:

www.bkconnection.com/welcome

When you claim your **free ebook**, you'll also be subscribed to our blog.

Our freshest insights

Access the best new tools and ideas for leaders at all levels on our blog at ideas.bkconnection.com.

Sincerely,

Your friends at Berrett-Koehler